ROMANTICISM,
RADICALISM,
AND THE
PRESS

D1255612

ROMANTICISM,
RADICALISM,
AND THE
PRESS

Edited by
STEPHEN C. BEHRENDT

WAYNE STATE UNIVERSITY PRESS   DETROIT

Copyright © 1997 by Wayne State University Press,
Detroit, Michigan 48202. All rights are reserved.
No part of this book may be reproduced without formal permission.
Manufactured in the United States of America.
01   00   99   98   97   5   4   3   2   1

Library of Congress Cataloging-in-Publication Data

Romanticism, radicalism, and the press / edited by Stephen C.
Behrendt.
p.   cm.
Includes bibliographical references and index.
ISBN 0-8143-2568-8 (pbk. : alk. paper)
1. English literature—19th century—History and criticism.
2. Politics and literature—Great Britain—History—19th century.
3. Politics and literature—Great Britain—History—18th century.
4. English literature—18th century—History and criticism.
5. Radicalism—Great Britain—History—19th century.   6. Radicalism—
Great Britain—History—18th century.   7. Journalism—Great
Britain—History—19th century.   8. Journalism—Great Britain—
History—18th century.   9. Romanticism—Great Britain.
I. Behrendt, Stephen C., 1947–   .
PR468.R33R66   1997
820.9'358—dc21   96-51736

FOR
PATRICIA FLANAGAN BEHRENDT

CONTENTS

7

CONTENTS

Mab and Mob: The Radical Press Community
in Regency England
David Worrall   137

Demonology, Ethos, and
Community in Cobbett and Shelley
Kevin Binfield   157

"Radical Trash":
American Emigrants in the *Quarterly Review*
Kim Wheatley   170

William Hone, John Murray, and the Uses of Byron
Kyle Grimes   192

The *Black Dwarf* as Satiric Performance; or, the
Instabilities of the "Public Square"
Steven Jones   203

CONTRIBUTORS

BRENDA BANKS, whose particular interest is William Wordsworth in the context of his times, is Assistant Registrar at Cornish College of the Arts, Seattle.

STEPHEN C. BEHRENDT, George Holmes Distinguished Professor of English at the University of Nebraska, has published books on Blake and the Shelleys and is presently working on British women writers of the Romantic period.

KEVIN BINFIELD is Assistant Professor of English at Gardner-Webb University; in addition to his ongoing work with P. B. Shelley, he is completing major projects on Joanna Southcott and on writings associated with the Luddites.

KYLE GRIMES, Associate Professor of English at the University of Alabama at Birmingham, centers his research in the social history of the Romantic period. He is currently completing a critical biography of William Hone.

STEVEN JONES is Assistant Professor of English at Loyola University of Chicago; in addition to his ongoing research in the Romantics, he presently serves as editor of the *Keats-Shelley Journal.*

VICTORIA MYERS, Professor of Humanities at Pepperdine University, is currently working on a book-length study of Coleridge.

THOMAS PFAU is Andrew W. Mellon Assistant Professor of English at Duke University, where his current projects include Wordsworth and nineteenth- and twentieth-century philosophy.

MICHAEL SCRIVENER, Professor of English at Wayne State University, is author of *Radical Shelley* (1982) and *Poetry and Reform: Periodical Verse from the English Democratic Press, 1792–1824* (1992).

9

KIM WHEATLEY is Assistant Professor of English at the College of William and Mary, where she pursues her research on both Percy Shelley and on Romantic poetry and its reception.

DAVID WORRALL, who teaches at St. Mary's University College, Strawberry Hill, is the author of *Radical Culture: Discourse, Resistance, and Surveillance, 1790–1820* (1992) and editor of Volume 6 of the new Blake Trust facsimile editions, *The Urizen Books* (1995).

ACKNOWLEDGMENTS

Any collaborative project requires the interest and enthusiasm of the participants, as well as their patience and good will. In preparing the present collection I have had the good fortune to find all of these in abundance among the good colleagues whose work is represented in the pages that follow. The timeliness of a collection of essays on the broad range of interactions among various aspects of Radical thought during the Romantic period in England, as indicated in an equally broad range of publishing activities, is underscored by the resurgence in interest in the historical framework for literary and extra-literary art of that remarkable era. The essays included here take various approaches to this fertile intersection of cultural activities, exploring how Radical culture and some of its representative figures inform a surprising number of texts, both by canonical writers and by those who have historically been marginalized, misrepresented, dismissed, or simply ignored. As is clear in these essays, the lines of demarcation between "polite" public activity (of which writing is but one representative phenomenon) and "impolite" (or impolitic) is often a vague and continually shifting one, and the role played by the remarkably vigorous and diverse press of the period further complicates the matter. The sort of indeterminacies and ambiguities that frequently emerge from this cultural mix help to account for the distinctive vitality of the writing (and other types of text-production) associated with the Romantic period, both among authors and artists who were located (or who located themselves) outside the socio-political and cultural mainstream and among those who situtated themselves (or whom literary-critical history has subsequently situated) firmly therein. Indeed, further consideration of the dramatically expanded body of "Romantic writing" that comes into view when we include in our consideration these non-canonical authors and texts is already producing a significant redefinition of what we mean by "Romanticism." To that ongoing redefinition the contributors to this collection have dedicated their efforts—as well as their continuing interest.

I want to thank, in addition to the colleagues who have contributed to this collection, the staff and editors of Wayne State University Press, and particularly the director, Arthur B. Evans, for the support and patience they have demonstrated throughout the process of preparing this collection. I thank also Dawn Vernooy for her assistance with compiling the index. Finally, and as always, to my wife, Patricia Flanagan Behrendt, I owe more than I can say; her unwavering support, in good times and in bad, is the greatest gift of all, and the dedication to this collection only begins to acknowledge in a small way all that she has given me over the course of our lives together.

Stephen C. Behrendt
University of Nebraska

Introduction

Stephen C. Behrendt

Revisionist scholarship of the past decade focusing on the British Romantic period has amply illustrated why we need to continue to examine carefully and systematically the historical contexts which at once shaped and were shaped by artifacts of culture—including literary works. The purpose is not to discover a past that will prove to be in some fashion continuous with the present, however. Indeed Marjorie Levinson warns us against any such course, insisting that the objective—at least from the perspective of New Historicism—is to focus not on perceived similarities but rather on actual, historical and cultural differences that separate us from our forebears.[1] Nevertheless, critical and theoretical discussion requires us to explore as much of the rich and various contextual material as our limited resources permit. This exploration necessarily entails a good deal of historical, cultural, and textual spadework, not to mention a willingness to rethink—often dramatically—both our assumptions and expectations about the materials we are considering and the ways in which we are accustomed to think about them. A particularly useful example may be seen in the important developments in feminist theory and feminist historiography, which are contributing to the recovery of women writers of the period and to a more historically accurate reconstituting of the context of a Romantic writing community. The present dramatic remapping of the Romantic literary and cultural landscape reminds us of the central position occupied by significant numbers of women on the literary scene and within the "writing culture." Moreover, it reminds us of how much remains still to do before we can begin to claim to have anything like an accurate and historically informed picture of the British Romantic period.

An important parallel to the recovery of British Romantic women writers exists with regard to the writings associated with English Radicalism during the Romantic period. Radical writers and publishers provided an important conduit for disseminating the programs and principles of the Opposition—loyal or otherwise—during the volatile Romantic period. A historically logical product of English Enlightenment views of an informed and articulate (even garrulous) citizenry, the Radical press had by the time of Great Britain's entry into the war with Revolutionary France assumed an important role in the evolution of British socio-political discourse. Radical publishers like Daniel Isaac Eaton, John Thelwall, Thomas Spence, and to a lesser extent Joseph Johnson, performed a risky but necessary service by keeping in the public eye and mind the existence of a strong opposition to government policy, both at home and abroad. This opposition was of particular concern to the political establishment because of its roots in an emerging bourgeois value system: its rejection of hereditary (and therefore unearned) privilege and its embrace of an alternative vision of a meritocracy epitomized in the trope of life as a "race" and in the powerfully multivalent word "industry." This latter term denotes both manufacture (or a system *and a site* of production) and an attitude toward labor that is at once economic and religious in orientation.[2] That these values held such sway with the fastest growing and most politically and economically volatile portion of the populace made containment and outright suppression a priority for the privileged classes, who rightly feared for their status.

From the start, Radical publishers exerted a powerful influence over the *literary* and pseudo-literary culture of England. (It is no coincidence, for instance, that William Wordsworth went to Joseph Johnson to publish "An Evening Walk" [1793], an ostensibly descriptive poem that contains a powerful embedded attack on the societal consequences of warmaking). The status attained by the Radical press owed in part to Radicalism's frank delight in post-Wilkesian agitation, in annoying and badgering the political and cultural establishment. And partly it owed to the convincing case that the Radicals could often make for their being regarded as the voice of "common sense" in the midst of factionalism, party patronage, and plain jingoism. Oppositional Radical rhetoric frequently sought to politicize the masses by linking their interests with ancient British (Saxon) traditions of individual and collective liberty ostensibly preserved in the House of Commons but increasingly imperiled by self-serving initiatives of the aristocracy and the monarchy.[3] These initiatives, whose political *and physical* burden was borne increasingly by a long-suffering populace that would be partially emblematized in the iconic popular-culture figure of John Bull, ranged from intrusive economic oppressions to warmaking. Radical writers and their publishers (who were often one and the same) endeavored to make common cause with an increasingly literate and economically viable public of *consumers,* whose patronage might place them in a mutually profitable, symbiotic relationship with the Radical establishment. And yet the ostensible solidarity with "the masses" is itself often less a fact than a rhetorical convenience. Especially among bourgeois Radicals like Priestley and Wollstonecraft we can discern a thinly-disguised contempt for the poor (in particular), who are often branded (directly or not) as undeserving of full equality and privilege (or "entitlement") precisely because, like the despised aristocracy, they are not "industrious"—because they labor little, contribute little, and therefore have no legitimate claim on the rewards accorded the victors in the "race of life."

Radical writing's appeal owed partly, too, to the sheer sensationalism of much of that writing, which often included in its armory a rich and varied vein of humor, sometimes broad and scatological, at other times subtle and refined. In short, the Radical press thrived because so much of the writing represented there was at once *readable* and *engaging;* it addressed an expanding and diversifying audience of newly literate readers who were coming to appreciate the power and prerogative they were beginning to acquire through that very vehicle of literacy. Jon Klancher's examination of the demographics of this emerging, diversified audience, in *The Making of English Reading Audiences, 1790–1832,*[4] explored and clarified many of the issues involved with Radical discourse's important relationship to the expansion of literacy. Earlier still, Marilyn Butler remarked on the innovatory nature of the writing associated with Radicalism of the 1790s, which effectively democratized language in reaching for "a written style appropriate for the literate but not classically educated lower middle and upper working class."[5] Coming at the matter from a somewhat different angle, David Worrall has more recently insisted on the pronounced "orality" of Radical discourse and its preference for speech over writing, a preference that stems from the fact that "the oral mode of textuality was less susceptible to scrutiny by the Government's surveillance system."[6] Indeed, one of the hallmarks of Radical writing—and of the rhetorical strategies that underlie it—is its uneasy, shifting positioning between written and oral discourse, a rhetorical positioning whose oscillations produce much of the immediacy and force we associate with it. In part because of this immediacy and the high profile it dictated, the Radical press was one of the most important and influential aspects of Romantic culture, especially—but not exclusively—in major population centers like London and Edinburgh. (In Norwich and Bristol, to mention only two other centers, Radicalism's ties with the Dissenters and other disenfranchised groups are likewise conspicuous and important.)

Insistently public both in nature and in intent, the Radical press provided a visible and therefore an important *target* for reactionary forces, who frequently "found it difficult to discriminate between the different types of perceived threat"[7] the Radicals posed, and who sought refuge—or at least the semblance of security—in repressive regulation of public discourse, most notably in 1794, 1795, 1797, 1799, 1801, 1817, and 1819. Paradoxically, this same vulnerability to attack from the establishment made the Radical press the more attractive to a liberal/Radical populace, who saw in its fate—and in the fate of its leading figures—a measure of its own fate at the hands of a governmental and social structure from which it was largely excluded. In this light, for example, both the Treason Trials of 1794 and the "Manchester massacre" (or "Peterloo") of 1819 held for Radicals and liberal reformers alike both legal and symbolic significance as indicators of the precipitousness and viciousness with which their efforts might be met. The 1794 trials proceeded in a climate of early nationalistic wartime fervor; that the second incident was immediately dubbed "Peterloo" merely underscored the extent to which that action in Manchester was portrayed as a treacherous transfer of the focus of warmaking from a foreign enemy to a domestic one.

In his introduction to a collection of essays on the tradition of British Radicalism, Michael Foot observes that the "official" history of parliamentary (and other social and political) institutions is marked by the spirit of creative compromise, which congratulates individuals of all parties for their moderation, their observance of a sense of how far they could safely go in advancing their agendas. Foot's point is that this official history relegates to the margins—when it does not entirely erase—"the others who have supplied so much of the engine power in [British] history—the rebels, the revolutionaries, the heretics who risked their necks, the prophets who understood more than the statesmen, the far-seeing, the eccentrics, and the men of no-compromise." Foot goes on to observe, however, that "the whole story can be written so differently," implying the often considerable differences between official history and actual history, a point that is underscored by the old truism about history generally being written by the victors, the dominant culture. The "different" version of history, Foot intimates, will need to be more generous and will need to "give us glimpses of great companies of men *and women* who struggled and fought and were beaten" and "whose names have been obliterated altogether" (my emphases).[8]

In fact, recent revisionist scholarship reveals that while many of these names and faces, like the works they left behind, have indeed been lost, not all of them have suffered that fate. This is as true for studies of writing as it is for studies of politics. Recent years have witnessed a new appreciation for the writings of marginalized, non-canonical authors of both sexes, and in all genres—including some, like popular journalism, the squib, and the formally published "letter" (as in the "letter to the editor"), which are traditionally regarded as largely extra-literary forms. Even canonical authors are being reassessed, at least in part to reveal—to generations that seem to have forgotten—how much a part of the volatile social and political milieu of their times they actually were. No mere ephemeral, inconsequential nature-lovers and dreamy idealists, they were engaged artists for whom Percy Bysshe Shelley spoke articulately and sincerely when he called poets (by which we may prop-

16

erly infer artists—including rhetoricians) the "unacknowledged legislators of the world." That "unacknowledged" status stems, it seems to me, less from their being invisible than it does from the fact that the best artist—certainly for Shelley—is the artist whose political, social, and intellectual agenda is so perfectly melded with her or his art that it is transparent. Not invisible, but transparent. In reading and accessing the "content" of a work by such an artist, one quite literally sees through the transparent ideological framework. The legislating is done largely without the reader's consent—or even consciousness—so that she or he comes gradually to see as the artist sees, believe as the artist believes. In this, the artist is the ultimate seducer, a word Shelley applied tellingly to Jesus Christ in his essay on Christianity.[9]

Edmund Burke, whose *Reflections on the Revolution in France* provided fuel for so many Radical fires, understood this, as we see in his comment in a letter to Philip Francis from February 1790. Writing about English Dissenters, Burke suggested that the *Reflections* was designed to expose just such seduction. The book would, he wrote, "set in a full view the danger from their wicked principles and their black hearts."[10] Not just the principles were "wicked"; so too were those who propagated them. That counterrevolutionary (and therefore, for the most part, counter-Radical) rhetoric of the period engages so frequently in *ad hominem* attacks reflects the Radicals' own rejection of the decorum which the privileged took for granted. Unacceptable people could only produce unacceptable utterances, in other words, and those utterances might most profitably be countered by exposing the vulgarity of those who pronounced (or printed) them. Rather than adopt (or adapt) the discourse of the elite they opposed in every other respect, Radicals responded by insisting on a language and discourse-system (which included extra-linguistic materials as well) that simply *bypassed* the forum of the elite and directed itself straight to its increasingly large, predominantly bourgeois audience. That the entire discourse-system could be turned upon itself with devastating effectiveness, as we see in the Treason Trials of 1794, simply underscored the fears of the establishment about its own susceptibility to subtle seduction.

"Seduction" usually implies an insidious and undermining activity, one that draws individuals away from activities ostensibly deemed "proper" because they are culturally-sanctioned. "Subversion," on the other hand, involves less a luring away from, than a revelation of the bankruptcy of, those supposedly sacrosanct priorities and the institutions that perpetuate them precisely because they benefit from them. The Radicalism that emerged in England late in the eighteenth century had in its constitution much of both seduction and subversion. Frequently hearkening back to the Revolution of 1688, itself a backward-looking insurgency, the Radical movement focused new attention on the usurpation of individual and collective prerogative of the citizenry by the imposed authority of a power elite that drew its mandate to rule more from custom (principally of the aristocracy) than from the people who were governed. Suffrage under these circumstances had to do not merely with the vote *per se,* but, more broadly, with the free exchange of information and opinion, with freedom of discussion, freedom of movement, and freedom of the press. It was a matter of the rights—the *natural* rights—of the governed as opposed to the privilege enjoyed by those who governed. Central to any compact between those who are governed and those who govern is the matter of consent, and this matter, not surprisingly, lies at the center of much of Radical discourse. Thomas Hardy, for instance, one of the first to be prosecuted with real vigor, posed an especial threat precisely because in originating the London Corresponding Society he set in motion a mechanism for the exchange of information—information that could incite the corresponding membership not just to recognize that they were ruled without their consent but also to discover means of acting in concert to rectify their intolerable position. That the London Corresponding Society was by design open to all underscored its egalitarian basis even as it modeled a parliamentary structure that was of particular interest to the Radicals.

This free exchange of *information* mandated a comparable liberation of language and discourse from their acquired narrowness and exclusivity. And here is where Radicalism ultimately looks forward—to a new social vision incorporating morality and economics in equal measure—more than backward. Responding with "a vigorous embrace of modernity," British Radicals of the Romantic period set out to seize and transform every aspect of English life, clearing away "the thick underbrush of outdated and useless institutions," simplifying government, and exposing prejudice, mystery, and disinformation to the cold light of pseudo-scientific objectivity.[11] This expansion of the field of discourse happened throughout British society during the roughly thirty years considered by the essays in this collection. That the press was a key player—indeed the central agent—in many respects suggests why this collection of essays sets out to reopen the inquiry into the complex relations among professed Radicals, their sympathizers and adherents, their adversaries, and the ever-expanding readerships to whom all parties directed their efforts. That the struggle for influence and ascendancy is, as often as not, visible also as a struggle for control of both the *terms* and the *field* of discourse attests further to the centrality of this entire matter to any properly informed understanding of the Romantic writing community.

Surprisingly, Radical writers and their considerable influence have been marginalized by traditional literary-historical studies, which have typically invoked narrow definitions of intellectual utility and aesthetic valuation in formulating the canon of Romantic writing. Inexplicably, even modern theorists like Jürgen Habermas have explicitly excluded "the *plebian* public sphere" from their formulations because they believe this sphere to have been, as Habermas puts it, "suppressed in the historical process."[12] And yet, as Kevin Gilmartin demonstrates, Radical culture was not only rooted in that plebian public sphere but in fact developed a widespread and sophisticated rhetorical network that came to have real public impact, whether through the print culture or through public activities like debating societies, political clubs, petition campaigns, and organized boycotts, all of whose actions were of course themselves reiterated in printed accounts that were read both privately and aloud in still other public contexts.[13] This very diversity of activity—and therefore of audiences— ensured the competition for control of public institutions that we recognize in so much of Radical activity. What has not been sufficiently appreciated in modern scholarship, then, is the extent to which the Radical press figured directly in the "writing culture" we associate with both the canonized and the marginalized writers of British Romanticism. I say "writing culture," rather than "literature" or "literary works," in order to broaden the field of relevant materials to include, along with works conceived as literature or pseudo-literature, also others whose nature is essentially extra-literary—works like dissertations on natural science, economics, and public policy. The Radical "writing culture" includes as well contributions to Radical periodicals and journals (from essays to letters), along with squibs and satires (which are sometimes verbal, sometimes visual, and sometimes a combination of the two, like Hone and Cruikshank's *The Political House that Jack Built* [1819]), and, during the Luddite agitation in particular, "inscriptions" ranging from chalkings to songs.

Radical discourse is often about discourse itself. Who, if anyone, "owns" language and other signifiers (like the white hat—and the *White Hat*—David Worrall describes in his essay in this collection, or the caricature prints Thomas Pfau discusses in his)? And how is the struggle for ownership—or even temporary possession—traced both in the press and in the courts (in actions like the trials of Thomas Hardy and John Horne Tooke and, later, of Richard Carlile)? Further, how are the rules and conduct of public and private discourse altered both by conditions of suppression and by acts of insurrection or subversion (especially verbal ones) that stem from those very conditions? The issues are not just those of linguistic or semantic propriety and "vulgarity" which have been admirably examined by scholars like Olivia Smith,[14] although these issues are certainly central to the acts of resistance initiated by both sides. They involve also the politics inherent in a complex negotiation among authors, publishers (when they are not one with the authors), perceived or intended readerships, actual readerships, and monitors or agents of surveillance in the hire of the opposition.

In large measure, the early Radical writers of the Romantic period had to invent their audiences, at least rhetorically. As Smith observes, when Daniel Isaac Eaton began his *Politics for the People* he appeared—to judge from what he wrote—to be "wary and uncertain of his audience," carefully controlling his material and releasing his information in a guarded manner because "the audience is not represented" in the writing. Since he does not directly and explicitly figure his audience within his writing, in other words, Eaton consequently lacks an appropriate language in which to articulate his thoughts. Later, Smith continues, Regency Radicals like Cobbett, Wooler, Hone, and Carlile "trusted their audience" and "could portray it convincingly" because they knew those readers—knew their political, social, ideological, and demographic profile—and so could write to and for them in "a bold vernacular language" that was largely impossible for earlier writers like Thelwall, Parkinson, and even Spence, who wrote under far different constraints and in a far less clearly delineated relationship with their readers. Indeed, at the end of the Regency and the beginning of the reign of George IV the Radical press—and in fact the whole print and popular media generally—became more aggressive and "wilfully, hilariously rude."[15] Of course, this is always one of the great fears of any entrenched power structure: the fear that its ability to frighten and intimidate will be stripped away by its being made ridiculous—the object of humor and ridicule. These matters bear important implications for our understanding of British Romantic writing, both because they inform that writing in interesting and historically often underappreciated ways and because they help us, some two centuries later, to situate Romantic discourse itself more precisely in its broader historical and cultural context.

The present collection of essays, then, provides a forum for examining some of the ways in which Radical ideas interacted with what we understand to be Romanticism through the medium of the Radical press. Leading figures early on include Daniel Isaac Eaton and Thomas Spence, both of whom were prosecuted in highly publicized trials, and during the Regency William Hone, Thomas Wooler, William Cobbett, and Richard Carlile, who likewise felt the wrath (and the legal machinations) of the established government. The volume takes some of its intellectual impetus from Clifford Siskin's observation in *The Historicity of Romantic Discourse* that in the Romantic period a fiction of communication was created as a basis for a new human community;[16] in fact, the period appears to have been driven—especially after 1800—by impulses toward the creation of *several,* often non-intersecting communities. Contributors to this collection examine the relationship of several key "traditional," canonical figures in Romantic literature (Wordsworth, Coleridge, Byron, P. B. Shelley), as well as some less familiar, non-canonical writers, to items on the Radical agenda and to their advocates among Radical writers and publishers. Other contributors examine particular aspects of the Radical press and its leading figures to flesh out that cultural context for the modern reader. Inevitably, the essays begin to inscribe in their dialogue a revealing picture of the confluence of Radical ideologies with literary endeavor.

Radical journalists typically directed relatively explicit appeals and programs to their readers, in the process foregrounding both the actual political, social, or economic agenda of their discourse and the rhetorical structures and postures by which they sought to advance that agenda. Writers who fashioned themselves more as literary artists (and whom subsequent critical opinion has accepted and even canonized in that way) naturally opted more often for a less direct approach, striving to stimulate and manipulate their readers' consciousnesses through the vehicle of imaginative literature. In both cases, though, the writers could count upon audiences whose ranks ranged from similar-minded enthusiasts to the only vaguely curious. The growth of reading public*s*, which was matched by a comparably exponential growth in publications (periodicals in particular), ensured both access and sympathetic readers. But it ensured also a fragmentation that would significantly alter the nature of Radical discourse—and the Radical press—during the Regency, when both the Radical interest groups and the opponents against whom their forces were deployed became increasingly diversified and hence less susceptible to appeals for unified public action.

The interconnected essays in this volume trace the rise, during the era of Price, Burke, Eaton, Godwin, Spence, and Thelwall, of the "professional intellectual" (who was frequently, like Coleridge, associated with or employed by the press) and the further evolution of this phenomenon during the Regency. While during the Regency period Radical journalists like Cobbett and Hone maintained a regard for the qualities of discrimination and discernment possessed by "the common reader," the cultural dynamics of this later period make clear that a dramatic change had taken place in the relations among authors, readers, and the press that mediated those relations. Specifically, by the time of P. B. Shelley's death in 1822 we can see that the new mass audience produced by advances in literacy and technology alike was increasingly subdividing into specialist readers to whom independent journalists catered. This change corresponds to the dissolution of one sort of "community" that had arisen in the eighteenth century *with the assistance of the press* (through what Benedict Anderson has called "print-capitalism"[17]) and the evolution of a plethora of subcommunities whose internal coherence was offset by the increasing inability of these subcommunities to communicate meaningfully with one another. The dangers of specialization that William Godwin had foreseen in *Political Justice* (1793) emerged with a vengeance in the decades that followed. Meanwhile, the structure of public society—and both the vehicles and the modes of discourse relating to it—had been transformed and the seeds of Victorianism planted.

Remarkably, relatively little attention has been paid to the productive intersection of Romanticism, Radicalism, and the Press in England. One particularly good study is Smith's *Politics of Language,* mentioned earlier. William Stafford's *Socialism, Radicalism, and Nostalgia*[18] focuses primarily upon Radical social criticism in an examination of ten key philosophical/political texts, none of which is a work of imaginative literature, while Iain McCalman's *Radical Underworld: Prophets, Revolutionaries and Pornographers in London, 1795–1840* takes a broader cultural perspective on these particular varieties of subversion and activism in that expanded hsitorical period.[19] Nearer in some respects to the concept of the present volume is Roger Sales's *English Literature in History, 1780–1830;*[20] that book, however, focuses on the relation of the pastoral mode in Romantic literature to political events like the Cato Street Conspiracy, the trial of Queen Caroline, and the like. Nevertheless, the interest in connections among social, political, intellectual, and aesthetic phenomena that informs Sales's inquiries prefigures some of the concerns of the contributors to the present collection. More immediately relevant is Jon Klancher's study, also mentioned earlier, of English readerships during the Romantic period. Klancher's analysis of the burgeoning print culture and the variously defined reading publics severally addressed and fed by a diversifying publishing industry—with or without state support (and interference)—provides one of the contextual backgrounds against which the essays in this volume are inscribed. Another, this one emphasizing the representative contemporary literary materials, is Michael Scrivener's edited collection, *Poetry and Reform: Periodical Verse from the English Democratic Press, 1792–1824,*[21] whose introduction and annotations address Radical concern with political reform and the significant implications of the ways in which the expression of that concern, in poetry, varies from the 1790s to the Regency. Scrivener's study, in fact, reflects and documents interests that drive his earlier study, *Radical Shelley,*[22] in which he demonstrates the intricate interplay among various levels of literary and cultural discourse in the work of a single great Romantic stylist in poetry and prose. David Worrall's *Radical Culture* offers yet another perspective on the complicated interaction that developed over the central thirty years of the Romantic period among Radical writers and their interested readers from all positions in the political and cultural landscape. Finally, the fullest and most sophisticated study to date of the relationship of the press to English Radicalism in this period is Kevin Gilmartin's *Print Politics: The Press and Radical Opposition in Early Nineteenth-Century England,*[23] which is scheduled to appear at about the same time as the present collection.

Given the continuing interest in historicizing the dynamics of Romantic discourse, and given too the emergence of ever more evidence of significant interaction among the artifacts of Romantic literary culture and that writing culture which is normally *not* considered a part of high art, we need to look again at how the Romantic writing community was and is constituted. The essays that follow investigate some of the fertile intersections during the Romantic period among Radical ideology and its evolving social, political, economic, and intellectual agenda; a literary culture that includes both traditionally recognized and canonized literary artists like Coleridge or P. B. Shelley and non-canonical ones like John Thelwall or Mary Robinson; another writing community less immediately "literary" in its primary preoccupations and which includes Radical journalists like Thomas Spence, William Cobbett, or Richard Carlile; and the broader social and cultural environment inscribed and recorded by the press in all its diversity of political and cultural positions. These essays investigate also some of the ways in which the British Romantic ethos, traditionally associated with the bardic, visionary postures of its masculinist poets, was significantly affected and informed by a decidedly more worldly element visible in the works of the active Radical writers and their publishers. To what extent did writers at all levels—and in all segments—of the Romantic writing community share common interests with the Radical movement? What intertextual interchanges among these writers signalled their awareness of one another's ideals and efforts, and what can we say about the effects upon both "Radical writing" (including Radical rhetoric) and "Romantic writing" of this cross-fertilization that was transpiring in the public forum of the press? What emerges in the essays gathered here is a portrait of a diverse writing community in which elements of the Radical social, political, and economic agenda are articulated and advanced both by writers whose aims are primarily literary and by writers whose principal motivation stems from more immediately politically and socially engaged commitments. That these efforts take place so often in full view of one another, and that they participate in a public dialogue mediated through the press, reveals at once the broad currency of the Radical agenda during the Romantic period and the extent to which Romantic writers who were once stereotyped as aloof or ethereal were in fact in touch with—and involved with—the pressing political, social, and economic issues at the very center of their contemporary culture.

The essays chart a roughly chronological course, although many of the figures and events (including literary events) that are discussed necessarily overlap one another within the two broadly inclusive periods of the 1790s and the Regency. What emerges from the constellation of essays as a whole is the startling *diversity* involved in the activities of Radicals and their followers as they related to the press, to publication, and to readerships. Thomas Pfau's careful treatment of the rhetorical strategies involved in the 1794 Treason Trials immediately complicates and problematizes some of the issues of discourse I have raised in this introduction. Pfau shows how in Thomas Hardy's trial for high treason the prosecution exploited imagination and the eminently human tendency to fictionalize by collapsing questions of fact with questions of law; the product of these efforts was a carefully-woven texture of discourse that accorded unprecedented legal and social consequences to a seemingly "harmless" and innocuous array of facts. The result is a Romantic model of critical interpretation that acknowledges and cultivates the continuity and interdependence among the legal system, the socio-logic of any and all discrete material facts (however innocuous), and the aesthetic design that is created as a means of concealing the political import of such facts. The early 1790s saw dramatic transformations in class relations, economics, and the law—as well as in the social and political structures they involved. Attributing an efficient cause to these transformations—making them the consequence of the treason of Hardy and nine other defendants—constitutes in Pfau's careful reading not just a paranoid delusion on the government's part but, more importantly, an initial conscious *projection* of causality that facilitates a fundamentally therapeutic process by acknowledging change in the form of a series of interrelated social and political effects.

Victoria Myers considers the struggle over language not in the discourse of the courts but rather in Coleridge's journalistic writings, where he expressed his concern over the threat to sincerity and truth posed by writings on both sides in the 1796–1800 dispute between ministerial hacks and Radical journalists. Terms like "fraud" and imposture," which were widely bandied about by journalists of all political stripes, constituted one plot of the disputed terrain of political valuation and devaluation, Myers argues, and so Coleridge set out to systematize accusations of imposture and insincerity into a language of analytical and poetically allusive power. This language he then redeployed against both the new French Constitution and the British refusal to negotiate peace with the nation governed by that constitution. Coleridge's procedures betray a self-consciousness about the equivocalness of analysis itself that suggests it is not amiss to locate in the political discourse of 1798–1800 (in which Coleridge was an informed and acute participant) one important germ of the Romantic transvaluation of "values" and a concomitant transformation of sentimental sincerity into (no less sentimental) irony.

My own essay, which focuses primarily upon the 1790s, considers the paradoxical situation in which women poets found themselves in relation to Radical principles. The nostalgic yearning professed by many male Radicals for a mythologized Golden Age associated in the popular mind with the Anglo-Saxon age in England (and in particular with the reign of Alfred the Great) offered little for women, whose situation had been no better in that mythic past than it was in the contemporary world. The oppositional impulses that inform these women's writing often center, therefore, on the threat posed by the government and its institutions to that most elemental unit of society, the family. Warmaking, in particular, devastates the family, sacrificing not just the lives of husbands, brothers, and sons but also those of their spouses, children, and parents to the designs of a government whose devotion to the interests of the privileged and the propertied—and thus to itself—reveals its signal lack of concern for the welfare of the individual family unit. Hence the reformulation of part of the Radical agenda in terms of anti-war poetry written by women in the 1790s (in particular) reveals yet another way in which discourse is redirected in this period in service to Radical ends.

Brenda Banks takes up the transitional moment represented in the period following the collapse of the Peace of Amiens, examining how the British press's largely univocal savaging of Napoleon provided an important context for William Wordsworth's efforts in 1804 to account for his seeming abandonment of earlier revolutionary ideals. This national alarmist discourse, which flourished in the verbal medium of the press and the visual medium of the caricature print, provided a backdrop for Wordsworth's efforts to distinguish between the Revolution in its early phases and what became of it with the ascendance of the Jacobins and later of Napoleon. Unlike the popular press, whose vilification of Napoleon gradually encouraged the English to replace their fear of Napoleon with laughter and ridicule, Wordsworth took the tack in *The Prelude* of likening Napoleon to the despotic Bourbon kings rather than the revolutionaries who supplanted them. In the process Wordsworth anticipated modern historians' recognition that Napoleon was in fact less a product of the Revolution than he was a product of Europe's reaction against it. Rejecting the powerful discourse of political authority articulated in the press on the British government's behalf, Banks argues, Wordsworth reasserted his continued political engagement with principles he had originally associated with the revolution while building a subtle defense against charges that he had simply turned his coat.

John Thelwall was a key player in Radical publishing throughout the period, and his work encompasses both the designedly journalistic and the calculatedly "literary." His poetry and prose appeared in documents of the London Corresponding Society and in publications of his own like the *Politician* and the *Tribune,* and his political songs appeared as broadsides and were sung at political meetings. And yet he also wrote for the middle-class, post-Enlightenment *Monthly Magazine,* whose audience was decidedly different. Michael Scrivener examines how this paradoxical positioning affected Thelwall's writing for several journals he edited, revealing a more complex Thelwall than we usually think of, a writer who for the most part maintained, even in difficult and rapidly changing circumstances, an idealistic faith in the continued existence of readers who were fellow intellectuals capable of integrating complex ideas and contributing meaningfully to the sort of ongoing, rational dialogue advocated by William Godwin in his *Political Justice.* Scrivener focuses especially on Thelwall's editorial work with the *Champion,* the mildly reformist paper he puchased in 1818 during the revival of the reform movement and then turned into a Radical reform organ, and the *Monthly Magazine,* which he edited briefly from the end of 1824 to the end of 1825. What emerges is an intriguing picture of a virtuoso intellectual who never lost his sense of the centrality of the periodical press to the shaping of both political and cultural issues.

In an essay that examines the conditions under which Radical publishers did their work during the Regency, David Worrall considers journals like Cannon's *Theological Inquirer,* Wooler's *Black Dwarf,* Richard Carlile's *Republican,* Robert Shorter's *Theological Comet,* and James Griffin's *Cap of Liberty.* His account of the political environment in which such journals were situated is buttressed by his detailed examination of Home Office papers documenting the surveillance to which Radical publishers were subjected. These considerations reveal much about the Regency climate for Radical publishing, of course, but they also help us to see where Percy Bysshe Shelley fits into the equation. In the course of his discussion, Worrall traces Shelley's relation to Cannon's *Theological Inquirer* and to the elusive William Clark, who was the first pirater of Shelley's *Queen Mab,* in 1821. Worrall's discussion offers yet another illustration of the extent to which canonical Romantic texts (and their authors) share the field of discourse with those of their more explicitly activist Radical contemporaries.

Kevin Binfield's discussion of Shelley and Cobbett examines the resurgence of Radicalism in the later Regency under a new set of circumstances in which wartime mentality is no longer an issue. Beginning with Cobbett and Shelley's shared concern with the notion of a rhetorical community, Binfield demonstrates how these two writers differed significantly in their assessments of their audiences and the most effective ways to motivate those audiences. By the later Regency the generalized rhetoric about brotherhood and the rights of man was being replaced by a more particularized and often more distinctively negative discourse aimed at eliciting practical popular *action.* The extent to which the Radical writer recognized and fulfilled this practical need to prod the audience into action effectively determined the success of his or her polemical writing. Focusing on the twin devices of demonology and martyrology, Binfield examines some of the reasons why the rhetorical immediacy of Cobbett's deliberately self-centered style suited it to the sort of direct political action he envisioned, while Shelley's political writing, which opted for a less self-centered and more Ciceronean stance grounded in reasoned argument and irreducible principles, missed the mark at which its author had aimed.

Cobbett also figures in Kim Wheatley's essay, which examines how the *Quarterly Review* attempted to discount the political and philosophical principles articulated in the writings of Morris Birkbeck and other British emigrants to America during the Regency (and afterward) by demonizing the emigrant authors. Wheatley details in particular the dynamics of what she terms the paranoid style adopted by the *Quarterly*'s reviewers when they discussed for their readers these emigrant writings on America. On those occasions, the *Quarterly* frequently treated emigration in terms of an ongoing narrative in which the Miltonic plot of the fall from heaven is Romantically and humorously rewritten, but not without a clear bias that reflects the *Quarterly*'s strong Tory ideology. In effect, the *Quarterly*'s strategy was to demand that the author be held personally responsible for the baleful effects of his texts (a strategy visible also in the *Quarterly*'s responses to P. B. Shelley's works, for example), which, the reviewers claimed, exerted a dangerous power to dupe and seduce innocent readers. Adopting a sort of conspiracy-theory model of history, the *Quarterly*'s reviewers approached literary discourse in terms of a

26

struggle between moral good and moral evil. Not surprisingly, discontented English citizens like Birkbeck (or Cobbett, or Henry Fearon, or Frances Wright), who traveled to America or otherwise espoused and articulated opinions favorable to America and American politics, were singled out for particular demonizing. Wheatley argues that the rhetorical stance of moral authority adopted by self-anointed custodians of public opinion (like the *Quarterly*'s reviewers) recast the emigrant writers in the role of satanic rebels and America as a parodic and debased new Eden. But that strategy proved ultimately disabling to both sides, for while it perhaps reduced the emigrants' influence in some quarters, it in fact perpetuated (by foregrounding it) the mythic structure of oppression against which the emigrants had themselves revolted and which they sought to highlight by tracing its comparative absence in the New World. In short, the bullets fired in all such attempts at character assassination tended to ricochet in surprising directions, including back at those who fired them.

In his essay, Kyle Grimes examines how in publishing *Don Juan, Canto the Third!* (1819) the Radical publisher William Hone coopted the comic-Byronic voice in service to a popular politics that allowed Hone at once to criticize the seeming cowardice of his publishing rival John Murray and simultaneously to elevate his own status as a Radical writer and publisher. As Grimes shows us, the complex cultural dynamic that permeates Hone's *Don Juan, Canto the Third!* reveals the tensions that existed between, on one hand, Radical writer/publishers like Hone, Carlile, and Wooler and, on the other hand, the "high literature" establishment embodied in figures like Murray, Byron, Scott, and other intellectuals. Hone's poem becomes in Grimes' analysis a field of cultural struggle where the battles for authority over text, language, and discourse represent in microcosm the struggle within the Radical community for access to and influence upon the reading public during the early stages of the emergence of a new "mass" audience catered to not by the literary elite but rather by the efforts of independent artisans of the press.

Finally, Steven Jones points out that Radical journals of the later Romantic period (and especially Wooler's *Black Dwarf*) depended heavily upon popular satiric modes that include parodic appropriation, burlesque, transvaluative inversion, (self-)demonization, and the shock effects of disgust and symbolic violence. These journals, Jones argues, participated in a mixed-media discourse that attempted both to appropriate and to subvert the rhetorical and symbolic conventions upon which such dialectical discourse is typically constructed. The result was a paradoxically unstable sort of discourse that is essentially carnivalesque in nature and that formed a potentially anarchic site where the relational or conjectural nature of social (and discursive) categories was opened up to Radical scrutiny. This scrutiny implicitly confronted the threat posed by a volatile class mixture to the apparent purity of binary distinctions like "high" or "low," even as it undermined its own status and authority by casting it as a threatening alterity whose very display in public jeopardized the established order.

Taken together, these essays attest to the truth of Kevin Gilmartin's suggestion that the Radical public sphere was during this remarkable period "both representation *and* practice, both an elusive phenomenon *and* a material body."[24] It was the site of a richly intertextual public discourse in which literature (and the arts generally) bore an often highly context-specific referentiality that is only now becoming fully apparent as we better familiarize ourselves with the day-to-day lives of an English public we are still endeavoring fully to know. As we revise our understanding of what "Romanticism" was (and is), then, we must continue to revise both our interpretations of history and the culturally-conditioned expectations we customarily bring to those acts of interpretation. In seeking to reveal more clearly the nature of the inevitable complications that await us at virtually every site of this revisionist enterprise, the essays that follow at the same time invite us continually to question anew how—and why—we go about our work. Unsettling though it may be, this enterprise cannot but be salutary.

NOTES

1. Marjorie Levinson, "The New Historicism: Back to the Future," *Rethinking Historicism: Critical Readings in Romantic History,* ed. Levinson (Oxford: Basil Blackwell, 1989), p. 50.

2. This trope and its ramifications are central to the insightful reading of bourgeois Radicalism offered by Isaac Kramnick, *Republicanism and Bourgeois Radicalism: Political Ideology in Late Eighteenth-Century England and America* (Ithaca: Cornell University Press, 1990).

3. Previous discussions of Radical culture are too numerous to itemize. They tend to fall into three basic categories (each with many variations). Most familiar is that represented by E. P. Thompson's enormously influential *The Making of the English Working Class* (New York: Vintage, 1963), the Marxist orientation of which links Radicalism to the emergence of an English proletariat and which develops its argument in terms of insistently pointed political, economic, social, or ideological dualisms. The second position is that represented, for instance, by J. G. A. Pocock in works like *Virtue, Commerce, and History* (Cambridge: Cambridge University Press, 1978), where Radical zeal is linked to a reactionary dread of modernity and a nostalgic fondness for classical republican values. Finally, there is the position represented by works like Kramnick's *Republicanism and Bourgeois Radicalism,* which largely rejects the notion of Radicalism as inherently nostalgic and characterizes it instead as an intensely forward-looking, liberal movement grounded in the conviction that "social mobility was possible and the rightful reward for ingenious people of talent and hard work" (p. 4).

4. Jon P. Klancher, *The Making of English Reading Audiences, 1790–1832* (Madison: University of Wisconsin Press, 1987).

5. Marilyn Butler, ed. *Burke, Paine, Godwin, and the Revolution Controversy* (Cambridge: Cambridge University Press, 1984), p. 14.

6. David Worrall, *Radical Culture: Discourse, Resistance and Surveillance, 1790–1820* (London: Harvester Wheatsheaf, 1992), p. 5.

7. Worrall, p. 5.

8. Michael Foot, "Introduction," *People for the People: Radical Ideas and Personalities in British History,* ed. David Rubinstein (London: Ithaca Press, 1973), pp. 14–15.

9. Percy Bysshe Shelley, "On Christianity," *The Prose Works of Percy Bysshe Shelley,* ed. E. B. Murray, 2 vols. (Oxford: Clarendon Press, 1993–) 1:262. Interestingly, Shelley cancelled "seduces" in his manuscript and replaced it with "induces" in describing Jesus's rhetorical strategy.

10. *The Correspondence of Edmund Burke,* ed. Alfred Cobban and Robert A. Smith, 9 vols. (Chicago: University of Chicago Press, 1958–1971), 6:92.

11. Kramnick, p. 32.

12. Jürgen Habermas, *The Structural Transformation of the Public Sphere: An Inquiry into a Category of Bourgeois Society,* trans. Thomas Burger, with Frederick Lawrence (Cambridge, Mass.: MIT Press, 1989), p. xviii.

13. Kevin Gilmartin, "Popular Radicalism and the Public Sphere," *Studies in Romanticsm* 33 (1994): 550–51.

14. Olivia Smith, *The Politics of Language, 1791–1819* (Oxford: Clarendon Press, 1984). The book's orientation is principally linguistic and its focus primarily upon the rhetoric of parliamentary debates, dictionaries, and grammar books—many of them directly relevant to the Radical agenda—rather than upon imaginative literature.

15. Smith, pp. 85, 154–55.

16. Clifford Siskin, *The Historicity of Romantic Discourse* (New York: Oxford University Press, 1988), p. 68.

17. Benedict Anderson, *Imagined Communities: Reflections on the Origin and Spread of Nationalism* (London: Verso, 1983), p. 47.

18. William Stafford, *Socialism, Radicalism, and Nostalgia: Social Criticism in Britain, 1775–1830* (Cambridge: Cambridge University Press, 1987).

19. Iain McCalman, *Radical Underworld: Prophets, Revolutionaries and Pornographers in London, 1795–1840* (Cambridge: Cambridge University Press, 1988).

20. Roger Sales, *English Literature in History, 1780–1830: Pastoral and Politics* (New York: St. Martin's Press, 1983).

21. Michael Scrivener, *Poetry and Reform: Periodical Verse from the English Democratic Press, 1792–1824* (Detroit: Wayne State University Press, 1992).

22. Michael Henry Scrivener, *Radical Shelley: The Philosophical Anarchism and Utopian Thought of Percy Bysshe Shelley* (Princeton: Princeton University Press, 1982).

23. Kevin Gilmartin, *Print Politics: The Press and Radical Opposition in Early Nineteenth-Century England* (Cambridge: Cambridge University Press, 1997).

24. Gilmartin, *Popular Radicalism,* p. 553.

PARANOIA HISTORICIZED:

Legal Fantasy, Social Change, and Satiric Meta-Commentary in the 1794 Treason Trials

THOMAS PFAU

The connexion of intention and the circumstances is plainly of such a nature, as more to depend on the sagacity of the observer, than on the excellence of any rule. The pains taken by the civilians on that subject have not been very fruitful; and the English law writers have, perhaps, as wisely, in a manner abandoned the pursuit. In truth, it seems a wild attempt to lay down any rule for the proof of intention by circumstantial evidence; all the acts of the party; all things that explain or throw light on these acts; all the acts of others relative to the affair, that come to his knowledge, and may influence him; his friendships and enmities, his promises, his threats, the truth of his discourses, the falsehood of his apologies, pretences, and explanations; his looks, his speech; his silence where he was called to speak; every thing which tends to establish the connexion between all these particulars;—every circumstance, precedent, concomitant and subsequent, become parts of circumstantial evidence.

Edmund Burke, Report from the Committee of the House of Commons (1794).

"Symptoms are meaningless traces, their meaning is not discovered, excavated from the hidden depth of the past, but constructed retroactively—the analysis produces the truth; that is, the signifying frame which gives the symptoms their symbolic place and meaning. . . . Thus things which mean nothing all of a sudden signify something but in a quite 'different domain.' What is a 'journey into the future' if not this 'overtaking' by means of which we suppose in advance the presence in the other of a certain knowledge—knowledge about the meaning of our symptoms—what is it, if not the *transference* itself? This knowledge is an illusion, it does not really exist in the other, the other does not really possess it, it is constituted afterwards, through our—the subject's—signifier's working; but it is at the same time a necessary illusion, because we can paradoxically elaborate this knowledge only by means of the illusion that the other already possesses it and that we are only discovering it."

Slavoj Žižek, The Sublime Object of Ideology

OPENING ARGUMENTS

This essay seeks to establish communications among three, structurally related issues. The first one, strictly historical in kind, involves the trial of Thomas Hardy for high treason in 1794 and focuses specifically on how the efforts throughout that trial to legally determine the allegiance between individual and government came to expose a significant theoretical crisis within the larger paradigm of the law. Considerations of the ideological pragmatics served by the formal composition of judicial argument take us to the next, closely related issue, namely, the role of transferential and self-privileging narratives as a model of historical comprehension during the early Romantic period. Both the formal and theoretical significance of the notably paranoid model of narrative here at issue—as well as the epistemological tensions inherent in it—first emerged as a theoretical and disciplinary problem in Freud, specifically in his reading of Daniel Paul Schreber's autobiographical account of a case of paranoia. In his efforts to develop a theoretical formulation for the general mechanism of paranoia, Freud encountered epistemic convolutions remarkably similar to those which produced the reversal of fortune in favor of the defendants during the 1794 treason trials; there the defense was able to expose the prosecution's self-confirming, "constructive," and distinctly narrative modes of inferential legal argumentation. Notwithstanding the local-historical context, the cogent analyses offered by Thomas Erskine's defense during the trial of Thomas Hardy open up the larger issue as to whether there are, can, or even should be "disciplines" and "methods" dedicated to reinterpreting a world axiomatically posited as "symptomatic" and "conspirational." To raise the question in *that* manner is to involve ourselves in the larger problem of "disciplinarity" in the humanities and social sciences today, specifically the problem of a lingering, structural and inextricable complicity between *any* method of interpretation and its proposed "objects" of analysis. To what extent do the currently dominant models of historicist scholarship, materialist analysis, and rhetorical (tropological) reading open up more authentic and historically "durable" vistas on the antagonistic, socio-political and aesthetic scene of Romanticism? Or is, alternatively, the disciplinary, methodological, and theoretical rigor and reflexivity characteristic of such approaches but another, distant echo of Romanticism's ideological dispensation? Do our scholarly and critical engagements of Romanticism constitute an authentic "overcoming" or but another repetition of Romanticism? Are our knowledges of Romanticism objective and abiding or pragmatic and transferential representations of that "past"?

From another perspective, these questions appear to converge with the particular causal accounts and ambitiously plotted narratives by means of which historical subjects—ourselves no less than individuals in England during the 1790s—represent their experiences of a contingent present. As I intend to show, it is precisely in their ambitious efforts at coping with comprehensive ideological transformations, of which they are only ever partially conscious, that specific individuals and communities of interpretation generate those rhetorical symptoms which now, belatedly, solicit our aesthetic and ideological "interest." Thus it is the formal and rhetorical organization of narratives, rather than their professed content, which emerges as the symptomatic material on which pivots our analytic relationship to Romanticism. The formal-rhetorical structure of these accounts *is* their historical content, which is to say, it is the *mode of appearance* of the consciousnesses produced by historical change. Logical and formal tensions and contradictions inherent in the legal narratives and counter-narratives produced, for example, by Sir James Eyre, Sir John Scott, Thomas Erskine, and William Godwin in the context of the 1794 treason trials thus reflect the affective and cognitive disequilibrium of subjectivities at once produced *by* and participating *in* their precarious historical moment. What accounts for their rhetoric being at once cogent *and* symptomatic is the significantly unconscious "knowledge" of their historically contingent and tenuous disposition, a moment of impending recognition to which both sides in the legal conflict at issue respond by revising existing or generating new rhetorical strategies capable of diffusing the ultimately unbearable "knowledge" of their historicity.

What complicates our analyses of the astonishingly productive and imaginative accounts produced by the "disciplines" of the law and psychoanalysis or, rather, what reflects our own irremediable involvement in these disciplines' mode of reasoning is the fact that like these historical communities retroactively produced by the earnest and urgent historicism of contemporary critique, we remain just as caught up in that web of transformations sometimes euphemized as the "present." For we, too, respond to these transformations by mobilizing, revising, and fine-tuning a rhetorical calculus comprised of terms like experience, perception, explanation, generalization, and justification. And in so doing, our methodologically hyper-reflexive modes of historical investigation—still dedicated to the project of defining and administering a distinctive and "functional" body of social and cultural knowledge—ultimately continue to operate as further displaced effects of the ultimate unattainability of such knowledge. The early phase of Romantic culture in England focuses this epistemological dilemma in the peculiar rhetorical form of anxiously prophetic accounts. Late eighteenth-century legal reasoning on treasonous conspiracy and early twentieth-century psychoanalytic reflections on paranoia substantially converge in their representation of historical change, namely, by objectifying such change in the bilateral temporality of narratives at once suspicious and prophetic. In order to compensate for the fundamentally unbearable knowledge of their historical instability, and so as to suspend the consciousness of a non-contradictory and fully aligned "self" and "culture" as irremediably illusory, subjects tend to represent their historical knowledges in prosecutorial form by projecting them as malignant intentions onto their Other. As we shall see, such narrative detours not only produce and effectively control that Other but, in a genuinely Hegelian mode, also enable the agents of representation to produce their historical "truth" without consciously having to "mean" it.

EXHIBIT A

Paranoid Justice: The Law of the Symptom and the Trial of Psychoanalysis in Freud's Reading of D. P. Schreber's Autobiography

Following his close reading of the strange case presented by the onetime superior court justice Daniel Paul Schreber with a characterization of the mechanism of paranoia, Freud made two general observations (of potentially very disruptive impact) on his overall conception of psychoanalysis as a discipline. First, he conceded that "the psychoanalytic investigation of paranoia would be altogether impossible if the patients themselves did not possess the peculiarity of betraying (in distorted form, it is true) precisely those things which other neurotics keep hidden as a secret."[1] Oddly enough, that is, the functional mechanism characterizing paranoia appears preemptive of the work of analysis; indeed, it seems all but structurally cognate with the investigative rigors of psychoanalysis. Sensing that their mode of production of psychological knowledge all too closely resembled the procedures of psychoanalysis, Freud declared cases of paranoia all but impossible to treat. Surely no one knew better than Freud how frequently and with what intensity the emergent "science" of psychoanalysis had been branded as paranoid and obsessional conspiracy against established psychiatry, a pseudo-science discovering ghosts, hidden connections and inscrutable machinations everywhere, devoid of any moral core, precariously cosmopolitan and dissociated in its sensibility; in short, to sum up the prejudice Freud encountered throughout much of his life and career, a Jewish science. For Freud, then, to take up the subject of paranoia in anticipation of his meta-psychological writings was to hazard a precarious reversal whereby paranoia, rather than functioning as the "object" of psychoanalysis, would emerge as the unconfessed origin of that science itself.[2] After all, his readers might well consider the "object" or "issues" of psychoanalysis to be but the effects of an elaborate explanatory practice which, in classically paranoid fashion, continually projects these "objects" (i.e., neuroses) onto its socio-cultural environment as the presumptive cause of its analytic industry. The question thus arises whether psychoanalysis constitutes the legitimate science of the Real *as symptom,* or whether it constitutes but another, as it were complementary symptom which it reproduces transferentially in the analysis of its so-called "cases," lest its authority be discredited and its institution disestablished.

33

Opening his general discussion of the subject, Freud noted that "the distinctive character of paranoia (or of *dementia paranoides*) must be sought . . . in the particular form assumed by the symptoms [*die besondere Erscheinungsform der Symptome*]," insofar as "the mechanism of symptom-formation in paranoia requires that internal perceptions, or feelings, shall be replaced [*ersetzt*] by external perceptions."[3] A close relative of the more general psychic function of displacement, "projection" constitutes "the most striking characteristic of symptom-formation in paranoia," a process in which "an internal perception is suppressed [*unterdrückt*], and, instead [*zum Ersatz*], its content, after undergoing a certain degree of distortion, enters consciousness in the form of an external perception" (*SA*, 189 / *CH*, 169). As Freud argued time and again about all cognates of displacement, their representational structure is organized by the overriding functional aim of "staving off consciousness," which also suggests that the "symptom" signifies only retroactively, compelling the inferential elaboration of a past from the exigencies of the future.[4] As Naomi Schor has argued, the Freudian concept of "displacement" (*Verdrängung*) assumes a point of contact between the consciousness forestalled by the operation of displacement as such and the details furnishing the material conditions for that operation in the first place. Freud's term for this contiguous element linking the psychic operation and its representational focus is *Anlehnung*. In a more general theoretical sense, that word may be translated as "contiguity," an essentially rhetorical device insuring the mediation-by-resemblance of the (traumatic) consciousness forestalled by "displacement" as such with the conscious subjectivity resulting from that operation of "displacement." *Anlehnung,* in other words, enables us to forget the difference between the consciousness that should have been and the consciousness that is, between the virtual and not-yet-recognized import of a past preemptively deferred/displaced into the future (whence it will return as a "symptom") and the specious integrity of a present predicated on that exclusion.

Still, to construe the relationship between the "feeling" displaced and the external, distorted pereception projected in its stead as one of *Anlehnung* is to ignore the substitutive meaning of *Ersatz* and *ersetzen,* the very words chosen by Freud to describe the dynamics of "projection" in cases of paranoia. While he conceives of the paranoiac's projections, his ideas and representations, as *metonymic* traces or marks of contiguity that relate in an essential or consubstantial sense to the repressed arché of the unconscious, *Ersatz* actually suggests that the "projection" mobilizes a fundamentally independent signifier and signifying frame (discourse).[5] Hence, notwithstanding his conceiving of the relationship between feeling and displacement in metonymic terms, Freud had no reason to assume that the representational surfaces of displacement are fully coextensive with, or even authentically related to, the psychic "content" allegedly displaced and, only on the grounds of that unproven assumption, invested by Freud himself with *a priori* authenticity. Not only is the relationship not totalizing, but it constitutes the grounding hypothesis that will guarantee the disciplinary and interpretive coherence of the "science" of psychoanalysis. Freud thus predicated his quasi-legal jurisdiction over the representational excess of the symptom (i.e., detail) on the assumption that the relation between "feeling" and "displacement" is metonymic rather than metaphoric, not a relationship between two heterogeneous orders—the silence of affect and the clamor of representation—but an allegiance between a legitimate (though displaced) authoritative signifier and a subsidiary signifier which has temporarily usurped the timeless office of the unconscious by means of its counterfeit representation. To posit *a priori,* as it were, a relation of "contiguity" (*Anlehnung*) between the truth of the unconscious and the metonymic representations preventing such truth from assuming its office, by emulating its appearance, is ultimately to insure the integrity of a discipline against the contingencies of reading, to shelter an institutionalized mode of epistemic production from the malodor of political and generally ideological expediency. Alternatively, to conceive of the symptom as a "free-floating" detail—a sign of contingent and open interpretive import rather than an integral component within a closed economy of knowledge—is to contest the disciplinary and scientific authority of psychoanalysis altogether, and to challenge its presumptive theoretical and descriptive authority over psychic phenomena. Indeed, to stress this aspect of non-closure in Freud's overall theory is also to suggest, at least implicitly, that in its deterministic attempts at excavating affective potentialities from empirical phenomena, this "discipline"—with all the connotations of *askesis* and *regimen*—represents but a supplemental effect or symptom of an irreducibly antagonistic Real which psychoanalysis continually seeks to dominate through its interpretive procedures. The scenario palpably resembles Lacan's descriptions of the open-ended, detotalized dynamics between patient and analyst who construct each other's subjectivities in a dialectic of speech; the symptom, in other words, produces the identity and epistemic authority of the addressee whom it has framed beforehand.[6]

Sensing that any further inquiry into the figural status of the displaced and the projected consciousness would likely compromise his entire overarching project of a meta-psychological theory, Freud abruptly dropped the question, noting that in any event projection "makes its appearance not only in paranoia but under other psychological conditions as well, and in fact has a regular share assigned to it in our attitude towards the external world. For when we refer the causes of certain sensations to the external world, instead of looking for them (as we do in the case of others) inside ourselves, this normal proceeding [*dieser normale Vorgang*] also deserves to be called projection" (*SA,* 189 / *CH,* 169). Having conceded all along that, contrary to cases of neurosis, paranoia is distinguished by the subject's tendency to betray rather than conceal, to excessively narrate and elaborate highly coherent plots rather than to be cryptic, erratic, and inchoate in its representations, Freud all but suggested that there is, in fact, nothing distinctly pathogenic or structurally unique about the operation called "projection." Indeed, even the otherwise sacrosanct premise of psychoanalysis that all neuroses are ultimately sexual in their aetiology does not appear secure either. With the "sexual aetiology by no means obvious, . . . strikingly prominent features in the causation of paranoia, especially among males, are social humiliations and slights" (*SA,* 183 / *CH,* 162). And so, resolving "to postpone the investigation" of projection and turning instead to "the mechanism of repression," Freud first unfolded the tripartite sequence of repression, subsequently amplified in his 1915 metapsychological essay on that concept. That sequence leads from "fixation" to "repression proper" and terminates in what he called "the most important phase . . . of miscarriage of repression, of irruption [*Durchbruch*], of the return of the repressed."[7] As Freud then suggested, the mechanisms of paranoia are, in fact, nothing but this third phase, the "return" of the repressed, writ large and formally organized as a symptomatic representation, a discursive and often enough conspicuously eloquent substitution (*Ersatz*), which is to say, not a story held to a subsidiary role by the affective powers which it displaces but, on the contrary, a whole new system of empirical perceptions, causal explanations, and ethical justifications.

Exhibit B

Law Mediating Politics: Sir James Eyre's and Sir John Scott's Art of Prosecutorial Narrative in the 1794 Trial

Having, perhaps, offered thus far little more than standard psychoanalytic fare, our review of Freud's session with justice Schreber will now go into recess until we have shown sufficient cause for our hearing yet again a case history that has already undergone plentiful critical review.[8] To show what this structural problem in psychoanalysis has to do with our stated topic, i.e., the representation of historical change, I turn now to the circumstances surrounding the arrest of Hardy, Thelwall, and other members of the London Corresponding Society on 12 May 1794, though these can only be rehearsed with the utmost brevity here. As the more substantial accounts of E. P. Thompson and Albert Goodwin have shown, the trials of Gerrald and Margarot in Scotland—which saw these emissaries of the London Corresponding Society to the Scottish National Convention sentenced to "transportation"— stimulated the corresponding societies in London, Sheffield, Norwich, Liverpool and other provincial towns into unprecedented activity. It was a climate highly charged with visions of political upheaval, as reflected in the particularly strident tone of resolutions adopted by the London Corresponding Society at its general meeting at Chalk Farm on 14 April 1794 under the leadership of John Thelwall. Rejecting the "arbitrary and flagitious proceedings of the court of justiciary in Scotland," the "Tyranny of Courts and Ministers," as well as the "Corruption of dependent Judges," Resolution 5 of that meeting concludes that such abuses "ought to be considered as dissolving entirely the social compact between the English nation and their Governors; and driving them to an immediate appeal to that incontrovertible maxim of eternal justice, *that the safety of the people is the* SUPREME, and in cases of necessity, the ONLY law."[9] Pitt's government responded on Monday, 12 May with a wave of arrests throughout the country that included the apprehension of Thomas Hardy, John Thelwall, John Horne Tooke, and other leaders of the reform movement. A vast number of papers were seized, particularly at Hardy's house. *Habeas corpus* was suspended on 22 May. Broadsheets headed "Treason, Treason, Treason" were sold, and ballad-singers were commissioned by Pitt's administration to strengthen what initially appeared to be widespread public acceptance of the government's charge—namely, that a pervasive and well-engineered conspiracy was being perpetrated by Radicals, millenarian visionaries and misguided reformers, all operating in collusion with French Jacobins, whose atheism and regicide did, after all, appear to constitute proof of the threat now posed to Crown and Constitution in England. In response, "Church and King" mobs attacked houses of the London Corresponding Society's members, including the dwelling of Thomas Hardy, whose wife died, according to the malignant surmise of one London newspaper, "in consequence of being haunted by visions of her dear Tommy's being hanged, drawn, and quartered."[10] Even so, after taking nearly half a year to review and connect all the written records and documents seized from the London Corresponding Society, the prosecution's case continued to look weak, not to say fabricated, for lack of the material or "overt" evidence required to sustain the state's indictment.

Opening the legal proceedings on 2 October with his "charge" to the grand jury, the presiding judge, Sir James Eyre, launched into an extensive discussion of statute 25 Edward III. and the legal principles that, in his view, ought to attend the adjudication of any charge of high treason. Proceeding with a soon familiar tenor of peremptory legal suspicion, Eyre affirmed that the seeming inscrutability of intent, the "wicked imagination of the heart," did not constitute an impasse for the adjudication of the statute in question. To the contrary, it entitled judge and jury alike to approach charges of high treason with extraordinary interpretive latitude: "with respect to the question, whether the fact has relation to the design, so as to constitute an overt act of this species of treason, . . . it is impossible that any certain rule should be laid down for your government; overt acts being in their nature all the possible means which may be used in the prosecution of the end proposed; they can be no otherwise defined, and must remain for ever infinitely various" (*STT,* 202). Eyre's Burkean refusal of "any certain rule" for the "government" of the grand jury, and his prejudicial characterization of evidence in matters of high treason as "infinitely various"—provided a narrative can be produced that will create a persuasive connection between "overt acts" and the legal fact in question—effectively demonstrate that he regarded the adjudication of treason as driven not by the inferences which the evidence might compel on its own, but by the "end proposed" relative to which such evidence is being narrativized as "always-already" imbedded in a holistic criminal "design." Acts represented by a particular prosecutorial narrative as favoring a certain outcome shall, he implied, be taken as evidence that such an (imaginary) outcome was already inherent, *a priori,* in the very intentions and purposes concluded to have produced these acts to begin with.[11] In Eyre's view, then, for the jury to regard empirical facts as a mere "veil, under which is concealed a traitorous conspiracy" (*STT,* 205) is to convert, by default, "matters of fact" into "matter of law" and to conclude that a traitorous intention sponsored these acts, even though such an intention could only be retroactively inferred *from* that act.

Eyre's, and subsequently Sir John Scott's, rhetoric displayed a fundamentally paranoid mode of reasoning, though to refer to it as paranoid is neither to dismiss it as false nor to pathologize it as deluded relative to otherwise unexamined criteria of objective truth and health. On the contrary, the conspirational surfeit in the state's case reveals the high degree of narrative productivity and epistemic coherence achieved *within* the prosecutorial rhetoric, the ultimate product of that effort being a (significantly delayed) consciousness of the inevitability of historical change on the part of its speakers. As Gordon Wood has argued, the term "conspiracy" and its cognates became rapidly more common and amorphous in its social usage during the last two decades of the eighteenth century, a phenomenon lucidly accounted for by Wood as the "last desperate effort to hold men personally and morally accountable for their actions" in a world that was palpably "outrunning man's capacity to explain it in personal terms."[12] In a world where "true motives had to be discovered indirectly, had to be deduced from actions," and where "causes had to be inferred from effects," historical knowledge was being produced in a dialectic manner, with social and political knowledge no longer constituted as a conscious proposition but as a highly mediated, elaborate, and counter-intuitive practice of narrative transference.[13] Which returns us to the 1794 trials and Sir James Eyre's proto-structuralist analysis of the British Constitution, a "constitution . . . so framed, that the imperial crown of the realm is the common centre of the whole; that all traitorous attempts upon any part of it are instantly communicated to that centre, and felt there" (*STT,* 204). In close correlation with his organic constitutional vision, Eyre exhorted the jurors to avail themselves of an organic mode of reasoning by "examin[ing] the evidence . . . very carefully, to sift it to the bottom; to consider every part of it in itself, and as it stands connected with other parts of it; and to draw the conclusion of fact, as to the existence, the nature, and the object of this project of a convention, from the whole" (*STT,* 207). This project of a national convention, comprised of delegates from chapters affiliated with the London Corresponding Society throughout England, was the very core of the government's case against Thomas Hardy and his co-defendants. Could a convention be called without those doing so thereby usurping the role of government? Could reform be demanded without such demands sounding like an ultimatum to the king and thus posing a direct threat to his office and person?

> If a conspiracy to depose or to imprison the king, to get his person into the power of the conspirators, or to procure an invasion of the kingdom, involves it in the compassing and imagining of his death and if steps taken in prosecution of such a conspiracy are rightly deemed overt acts of the treason of imagining and compassing the king's death: need I add, that if it should appear that it has entered into the heart of any man who is a subject of this country, to design, to overthrow the whole government of the country, to pull down and to subvert from its very foundations the British monarchy, that glorious fabric which it has been the work of ages to erect, maintain, and support, which has been cemented with the best blood of our ancestors; to design such a horrible ruin and devastation, which no king could survive, a crime of such a magnitude that no lawgiver in this country hath ever ventured to contemplate it in its whole extent; need I add, I say, that the complication and the enormous extent of such a design will not prevent its being distinctly seen, that the compassing and imagining the death of the king is involved in it, is, in truth, of its very essence. (*STT*, 203–4)

The cumulative thrust of this instance of extended legal parataxis symptomatizes, in its very rhetorical design, how the hermeneutics of suspicion constitutive of the law as discipline objectifies itself rhetorically in distinctly narrative or metonymic forms. Furthermore, it shows how such an infinitely ramified legal syntax reproduces the dominant (essentially Burkean) state-ideology of an organic, intricate ("that glorious fabric"), and—on those grounds— profoundly vulnerable British constitution. Implicit in Eyre's reasoning lies the charge that to contemplate *any* reform under the prevailing constitutional arrangements by necessary consequence—however unintended such consequence may be—will also "subvert from its very foundations the British monarchy" and, by further inference, would have to result in the "death of the king."[14] If Eyre's legal reasoning appears forced, this was quite possibly to compel the Grand Jury to find for a "true bill" of indictment in a case where several legal advisors had already expressed misgivings to the prosecutor, Sir John Scott, about his possibly having "over-charged" the defendants; anxiety about the outcome of the trial ran high in government circles, and many felt that a conviction was more likely to be obtained on the lesser charge of sedition.

Maintaining, nonetheless, the more ambitious charge of high treason, the prosecuting attorney general, Sir John Scott, proceeded to build his case against the defendants by elaborating a plot of deceptively simple design. Focusing on the London Corresponding Society's plans to hold a national convention as his central piece of evidence—the "overt act" that should prove the "principal" fact or criminal intention of high treason itself—Scott reiterated Eyre's organic view of the British Constitution by arguing once more that given the extraordinary connectedness and coherence of Parliament, the laws, the electoral system, and the monarchy, *any* challenge issued to *any* one of these institutions would, by logical extension, instantiate a threat to the office and, by further implication, to the natural person of the king; as Erskine was to exclaim, later in the trial, "how are men to express themselves who desire a constitutional reform?" (*STT,* 936). For Sir John Scott, however, the matter was settled altogether:

> It seems to me to follow, . . . not only that those who conspire to remove the king out of the government altogether, but that those who conspire to remove him, unless he will govern the people according to laws, which are not statutes in Parliament agreed upon, and the laws and customs of the same, or as the head of a government framed and modified by any authority not derived from that Parliament, do conspire to depose him from *that royal state, title, power, and government, which the indictment mentions,* and to subvert and alter the rule and government *now established* in these kingdoms. He *ought not* so to govern—I say he cannot so govern—he is bound to resist such a project at the hazard of all its consequences; he must resist the attempt; resistance necessarily produces deposition, it endangers his life. (*STT,* 245)

Scott's presentation appears curiously unconcerned with the heavily inferential, not to say transferential, logic of his case, a case substantially rooted in the narrative imaginary of the attorney general, who effectively "constructs" the traitorous conspiracy and the legal "fact" of high treason by first outlining a nightmare vision of comprehensive political and social change too sweeping to be consciously entertained as an acceptable political hypothesis by the state and therefore discursively objictified as the *legal* matter of high treason (what Blackstone had called the "highest civil crime"). What produces the crime, in other words, is precisely this narrative act of prosecutorial transference in which the state projects its unbearable knowledge of the British Constitution as historically contingent and temporal—which is to say, its own political unconscious—onto defendants charged with the "crime" of having had that knowledge all along. Yet precisely because the state cannot countenance the "knowledge" of its ideological dispensation as tenuous and changeable, it now mediates this knowledge through a shoemaker, a pamphleteer, and a linguist as the alleged conspirators charged with having *intended* that knowledge in the form of a highly sophisticated and concealed plot. As Erskine's defense pointed out time and again, "a supposed attack upon the king's civil authority has been transmuted, by construction, into a murderous conspiracy against his natural person; in the same manner, and by the same arguments, a conspiracy to overturn that civil authority, by direct force, has again been assimilated, *by farther construction,* to a design to undermine the monarchy by changes wrought through public opinion, enlarging gradually into universal will" (*STT,* 882).

In what proved an inevitably circumstantial case, the prosecution's construction of such a plot hinged on the interpretation of written evidence, specifically on establishing points of contact between resolutions and letters drafted by leading members of the London Corresponding Society and the notorious published writings of John Thelwall and Thomas Paine, writings from which, in an instance of profound irony, the prosecution proceeded to quote and enter into record hundreds of paragraphs. Referring to writings both published and unpublished, and including deliberately inflammatory letters written by government infiltrators of the London Corresponding Society to some of its members and charged against these members—the defendants—as proof of *their* treasonous intentions, Sir John Scott opens his case by stressing "the principles upon which construction is to be given to the written evidence that will be adduced," namely, that "the language they use, ought to be considered according to its obvious sense. If the language admits, and naturally admits, of a double interpretation, it must then be considered according to the nature of the *principle* which that language is calculated to carry into execution" (*STT,* 276). To be a good juror, in other words, is to operate preemptively within the notion of an "obvious sense" or in what, elsewhere, Scott referred to as "the ordinary course of things," and the "common experience of mankind" (*STT,* 254; 256).[15] The prosecution's narrative of a constitution beleaguered by regicidal conspirators had to be established in the jury's collective mind from the outset, lest the evidence submitted to the jury should be taken in good faith and according to its quite possibly innocuous mode of appearance. For Scott, however, the conspirators' "publications are either brought into the world with such a secrecy as baffles all prosecution,—published without names of authors or of printers,—published by contrivance, . . . in the dead of night" or, alternatively, in quantities that confound all government regulation. The point I wish to emphasize here is that such a paranoid mode of argumentation closely corresponds to Freud's (likewise text-based) analysis of paranoia as a conspicuously productive mode of interpretation; not surprisingly, then, Sir John Scott proceeded to engulf the jury in a blizzard of written matter which, as Thomas Erskine wearily noted in his opening statement for the defense, "consumed four days in the reading . . . the unconnected writings of men unknown to one another, upon a hundred different subjects" (*STT,* 891). Only so, the prosecution concluded, would it be possible to overcome the resistance *within* the writing entered into record—"all this handsome language" (*STT,* 296) as Scott characterized it—to yielding up its evidentiary import. In an effort to demonstrate the external existence of a conspiracy (the very imagining of which occasions and formally shapes the prosecutorial art of telling) Scott repeatedly stressed the need for a correspondingly metonymic imagination on the part of the jurors: "each paper must be considered with

41

reference to the context of the same paper, and with reference to the contents of all other papers that form the evidence of the same system, which the paper produced is meant to prove" (*STT,* 276). And what connects papers in "spirit and letter" is inferentially to be taken as evidence of a conspirational connection among all individuals somehow associated with *any one* of these papers, be it as their author, recipient, or merely as a member of the organization in whose name such papers were drafted: "In a conspiracy as widely extended as this is, I shall undoubtedly insist, before you and the Court, that the acts of individuals . . . [and] what they do in reference to these acts is evidence against all of them; and likewise that letters which the persons write relative to the same addresses, are evidence against each of them whether written by the particular individual or no, as being in prosecution of the same purpose" (*STT,* 320).[16] Rosalind's testy affirmation in *As You Like It,* that "Treason is not inherited, my lord; / Or, if we did derive it from our friends, / What's that to me?" (I, 3, lines 59–61), no longer applies.

Exhibit C

Reading the State's Case History: Godwin's and Erskine's Analysis of Prosecutorial Narrative as Social Symptom

In its strenuous resistance to any formal and theoretically motivated constraints on the admissibility and connectibility of evidence, Eyre's "charge to the jury" and Scott's case for the prosecution reproduce a cognate dilemma confronted by Edmund Burke during his attempted impeachment of Warren Hastings, the former governor-general of British India, whose trial extended from 1788 to 1795. Frustrated by six years of compulsive yet inconclusive gathering of evidence and legal maneuvering, Burke made a passionate plea for narrative latitude and challenged the then operative rules of evidence laid down by Blackstone in his *Commentaries,* which prohibited hearsay (albeit with some exceptions) and insisted on the independent integrity of each item of evidence. In particular, Burke objected to what he considered a deliberate fragmentation of his narrative account by the defense counsel, who, at every step of the way, constrained Burke to justify each piece of evidence *separately* as truly pertinent to the crimes alleged. To do so, Burke contended, is "to break to pieces and garble those facts, upon the multitude of which, their combination, and the relation of all component parts to each other, and to the culprit the whole force and virtue of . . . evidence depends."[17] As Alexander Welsh has shown in his lucid exposition of the rise of circumstantial/inferential legal reasoning, to ground the paradigm of criminality and of the judicial process in what Burke calls the "collective effect" of narrative representation is to be "already committed to a closed narrative of human affairs."[18] Fundamentally skeptical with regard to such a "constructive" and highly narrativized paradigm of legal representation, Jeremy Bentham, in his *Rationale of*

Judicial Evidence (1827), exposed the self-privileging logic of such legal procedure, pointing out how in the Burkean model evidence is not so much introduced *into,* as it is produced *by* the prosecution's narrative, and how the distinction between indirect and direct evidence is not one in kind but the result of "their position in the argument." As Bentham put it, "in this way a chain of facts, of any length, may be easily conceived, and chains of different lengths will be frequently exemplified: each such link being, at the same time, with reference to the preceding link, a principal fact, and with reference to a succeeding one, an evidentiary fact."[19] Arguably more concerned with the disciplinary quest for an utterly rational and transparent judicial process, and less with accomplishing a spectacular political feat, Bentham effectively conceded a point of crucial importance during the 1794 treason trials—namely, that evidence is always, as it were categorically, *indirect,* and therefore is to be kept separate from the actual crime, which, inhering solely in the criminal intention, remains inaccessible save by means of a cautious inferential process (excluding, for the sake of argument, the possibility of outright confession).

The question of the prejudicial legal hermeneutics at work in the narrative reshaping of empirical into evidentiary facts, and the consequent representation of the "legal facts" thus produced as fully coincident with the criminal charge itself, significantly occupied the young William Godwin. With his close friend Thomas Holcroft among those named in the indictment against members of the London Corresponding Society, Godwin hastened to London and, in an essay published in the *Morning Chronicle* of 20 October 1794, offered a first and highly trenchant response to Eyre's tendentious "charge," entitled "Cursory Strictures." The essay issued a direct challenge to Eyre's circular, *post hoc ergo propter hoc* mode of legal reasoning by suggesting that such argumentation is itself an anticipation, in the sense of a symptomatic style, of the deeper historical "truth" of those socio-political changes which Eyre and the prosecutor's indictment were charging the corresponding societies with contemplating (in particular, of course, the much-discussed project of a national convention). In questioning whether Eyre's "charge" is "reasoning respecting law, or respecting a state of society" (*STT,* 214), Godwin reversed the charge to the point where the "treason, real or imaginative" is the justice's and, by extension, the state's "own mere creation" (*STT,* 220[20]). He left conspicuously open the question of whether the principle of "constructive treason" set out in the "charge" in "the most unblushing and undisguised manner" (*STT,* 222) amounted to a deliberate narrative distortion of the facts and the law—based on "forced constructions, . . . ambiguous and deceitful words"—or to the more deeply seeded "delusions of a practiced sophister" (*STT,* 220). Godwin brilliantly analyzed Eyre's and the state's legal reasoning as proceeding "not forward from general rules of action to the guilt or innocence of particular men, but backward from actions already performed to the question, whether or no they shall fall under such or such provisions of

43

the law" (*STT*, 219–20). This is the narrative license practiced in Eyre's "Charge," with its continual invention "of a kind of accumulative or constructive evidence, by which many actions, either totally innocent in themselves, or criminal in a much inferior degree, shall, when united amount to treason" (*STT*, 222). For Godwin to expose how a presumptive ideological consensus is being enforced in the seemingly objective and dispassionate explication of the statute on high treason requires him to scan the rhetorical and, more specifically, metonymic compulsions of the state's legal reasoning, a "profusion of fiction, hypothesis, and prejudication . . . to bewilder the imaginations" of the jury and the nation (*STT*, 225). The law's presumptive disciplinary integrity and objectivity reveal its transference of an ideological trauma by continually projecting, "in the nature of an *ex post facto* law" (*STT*, 230), that trauma onto the defendants in the form of a malignant intention. The rhetoric of legal knowledge, the "accumulative" presentation of evidence—the equivalent of *Anlehnung* in Freud's discussion of paranoia and otherwise known as metonymy in narratology and poetics—thus is reconstructed by Godwin's critique as a social symptom:

> There is a figure of speech, of the highest use to a designing and treacherous orator, which has not yet perhaps received a name in the labours of Aristotle, Quintillian, or Farnaby. I would call this figure encroachment. It is a proceeding, by which an affirmation is modestly insinuated at first, accompanied with considerable doubt and qualification; repeated afterwards, unaccompanied with these qualifications; and at last asserted in the most peremptory and arrogant terms. (*STT*, 224)

To be sure, Godwin's fervently rational analysis succeeds in exposing the state's self-confirming narrativization of evidence, exposing the tendency to produce and infuse treasonous intent into otherwise quite possibly innocuous actions of the defendants. And yet, at least in the closely related world of his own political fiction, Godwin appeared to suggest that the prepossession of the Real by increasingly self-confirming disciplinary narratives, the law being only the most prominent of these, is here to stay and cannot be effectively countered except by opposed and preferably more persuasive narratives. As Forester advised Caleb Williams, "make the best story you can for yourself—true, if truth, as I hope, will serve your purpose; but, if not, the most plausible and ingenious you can invent. That is what self-defence requires from every man, where, as it always happens to a man upon his trial, he has the whole world against him, and has his own battle to fight against the world."[21] As James Epstein puts it, "it was not the 'happiness of nations' but the sacred act of narrating the story of a particular nation's happiness that was persuasive."[22] Godwin's "Cursory Strictures," meanwhile, remain in the older, if updated, constitutionalist idiom, a dialogic wrestling for the interpretation of a supposedly venerable and (in his view) perfectable body of legal and political rules.

Quoting, *via* Hume, the words of Strafforde against constructive treason—
"Let us be content with what our fathers left us; not our ambition carry us to
be more learned than they were" (*STT*, 219)—Godwin clearly appealed to the
more traditional sensibility of potential jurors, politicians, and (most importantly) the defense counsel (Erskine, Gibbs). His reasoning thus differed
markedly from the Painite, republican rhetoric that dismissed the constitution
outright as a fiction, as non-existent, and as in need of being written for the
first time.

Substantially cued by Godwin's essay, Erskine's brilliant defense began
with a nine-hour opening argument that not only exhausted all pertinent aspects of the law but, by all accounts, also the jury and spectators. Expanding
on the core-implication of "Cursory Strictures," Erskine again "protests . . .
against all appeals to speculations, concerning *consequences,* when the law
commands us to look only to intentions" (*STT*, 878), "the crime created by
the statute not being the perpetration of any act, but being, in the rigorous
severity of the law, the very contemplation, intention, and contrivance of a
purpose directed to an act" (*STT*, 897). The rhetorical symptom of the state's
paranoid case-history against the defendants analytically captured by Godwin
under the master-trope of "encroachment" was recalled by Erskine as a direct
threat to "the judgment" of a jury "in danger of being swept away into the
fathomless abyss of a thousand volumes" (*STT*, 892). For Erskine it proved of
paramount importance that the jury be put in control over matters of fact and
matters of law—in other words, that it be the jury's responsibility to affirm,
or dispute, whether an alleged "overt fact" bore a provable, direct, and com-
petent relation to the criminal intention alleged; which is to say, to insure
"that the province of the jury over the effect of evidence ought not to be . . .
transferred to the judges, and converted into matter of law" (*STT*, 895). As he
stressed on numerous occasions, "it is the act with the *specific intention,* and
not the act alone which constitutes the charge. The act of conspiring to depose
the King, may indeed be *evidence,* according to circumstances, of an intention
to destroy his natural existence, but never, as a proposition of *law,* can constitute the intention itself.—Where an act is done in pursuance of an intention,
surely the intention must first exist; a man cannot do a thing in fulfilment of
an intention, unless his mind first conceives that intention" (*STT*, 880). What
should matter to the jury, then, is "whether, even if you believed the overt
act, you believe also that it proceeded from a traitorous machination against
the life of the king.—I am only contending that these two beliefs must coincide to establish a verdict of guilty . . . and that the establishment of the overt
act, even if it were established, does not establish the treason against the king's
life, BY A CONSEQUENCE OF LAW" (*ST*, 895–96).[23]

It is, in other words, impossible "to pronounce *as a matter of law,* what
another man intends" (*STT*, 899); or, to quote from *The Rape of Lucrece,*

45

"thoughts are but dreams till their effects be tried" (line 353). It having been affirmed by the defendants themselves that they intended to hold a national convention, it was incumbent upon the jury to ascertain that such plans were contrived as direct expedients *"for the purpose alleged, of assuming all the authority of the state, and in fulfilment of the main intention against the life of the king."* Unless "this double intention" could be verified, Erskine time and again contended, the indictment cannot be maintained. Referring to his successful defense of Lord Gordon in 1782, Erskine recalled how even in cases of pervasive civic unrest "it is the end therefore for which the war is to be levied, and not the conspiracy to do any act which the law considers as a levying of war, that constitutes an overt act of treason" (*STT*, 906); once again, that is, intent must not be inferred retroactively as the presumptive cause for the "overt" material acts, acts which in the Gordon case were far more conspicuous than in the present instance, where

> the conspiracy imputed was not to effect reform by violence, but . . . by pamphlets and speeches, which might produce universal suffrage, which universal suffrage might eat out and destroy aristocracy, which destruction might lead to the fall of monarchy, and, in the end, to the death of the king.—Gentlemen, if the cause were not too serious, I should liken it to the play with which we amuse our children. "This is the cow with the crumpled horn, which gored the dog, that worried the cat, that ate the rat," &c. ending in the "house which Jack built." (*STT*, 906)

Inverting the narrative sequence of the children's rhyme, Erskine satirized the retroactive projection of treasonous intent by the prosecution and, in so doing, exposed the state's case history as simultaneously imaginative and paranoid, exhibiting a logic of retroactive prophecy driven by the desire to reconstruct heterogeneous and unrelated events as the supposedly coherent effects of one hidden cause.[24] To confirm their fears of a comprehensive transformation of the present ideological dispensation, then, the "alarmists" in Pitt's government might, for example, infiltrate the London Corresponding Society with *agents provocateurs* (which they did: Lynham, Watts, and Groves among them).[25] In their persistent efforts at steering the organization toward issuing more Radical resolutions and instigating what, subsequently, might be interpreted in court as the taking of material steps ("overt acts") toward the implementation of a treasonous intent, these *agents* functioned not so much as means of verifying that a past event *had* occurred (i.e., that the treasonous intent had already and independently been conceived by Hardy, Thelwall, and Tooke); rather, they produced what Michael Dummett has analyzed as the more excentric situation of "bring[ing] about an event in order that a *past* should have occurred." The motive behind the state's case, in other words, is not one of empirical verification of the past but the unselfconscious and retroactive positing of *a* past as harboring the kind of pervasive conspiracy that will legitimate the state's reactionary dealings with the ideological dissensions of the present.

Erskine's defense, then, went precisely to the heart of the state's case history, exposing the legal indictment of the state's alleged ideological Other as the paranoid projection into the empirical world of a wish for change entertained on the part of the government and the ruling class themselves. As Erskine noted, the conspirational paradigm proves fundamentally absurd, for it presumes intent and conscious manipulation where such behavior would serve no purpose. Challenging the evidentiary merit of private correspondence among various members of the London Corresponding Society—intercepted or seized by the state upon the arrests of Hardy and Thelwall and alleged to have been written with such ambiguity as to evade the charge of treason (analogous to Blackstone's example of flawed counterfeit)—Erskine commented:

> When the language of the letter, which is branded as ambiguous, thus stares them in the face as an undeniable answer to the charge, they then have recourse to the old refuge of *mala fides;* all this they say is but a cover for hidden treason;—but I ask you, . . . what reason upon earth there is to suppose, that the writers of this letter did not mean what they expressed? . . . [I]f this correspondence was calculated for deception, the deception must have been understood and agreed upon by all parties concerned; for otherwise you have a conspiracy amongst people who are at cross purposes with one another: consequently the conspiracy, if this be a branch of it, is a conspiracy of thousands and thousands, from one end of the kingdom to the other. (*STT,* 935)

To consider the correspondence in question an ideological symptom and to introduce it as legal evidence in the double sense of an "overt act" and as the concealment of the very intention which that act would otherwise confirm is, as Erskine notes, to presuppose that the state and the treasonous conspirators share one and the same imaginary; that is, ideological struggles and the historical transformations evidenced by such struggles do not eventuate between discrete empirical formations, classes, or communities—venerable aristocrats, guileless constitutionalists, and conspiring artisans. On the contrary, the analytic work performed by Erskine's defense on the case history of Sir John Scott suggests that any ideological struggle, objectified as the "legal fact" of allegedly treasonable language, takes the form of a pervasive transference whose discrete rhetorical manifestations project or construct identities subsequently held to be in competition with one another. By rereading the prosecution's case history, Erskine compelled the state, in the words of Lacan, to "recognize [its] unconscious as [its] history," which is to say, to help it "to perfect the contemporary historicization of the facts which have already determined a certain number of the historical 'turning points' in [its] existence" up to the present.[26] In reading the state's case history as the transferential projection of a wish for change entertained on the part of the political establishment,

Erskine's most effective evidence was provided, not suprisingly, by a representative of the state. Calling the Duke of Richmond to the witness stand, Erskine had him read extensively from documents attesting that the Tory administration itself had been contemplating for some twelve years precisely the kind of political and electoral reform now demanded by the corresponding societies.[27] In further questioning this extraordinary and (to make matters worse) perfectly obliging witness, Erskine followed up on his earlier, shrewdly elliptic admonition to the prosecution that they "ought . . . to proceed with more abundant caution, lest they should be surprised by their resentments and their fears" (*STT,* 892).

EXHIBIT D

Imaging the Metastases of Paranoia: Refracted Ideology in the Political Caricatures of Gillray and Sayers, 1791–1796

Erskine's articulate concept of historical change as encompassing the national imaginary as a whole and projecting itself in various transferential rhetorical and institutional manner onto individuals and communities—which is to say, his conception of social process as governed by a structural and necessary (rather than gratuitous and pathogenic) concept of displacement—became more articulated as he advanced his case for the defense. He framed his caveat regarding the government's tendency to rely on the abstract, calculated, and dispassionate enforcement of the law and the state's ideological apparatuses by stressing that these institutions are, ultimately, only capable of directing the current of social affect. They cannot, ultimately, control the nation's complex imaginary altogether:

> In times, when the whole habitable earth is in a state of change and fluctuation,—when deserts are starting up into civilized empires around you,—and when men, no longer slaves to the prejudices of particular countries, much less to the abuses of particular governments, enlist themselves, like the citizens of an enlightened world, into whatever communities in which their civil liberties may be best protected; it can never be for the advantage of this country to prove, that the strict, unextended letter of her laws, is no security to its inhabitants.—On the contrary, when so dangerous a lure is every where holding out to emigration, it will be found to be the wisest policy of Great Britain to set up her happy constitution,—the strict letter of her guardian laws, and the proud condition of equal freedom, which her highest and her lowest subjects ought alike to enjoy; it will be her wisest policy to set up these first of human blessings against those charms of change and novelty which the varying condition of the world is hourly displaying and which may deeply affect the population and prosperity of our country. (*STT,* 967)

Erskine's ardently humane caveat urged the judiciary and the jury to become aware of the acutely transferential dialectic at work in legal and partisan poli-

48

tics throughout the 1790s. Weary of the rapid disciplinary ascendancy and epistemic hegemony of the law as *the* dominant symbolic instrument in the production of political knowledge, Erskine pointed time and again to the treason statute's authority as grounded in the essentially unproven and unprovable hypothesis of criminality—a hypothesis procedurally obscured by the law's peremptory (narrative) claim to exercise jurisdiction over the Real. Erskine's vivid portrayal of a world caught up in constant "change and fluctuation" and a collective psyche forever divided between its allegiance to the indeterminate "blessings" of the present and the elusive "charms of change and novelty" of imaginary futures also organizes the highly performative medium of satiric prints and political caricature during the 1790s and the Romantic period more generally.

Etymologically linked to subterranean, conspirational, and (at least in a colloquial sense) unconscious forces, the "grotesque" style of widely popular satiric representations brilliantly executed by Sayers, Gillray, Rowlandson, and Cruikshank instantiated an interpretive dynamic substantially cognate with Erskine's defense strategy of drawing out the paranoid logic of peremptory suspicion that shaped the state's legal proceedings against the corresponding societies. At the same time, however, the undecidability of Sayer's and Gillray's work in particular also resurrects the aesthetics of excessive fixation and elaboration long identified with the practice and etyomology of *caricare*.[28] Like the narratives of legal suspicion and counter-suspicion examined thus far, the work of satiric prints strains the conventions of *mimesis* by its sheer visual excess or its gratuitous fixation on a particular feature, with the disingenuous implication being that a more profound grasp of the Real will demand a fuller (and thus far unachieved) consideration of that feature and—in thus suspending the mimetic contract of more traditional models of representation—produce a lesser reality, a "nature . . . worse than the actuality."[29] Many of the satiric prints published during the 1790s thus appear to compromise hermeneutic expectations of a public characterized by considerable political and aesthetic literacy; yet they were also viewed with distrust by engravers, satirists, and the first generation of Romantic poets alike on account of their conspicuous political dullness and aesthetic consumerism. What a usually rather obtuse-looking John Bull appeared most in need of was, in the view of Gillray and Sayers (whose position on this issue notably resembles the poetics of the early Blake and Wordsworth), to be visually and viscerally confronted with *the very consciousness of an excess that is the political.* Hence their satiric prints do not so much impose the excess of political image and speech (*a posteriori* as it were) into a socio-political sphere otherwise deemed sober and rational; on the contrary, in relentlessly exposing the obsessive, disingenuous, histrionic, and dissolute mentality of political agents and motifs, Gillray's and Sayer's satiric visions throw into relief the unselfcon-

scious, performative, and deeply antagonistic logic of the "Real," an aggrega-
tion of numerous competing discourses and disciplines.

For our first exhibit, we turn to James Sayer's 12 May 1791 print, titled
"Mr. Burke's Pair of Spectacles for Shortsighted Politicians" (fig. 1). Within
the ovals of Burke's spectacles—themselves an icon in prints of the period—we find Fox (l.) and Sheridan (r.) with conspirational expressions on
their faces. This print, which could be alternatively titled "The World according to Burke," features most of the prominent political figures of the 1790s,
the majority of them depicted in association with their writings. Priestley,
astride a demon sailing through the sky, holds *Priestley on Civil Government.*
Richard Price, just passed away and already rising from the dead, is predictably linked with a quote from his notorious *Discourse on the Love of our
Country.* And a demon is tempting the Duke of Portland with the French
Constitution, inscribed with blunt, Burkean shorthand as "Atheists, Demagogues, the Mob." While the real and the imaginary titles of Thomas Paine
(*Rights of Man* and *Treasonable, Seditious Sermons*) provide the devil with a
seat, Sheridan extinguishes the religious symbol of Anglicanism and Fox pre-
pares to chop down the British Oak. As a condensed visual meta-critique
on the already lurid imagery of Burke's *Reflections,* the print is significantly
complicated by its reflexive attitude to "vision" as empirical beholding and
paranoid projection, respectively. Such reflexivity is guaranteed above all by
the looming presence of Burke's spectacles, disproportionate in scale and utterly filled out with Burke's projections of his enemies. Associated, more than
ever, with rhetorical and ideological excess—which Mary Wollstonecraft,
Catharine Macaulay, Thomas Paine, James Mackintosh, and others had exposed as the very core-affect of his *Reflections*—Burke's peculiarly angled
and uneven mental topography is reconstructed as a Gothic spectacle, a stage
overloaded with countless displacements of personal and political enemies,
allegedly seditious or treasonable writings, and ideological phobias and fixa-
tions. A holographic portrait of Burke's utterly personal and uncompromising
view of good and evil, the print views Burke's mind as a space crowded by
agents teeming with traitorous designs and seemingly devoid of all rational
motivation.

Sayers' print "Thoughts on a Regicide Peace" (14 October 1796) (fig. 2)
shows the now retired and aged Burke asleep in his seat, his head spewing
smoke and flames, as well as assorted lines from *Richard II* (Act 2, i, 40ff.).
It includes a resigned Dutchman (or, rather, frog) on the left, kept in line by
the classic Sansculotte—who, in turn, is being treated to the competing tunes
of the British lion's roar and the latest opera (which begins with a "Peace
Overture"). All these are condensed into the nightmare world that produced
Burke's recent publication and is now being refracted in the print. That is, the
rigid ideological divide that characterizes the waking life and mental reality
of Edmund Burke appears, as it were, an imaginary realm guaranteed by the

50

Fig. 1. James Sayers. *Mr Burke's Pair of Spectacles for Shortsighted Politicians.*
1791.

Fig. 2. James Sayers. *Thoughts on a Regicide Peace.* 1796.

dream or nightmare of its potential and quite possibly imminent disintegration. The central historical reference here (the passport- and olive branch-carrying dove) concerns Malmesbury's mission to negotiate peace with the French Directoire, a mission to which Burke's widely anticipated pamphlet of 19 October 1796 was about to respond. Implicitly construing Burke's harangue as the textual projection of an ideological nightmare, the print dramatizes Burke's unconscious so as to locate the Tories' profound ambivalence regarding any prospects for peace with their revolutionary Other. Burke's dream—which the print holds to be his pamphlet's content—projects such peace as the disastrous prospect of an actual end to the ideological oppositions that support Burke's and England's political reality, indeed, *are* that reality. In its deeply paranoid argumentation—rivalled only by the prosecution's narrative during the 1794 trials—the print presents Burke's pamphlet as an act of unconscious ideological censorship, an attempt to forestall Burke and his Tory allies from becoming conscious of the full extent to which their identity is mediated and thus guaranteed by the stability of their ideological Other.

Hovering somewhere between the neat, albeit richly textured geometry of Hogarth's sketches of London life and the equally centered images of apocalypse and revelation in Blake's *Jerusalem* and *The Four Zoas,* Gillray's "Promis'd Horrors of the French Invasion—or—Forcible Reasons for Negotiating a Regicide Peace" (20 October 1796) (fig. 3) likewise confounds the static ideological opposition with its extremely imbalanced text/image ratio. The print strongly suggests that political reality and the choices to which that reality is preemptively reduced are founded on paranoid speculations about the apocalyptic prospects of a possible, even imminent future. If we recall the satiric prints depicting Burke as the paranoid dreamer of his "Letters on a Regicide Peace" in 1796, the question becomes: is the regicide peace a political choice designed to stave off the real consequence of a French invasion, of an introduction of French atheism and anarchy into England? Or might considerations of such a peace amount to a (perhaps necessary) form of therapy that will spare the Burkes and orthodox Tories of this world from having to retell (like Coleridge's Mariner) the same paranoid vision of social apocalypse over and over again?[30] A related matter is the question of whether they can actually bear to wake up from the dream of an eternal conflict with an eternal Other—or whether they can afford *not* to wake up from it? Is peace being simultaneously explored by some and opposed by other Tories because there is no longer a consensus as to whether continuing to project that revolutionary Other—a projection historically objectified in nearly twenty-two years of uninterrupted warfare against Revolutionary and Napoleonic France— might in the end not turn out to be more exhausting and unbearable than having to wake up from it? Do Burke and Pitt sleep better dreaming that dream or not dreaming it? Will a regicide peace give them a purchase on calmer sleep, and, if so, won't it, by the same token, also bring them closer to

Fig. 3. James Gillray. *Promis'd Horrors of the French Invasion—or—Forcible Reasons for Negotiating a Regicide Peace.* 1796.

those whom they must loathe and continue to represent as the most pernicious threat to everything British? Eventually, these questions all collapse into the issue of the status of this print as representation. Does it send a distinct political message or does it invoke and then confound countless interpretive scenarios so as to render ultimately *any* political message suspect? Does politics in this print constitute an integral component of the Real or does it, however inadvertently, produce discrete textual and visual symptoms of its own intrinsic irreality?

Similarly overdetermined is Gillray's "Opening of the Budget or: John Bull giving his Breeches to save his Bacon" (17 November 1796) (fig. 4), which assesses the issue of seemingly unbearable taxation through two competing projections or models of historical causation. Ronald Paulson's view that Charles James Fox is "the object of the artist's indignation" on account of Fox's ostensibly signalling to the French invasion fleet at Brest, though

Fig. 4. James Gillray. *Opening of the Budget;—or—
John Bull giving his Breeches to save his Bacon.* 1796.

tenable as a partial reading, arguably abridges the print's far more intricate performance.[31] An inversion of Paulson's empirical reading is just as plausible, namely, that the depiction of Fox's treason might constitute a projection, a pseudo-cause floated in public so as to sanction "Master Bill's" (Pitt's) heavy taxation. Is Fox *really* signalling the fleet, and, if so, is his doing so the cause for Pitt's levying heavy taxes in order to defend a predictably dull-looking John Bull from the treasonous Whigs and their French associates? What, after all, are we to make of John Bull's quizzical expression and his obtuse pledge ("—a-coming?—are they?—nay then take all I've got at once") being so monotonously echoed by Pitt and his associates ("Ay! They're a coming . . ."), obviously a reference to taxes levied and collected in unprecedented quantity? If we take Fox's signalling the French fleet as a probable, or at least plausible event, do his treasonous actions seek to prevent the adverse effects of taxes levied on John Bull by a Tory administration continually, though disingenuously, claiming to be in need of revenue for the defense of England against an allegedly impending French invasion? Suspended between these mutually cancelling readings, the print reproduces the competing inter-

55

pretive positions of subjective-pathological and objective-disciplinary paranoia, the latter roughly conforming to what Paul Smith calls a "kind of 'meta-
paranoia' in humanist practice" where the agency of interpretation proves
"unable and/or unwilling to recognize the condition of its own interpretations
as constructs, fictions, imaginary narratives. Such a subject not only 'constructs' the order of reality in which it wants to live, but also has to defend
itself against the otherness of that very world."[32] Similarly bent on exposing
the fictitious and imaginary logic of political practice, Gillray's satiric representation scrambles the cause-effect logic and thus exposes the contingent
ideological perspective from which any given political argumentation and position issues, as well as the mechanisms of resistance built into each such
position against recognizing its irreducibly contingent disposition. Gillray's
holograph of competing and mutually incompatible political causalities thus
proceeds from a first, "innocent" reading of the present political actions
(Pitt's taxation and Fox's treason) as *real* effects of a likewise *real* cause
(the French Revolutionary threat) toward a more reflexive and "experienced"
reading that posits the "Real" (i.e., the antagonisms of English political life)
as the concealment of a more deeply-seated and profoundly imaginary dialectic of Tory fear and Whig desires (invasion) and Tory desires and Whig fears
(taxation). In highlighting the physiological, raw, and self-absorbed interest-
edness of *any* political subject—French or British, Foxite or Pittite, Whig
or Tory, artisan or noble, rural, provincial, or metropolitan—Gillray's satire
invariably undercuts the transcendent, elating, and universalizing habits of
political rhetoric. Consequently, it calls into question the possibility of *any*
significant and organized development of national and cultural life. The undecidability so typically commented upon in discussions of Gillray is generated
by the continued interference between image and text, between situation and
rhetoric, between the contingencies of the body and the face, all of which are
certain to betray the ideological mask of aesthetic and rhetorical form.

Closing Statement

All this brings us back to Freud's case history of superior court judge
Daniel Paul Schreber. By now we can more fully appreciate how what seemed
but another dull and procedure-ridden deposition of that compulsive confessor
might nonetheless result in a surprise vindication; having heard the case,
Freud rendered his psychoanalytic verdict: "not pathogenic." As Freud observed, the prolonged narrative formalization known as "projection"—the
paranoiac's drawn-out staging of the process otherwise known as the "return
of the repressed," characterized by highly imaginative, coherent, and analytical representations of the Real—identifies an ongoing effort to reconstitute an
"inner" affective catastrophe as the spectre of a disastrous, empirical perception. And yet, in his articulate description of schemes supposedly devised to

hasten the utter collapse of a cherished social and cultural order to which the paranoiac retains a strong allegiance—"the end of the world is the projection of [an] inner catastrophe"—he also recovers from this fear. It is precisely in the narrative practice of his projections that the paranoiac recovers that world and his subjectivity, not in any more authentic or definitive sense, to be sure, but undoubtedly in a more functional one; he rebuilds his world,

> not more splendid, it is true, but at least so that he can once more live in it. He builds it up by the work of his delusions. *The delusion-formation, which we take to be a pathological product, is in reality an attempt at recovery, a process of reconstruction.* . . . We may conclude, then, that the process of repression proper consists in a detachment of the libido from people—and things—that were previously loved. It happens silently; we received no intelligence of it, *but can only infer it from subsequent events.* What forces itself so noisily upon our attention is the process of recovery, which undoes the work of repression and brings back the libido again to the people it had abandoned. In paranoia, this process is carried out by the method of projection. It was incorrect of us to say that the perception which was suppressed internally was projected outwards; the truth is rather, as we now see, that what was abolished internally returns from without (*SA,* 193 / *CH,* 173–5; second italics mine).

As Freud realized, the symptom cannot be discounted as the mere (albeit distorted) effect of an authentic (albeit absent) past—what we might call the "genealogical" and conspirational construction of the political unconscious—primarily because the symptom is itself fundamentally dynamic and productive. More crucial yet, with regard to its epistemological status, the symptom precedes both the interpretive efforts of psychoanalysis and the arché of an unconscious primary repression (*Urverdrängung*) which such analysis will subsequently hypostatize as the originary cause of that symptom. Hence, to argue that the subject's narrative practice is a metonymic displacement of a primordial, unconscious cause constitutes a hypothesis fundamentally triggered by the dynamic structure of the symptom itself. What was being explored as the paranoiac's distorted representations by Freud and indicted as the treasonous Other by the state-judiciary in 1794 thus amounts to a hypothetical entity whose existence, as a lucid conspirational threat retroactively anchored in the past, in effect activates the interpretive curiosity and subsequently underwrites the disciplinary authority of psychoanalysis and the law, respectively. For it is only on the grounds of that hypothesis—schematized as a progressive temporal movement leading from past repression to present distortion to future recovery—that the disciplinary mechanisms of legal and psychoanalytic interpretation can proceed to adjudicate the allegedly misrecognized past as harboring potential disaster.

What is systematically obscured by Enlightenment progression from unconscious causes ("feelings") to eccentric, conscious effects ("representation") is precisely the fact that the inference-based ("scientific") consciousness of such a cause, what Freud elsewhere calls *Urverdrängung,* exists only because it was produced by what has thus far been peremptorily classified (and disqualified) as merely a (pathogenic) effect or symptom. Freud's explication of the paranoiac's representation as a pathogenic and exaggerated structure of causal attributions will succeed only by reproducing, albeit in reverse order, the very explanatory mechanisms alleged to characterize the paranoiac himself. Where contradictory affect was projected into symptomatic external perceptions, the work of analysis purports to redress the effects of the operation of displacement itself, namely, by redirecting the subject's articulate representation to the rightful authority of the unconscious which they sought to evade. In a revealing turn of phrase, Freud conceded, however, that we "can only infer [the fact that the process of repression proper consists in a detachment of the libido from people—and things—] from subsequent events." What is institutionally objectified as the ornate, interpretive proceduralism of psychoanalysis and as the post-Blackstonian vision of a rational and coherent body of laws, respectively, and what is embodied by the analyst examining an autobiographical account of paranoia and by a judge and attorney general inferentially reconstructing the existence of a pervasive treasonous conspiracy, *is the consciousness of the symptom; and it is itself the product of that symptom.* The hermeneutic convolution here at issue has been succinctly characterized by Barbara Herrnstein-Smith as "a method for begging the question on a grand scale," which is to say, a "method for proving things, independent of empirical appeals, by demonstrating that they are self-evidently presupposed by what is (supposedly) self-evident."[33] Thus, in a fundamental sense, both the patient's and the analyst's narrative practice prove structurally and functionally cognate; each agent's analytic efforts are stimulated by a quasi-axiomatic sense of distress at the phenomenal organization of a present replete with eccentric and antagonistic empirical determinants, a present which both wish to be unified and non-contradictory. Inasmuch as the antagonistic structure of the present forecasts the future as irreducibly contingent and uncontrollable by *any one* ideological consensus, it is traumatic, unthinkable, except insofar as its heterogeneous determinants can be represented as the symptoms or distorted effects of an as yet undisclosed causality. Unconscious of the motives that shaped their narrative and analytic industriouess, Daniel Paul Schreber, Sir James Eyre, John Scott, and to a significant extent even Freud, thus shaped the institutional and disciplinary structure of legal and psychoanalytic interpretation precisely so as to secure their hypothesis (however unproven and unprovable) of an originary conspirational agency located in a near-ineffable past.

For these disciplines to salvage an embattled present from the presumptive subterranean conspirational machinations ascribed to the past is to fulfill the Enlightenment fantasy of a non-contingent future. To qualify or disqualify *any* representation as pathogenic thus constitutes an irremediably contingent event, a grasping for ideological hegemony whose contingent and self-privi-leging nature no amount of scientific method and no legal rationale can ever overcome. Indeed, such contingency is certain to infect these sciences them-selves, for it was an attempt to stave off the consciousness of an inescapably open and contingent future which produced these sciences in the first place. What appeared to be a symptom of a psycho-pathological affliction clinically referred to as *dementia paranoides* thus turns out to be a quasi-Blakean "con-trary" to the self-confirming conceptual logic of health and disease. The symptom is its own cure and, as such, resists either interpretive delimitation as suffering or recovery. This situation is roughly consistent with the postmodern notion of an irremediably scrambled causality elsewhere elaborated by Slavoj Žižek (cf. epigraph). Under such circumstances it becomes imperative that we abandon the cause/effect model as a valid explanatory mechanism for the adjudication of either psychoanalytic symptoms or legal evidence. For the romance of recovery—taking "recovery" here in the double sense of archeo-logical technique and spiritual restoration—that motivates and structures the practices of analyst and prosecutor alike *was itself produced by their peremp-tory or* (dare we retain the word) *paranoid reading of their respective worlds as a fundamentally antagonistic environment, fraught with hyper-charged de-tails that defy mastery unless they can all be referred back to the plenitude of an originary (if intricately concealed) plot.* To abandon the metonymic para-digm of *Anlehnung*—the phenomenalism of a material correspondence be-tween the unconscious and the projection which, for Freud, constitutes the final phase of repression—is to enter into an open economy of interpretation capable only of relating one order of effects to another and in which symptom and signifier are terms at once interchangeable and of equal validity, signifiers whose tropological status no longer differs in any *a prioristic* sense from any other set of significations.

What the 1794 trials exhibit "in progress," as it were, is the rapid ascen-dancy of speculative and theoretical argument *as a social and political prac-tice in its own right,* the most significant entailment of which may well be the claim of legal, political, and esthetic representations to an interpretive monop-oly over the Real. Burke's, Eyre's, and Scott's preference was decidedly in favor of cultivating the rhetorical integrity of their narrative presentation, rather than the integrity of their evidentiary material. That is, they conceived of narrative representation as a holistic, autonomous, and essentially perform-ative mode of epistemic production that progressively unfolds a chain of cir-cumstances in which each new piece of discrete evidence is instantly confirmed by all those narrative claims made earlier; having been authenti-cated by the narrative already in place, the production makes its own contribu-tion as a legitimate element of the narrative itself. The precarious evidentiary logic undergirding the legal reasoning on the statute of high treason and at the very heart of Burke's passionate plea for narrative license can thus be seen as but one reflex of a far more capacious transformation in the mode of epistemological productivity. Theory, it can be argued, emerges increasingly as a constitutively imaginative practice, a mode of discursive production that is at once self-launching, self-confirming, and intrinsically narrative in kind. It is also preemptively suspicious of any future threat to its claims for *a priori* autonomy—so much so that it has, in effect, made it its very business to head off or prepossess such potential encroachments by pathologizing the Real in the forms of legal, epistemological, and psychoanalytic suspicions.[34] As the Romantic texts and contexts examined here suggest, the only discourse to *defend* us against the traumatic recognition of an irreducibly contingent future is that of a "pure" theory unrelentingly enacting the dream of our having been all along awake, lucid, and reflexive. As Novalis was to put it, somewhat more cautiously, in one of his poetic/philosophical aphorisms of 1798: "We are close to awakening when we dream that we are dreaming."[35]

NOTES

For their encouraging and helpful comments on earlier drafts of this essay I wish to thank my colleague David Aers, as well as Nicholas Roe, Jerrold Hogle, and the highly engaged and probing gathering of students and faculty at Cornell University to whom I was able to present parts of this argument in Spring 1995.

1. Freud, *Three Case Histories* (New York: Macmillan, 1963), p. 104.

2. As Peter Gay has argued, Freud's work on the Schreber case was notably accompanied by an intense consciousness of his own transferences, particularly those referring back to Fliess; *Freud: A Life for Our Time* (New York: Norton, 1988), pp. 278–80. Gay's account does not address, however, the structural resemblance of the work of projection to that of analysis.

3. Sigmund Freud, *Studienausgabe* (Frankfurt: Fischer, 1973), 7:183, 186. The English text here quoted follows Sigmund Freud, *Three Case Histories,* pp. 161, 166. Subsequent citations will be parenthetical, with *SA* referring to the German and *CH* referring to the English text of this case history.

4. The phrase is from Freud's essay on repression: "Psychoanalytic experience of the transference neuroses, moreover, forces us to the conclusion that repression is not a defence-mechanism present from the very beginning, and that it cannot occur until a sharp distinction has been established between what is conscious and what is unconscious: that *the essence of repression lies simply in the function of rejecting and keeping something out of consciousness*"; Freud, *General Psychological Theory* (New York: Macmillan, 1963), p. 105; the German original is more categorical, speaking not of "keeping *something* out of consciousness" but rather of the "exclusion and rejection of consciousness" per se (*"daß ihr Wesen nur in der Abweisung und Fernhaltung vom Bewußten besteht"*). *SA,* 3:108.

5. As Naomi Schor puts it, "if the detail is not seen as referring metonymically back to a whole from which it has become detached, but rather as substituting metaphorically for another detail which it resembles, then we move from the typically Freudian valorization of totalization . . . to a notion of a detotalized detail, which would

make Freud a precursor of modernity, even of the post-modern"; *Reading in Detail: Aesthetics and the Feminine* (New York: Routledge, 1987), p. 72.

6. As Slavoj Žižek remarks, "the symptom can not only be interpreted but is, so to speak, already formed with an eye to its interpretation: it is addressed to the big Other presumed to contain its meaning. In other words, there is no symptom without its addressee . . . without transference, without the position of some subject presumed to know its meaning"; *The Sublime Object of Ideology* (New York: Verso, 1989), p. 73.

7. *SA,* 3:190–91; *General Psychological Theory,* pp. 170–71.

8. See Han Israëls, *Schreber: Father and Son* (New York: International Universities Press, 1989); and "The Schreber Case: Psychoanalytic Profile of a Paranoid Personality," in *Freud and His Patients,* ed. Mark Kanzer and Jules Glenn (New York: J. Aronson, 1980).

9. Quoted in Albert Goodwin, *The Friends of Liberty: The English Democratic Movement in the Age of the French Revolution* (Cambridge, Mass.: Harvard University Press, 1979), p. 329. For the developments of 1793–1794, see Goodwin, pp. 307–58, and E. P. Thompson, *The Making of the English Working Class* (New York: Vintage, 1966), pp. 102–85. See also Olivia Smith, *The Politics of Language, 1791–1819* (New York: Oxford University Press, 1984), pp. 68–109; and, on the general shape of British intellectual politics during the 1790s, David Simpson, *Romanticism, Nationalism, and the Revolt against Theory* (Chicago: University of Chicago Press, 1993), pp. 40–63. A broad outline of legal developments during the 1790s has been offered by Clive Emsley, "Repression, 'terror' and the rule of law in England during the decade of the French Revolution," *English Historical Review* 100 (1985): 801–25.

10. See Thompson, *The Making of the English Working Class,* pp. 132–33; Goodwin, *The Friends of Liberty,* pp. 332–37. To a significant extent, however, the evidence produced at the trial was either ludicrously unconnected with the crime charged or, in the case of Robert Watt and "Citizen" Groves, had been manufactured by government spies and *agents provocateurs* who, in a development of poignant irony, were subsequently called as witnesses by both the prosecution and the defense. See also Mary Thale, *Selections from the Papers of the London Corresponding Society* (Cambridge: Cambridge University Press, 1983).

11. Eyre was to go so far as to abandon the already questionable practice of retroactively inferring treasonous intent and, in its stead, to reason in rather mechanical fashion from the presumptive consequence of acts back to statutes; as regards plans by the London Corresponding Society for a national convention, Eyre thus holds that "the government cannot be said to exist, if the functions of legislation are usurped for a moment; and it then becomes of little consequence indeed, that the original conspirators, perhaps, had only meditated a plan of moderate reform: it is *in the nature of things,* that the power should go out of their hands, and be beyond their control" (*STT,* 208).

12. "Conspiracy and the Paranoid Style: Causality and Deceit in the Eighteenth Century," *William & Mary Quarterly* 39 (1982): 401–41; quote from p. 411. The replication of necessarily and (once again) by no means *simply* paranoid modes of socio-historical explanation during the 1790s within the scene of contemporary criticism has been very lucidly discussed by Paul Smith, *Discerning the Subject* (Minneapolis: University of Minnesota Press, 1988), pp. 83–99. I shall return to this complex figure of interpretation below.

13. Gordon Wood, "Conspiracy and the Paranoid Style," p. 423. Both the epigraph to this essay by Slavoj Žižek and the analytic writings of contemporary philosopher Michael Dummett apply here; see especially Dummett's essay entitled "Can an Effect Precede Its Cause?" in *Truth and Other Enigmas* (Cambridge, Mass.: Harvard University Press, 1978) and his example, in that essay, of the opening shot in billiards and the logical possibilities of representing that moment's dissemination of force into structured configurations of increased complexity *in reverse;* pp. 321, 324.

14. The bill of indictment, found to be a true one by the grand jury of Middlesex and consequently produced as the government's charge at the trial expressly frames Eyre's metonymic legal argumentation, viz. "to subvert and alter the legislature rule and government now duly and happily established within this kingdom of Great Britain . . . [and] to cause and procure a convention and meeting of divers subjects of our said lord the king to be assembled and held within this kingdom with intent and in order that the persons to be assembled at such convention and meeting should and might wickedly and traitorously without and in defiance of the authority and against the will of the parliament of this kingdom subvert and alter and cause to be subverted and altered the legislature rule . . ." (*STT,* 231–32).

15. As Barbara Herrnstein-Smith puts it, "the extent to which a circular argument is persuasive *for some audience* seems to depend on, among other things, the extent to which the concepts and conceptual syntax that the argument 'begs'—that is, employs and takes for granted—are also taken for granted by that particular audience"; "Resistance and Belief: A Symmetrical Account," *Critical Inquiry* 18 (1991): 125–39; quote from p. 130.

16. As Erskine insisted, during his otherwise minimal cross-examination and in one of very few direct challenges to the prosecution, "upon the evidence that is before the Court, every man who has been a member of these Corresponding Societies; who has been a member of this Constitutional Society; every man who has been connected with those acts, if the acts constitute a conspiracy to subvert the government, is liable to be put into the same situation with Mr. Hardy; and any thing that is written by any one person belonging to either of these societies would be equally evidence against him" (*STT,* 472).

17. Quoted in Alexander Welsh, *Strong Representations* (Baltimore: Johns Hopkins University Press, 1992), p. 34.

18. Welsh, *Strong Representations,* pp. 34–5.

19. Quoted in Welsh, *Strong Representations,* p. 37.

20. Evidently by a mistake of the printer, Howell's *State Trials,* vol. 24, repeats both pages 219 and 220, albeit with different text columns. The quote here is from the "first" page 220.

21. *Caleb Williams* (London: Oxford University Press, 1970), pp. 162–63.

22. James Epstein, *Radical Expression: Political Language, Ritual, and Symbol in England, 1790–1850* (New York: Oxford University Press, 1994), p. 31.

23. See also Erskine's equally apodictic defense of intentionalism as the exclusive source of all crime and his subsequent contention that the jury alone, and no amount of legal authority and reasoning, may adjudicate the relationship between the criminal intention alleged and the overt acts adduced in support of that charge; *Speeches of Lord Erskine,* ed. James L. High, 3 vols. (Chicago: Callaghan & Co., 1876), 1:283, 290.

24. The situation recalls Michael Dummett's recent analytic work on causality; referring to the possibility of taking a film of a game of billiards and repeatedly playing it in reverse, Dummett notes that it would be possible to "give a quasi-causal account of the normal behaviour of billiard balls. The balls, we should say, start moving at moments, in direction and with velocities such that one of them *will* strike the cue with the appropriate force and in the appropriate direction." It might thus be sensible, under certain circumstances, "to bring about the occurrence of some event with the intention of guaranteeing the occurrence of a previous event," he notes, such as "to set an alarm-clock one evening with the intention that someone might wake up the following morning before the alarm went off"; "Can an Effect Precede Its Cause?" pp. 324–25.

25. See Mary Thale, *Selections from the Papers of the London Corresponding Society.*

26. *Speech and Language in Psychoanalysis,* trans. and ed. Anthony Wilden (Baltimore: Johns Hopkins University Press, 1968), p. 23. Or, as Paul Smith puts it, the task of paranoid narrative is to construct "a fixed and reliable 'subject' who will in a sense endorse or stand behind the fictions as their guarantor. That 'subject' . . . controls the intention and interpretation of the world it has created in such a way as both to protect its own coherence and autonomy and also to fulfill the juridical demands of the symbolic system in which the utterances may be understood"; *Discerning the Subject,* p. 98.

27. Godwin's recollection that "twelve or fourteen years ago, many of his majesty's present ministers were deeply engaged in a project of this nature [viz. of constitutional reform]" (*STT,* 221) may have offered a significant cue to Erskine's defense strategy at the trial; not surprisingly, the decision to call the Duke of Richmond set off the trial's most intense and hard-fought debate regarding the admissibility of evidence (*STT,* 1048 ff.). As soon became apparent, this debate was truly paradigmatic in kind, for at issue was the general matter of what constitutes "proper" evidence in a trial where the charge is merely an "unconsummated intention" as Erskine had expressed it; put differently, the question at issue was how far to enlarge the sphere of "circumstantiality," and on this count the prosecution was in a weak position, since its strategy had been all along to bury the jury in a blizzard of discrete and, in the view of many observers, unconnected shreds of letters, pamphlets, and reports of hearsay. Having thus inflated the pool of eligible materials from the outset, it now proved all but impossible to hold the defense to a narrower range of evidence (see *STT,* 1075, 1081).

28. On the association between the grotesque and the unconscious, the etymological provenance of *caricare,* and generally on the visual excess of engraved and illuminated satiric prints with their characteristically imbalanced text / image ratio, see Ronald Paulson, *Representations of Revolution* (New Haven: Yale University Press, 1988), pp. 168–211.

29. Paulson, *Representations of Revolution,* p. 182.

30. For another brief discussion of this print, see Marcus Wood, *Radical Satire and Print Culture, 1790–1822* (Oxford: Clarendon Press, 1994), pp. 60–62; regretably, Wood's book came to my attention too late to be given due consideration relative to my own argument.

31. *Representations of Revolution,* p. 185.

32. *Discerning the Subject,* p. 97.

33. "Belief and Resistance: A Symmetrical Account," p. 128.

34. To call on but one instance of this tendency, Kant's transformation of traditional epistemology, what in Kant's theoretical architectonics insures the transcendental synthesis—which is to say the coherence of the Kantian subject *per se*—is the "schematism," identified by Kant as the source of all imaginary activity, a "product and, as it were, a monogram, of pure *a priori* imagination." Further characterizing this conceptual axiom, and simultaneously vesting in it all justification of his epistemological argument, Kant describes the transcendental schema "in its application to appearances and their mere form . . . [as] an art concealed in the depth of the human soul, whose real modes of activity nature is hardly likely ever to allow us to uncover, and to have open to our gaze." Kant's theoretical procedure replicates the eighteenth century's pervasive reliance on an essentially self-privileging concept of the passions, here potentiated into a "transcendental" theory of "pure intuition" (*reine Anschauung*) where all justifications are internal and sanctioned by what Kant sometimes calls the schematism or, in *The Critique of Judgment,* refers to as "spontaneity." As Stanley Rosen puts it, Kant "*constructs* theoretical entities that serve his purpose. There is no independent confirmation of Kant's hypothesis, however, since what counts as experience, and also as confirmation, is created by our acceptance of the hypothesis"; *Hermeneutics as Politics* (New York: Cambridge University Press, 1987), p. 25.

35. *Blüthenstaub,* in *Werke, Tagebücher und Briefe,* ed. Hans-Joachim Mähl (Munich: Hanser, 1978), p. 232 (translation mine).

THE OTHER FRAUD:

Coleridge's The Plot Discovered *and the Rhetoric of Political Discourse*

VICTORIA MYERS

From the time that Coleridge took up public speaking and journalistic writing in the 1790s, he showed a consciousness of rhetorical technique as applied to these media that could be called systematic and ideological.[1] In so doing, he used the idiom which was current, sounding his voice upon the rhetorical consciousness of those already practicing the art of polemic.[2] It was during this time that accusations of insincerity, pretense, imposture, and fraud reached greatest intensity and metaphorical scope. Such accusations were launched from both sides of the political divide—ministerial writers against Jacobin "patriots" as well as Radical and Whig journalists against the ministerial "hacks"—and Coleridge had the task of negotiating a position among the very real dangers these accusations posed in an environment of prosecutions against the press, of treason trials, and of parliamentary attacks upon the constitution.

This essay proposes that there was an active contest during the 1790s for control over the accusation of "fraud," as there was over the meaning of such terms as "nature," "constitution," and "rights." The word "fraud" and like terms often occur in contexts in which speakers or writers invoke Lockean (or apparently Lockean) premises regarding the desiderata of communication and partake of Lockean apprehensions about the danger of rhetoric to civil liberty, especially distrust of nonliteral language. Even writers hostile to the more Radical interpretations of Locke's *Two Treatises on Government* and suspicious of the religious implications of his *Essay concerning Human Understanding* inscribed their polemic upon Locke's terms of evaluation: references to clarity, plainness, obscurity, ambiguity, and equivocation abound. Moreover, apparently backed by Locke's standards, writers of various political persuasions developed techniques for prying the cover off political speech acts, thereby undermining politically motivated claims to sincerity and authority. This essay attempts to elicit the complexity of this technique as it passes from hand to hand and to show how Coleridge joined in the general contest. I have placed my discussion of Coleridge at the end of what looks like a disproportionate introduction in order to develop a verbal environment sufficiently complex to gloss the terms and modes of argument in his 1795 essay *The Plot Discovered*, thereby revealing not only its relation to the political rhetoric of the day, but also the distinct solution he offered to the war of words.

In the state trials of late 1794, extensively reported in the daily papers, Coleridge could observe the perennial contest for property in speech acts take a dangerous turn.[3] The presence of spies and informers at meetings of the reform societies had already induced members to moderate their references to Paineite doctrines, and the prosecution of Paine's *Rights of Man* in December 1792, and of a number of Radical publishers thereafter, warned the press to be circumspect in its criticism of government.[4] What I am speaking of with reference to the state trials, however, is something different; the strategy used in prosecuting Thomas Hardy, John Horne Tooke, and John Thelwall for treason threatened not simply to exclude certain kinds of utterances from public discourse, but to subject utterances to violent interpretation—in Bakhtin's terms, to colonize and subvert them.

In his opening remarks at the trial of Thomas Hardy, the attorney general, Sir John Scott (later Lord Eldon), assured the jury of his intention to proceed plainly and unequivocally, it being no less necessary to protect "the security of the subject" than to defend the nation and the king "that the crime of high treason should not be indeterminate, that it should not be unascertained, or undefined, either in the law itself, or in the construction to be made of that law" (Erskine 2.301).[5] His criteria here seem unimpeachably Lockean. Locke linked "obscurity" and "ambiguity" with motives of "ambition" and party interest (3.11.7); conversely, he connected "plain and direct" language with political honesty. He saw equivocation, affected obscurity, and departing from conventional meanings as signs of political corruption (3.10.5–12). Even commentaries on authoritative texts can prove to be instruments of political maneuvering, for they often render obscure what was plain and thus "unsettle People's Rights" (3.10.13).[6] Hence, the attorney general's adherence to Lockean standards is evident in his approving quotation of Matthew Hale's judgment:

"... how dangerous it is to depart from the letter of that statute [25 Edward III], and to multiply and enhance crimes into treason by ambiguous and general words ... and ... how dangerous it is by construction and analogy to make treasons, where the letter of the law has not done it, for such a method admits of no limits

66

or bounds, but runs as far as the wit and invention of accusers, and the odiousness and detestation of persons accused, will carry men." (Erskine 2.308–9)

Apparently, so thorough was his allegiance to such standards that his strategy against the accused was completely guided by them. He described the people of England as overwhelmingly loyal to the government and constitution; hence, he said, the conspirators needed to use duplicity and ambiguity to seduce them, "taking advantage of well-meaning ignorance, under *pretence* of instructing it" (Erskine 2.345; my emphasis). He accused the supposed conspirators not merely of indirection, but of an elaborate and fraudulent equivocation, of using one utterance to convey two meanings, each to a different audience, a band of Radical conspirators on the one hand and well-meaning reformers on the other:

> To them [the latter], therefore, the form of the government was not spoken of in terms which they might understand to be a condemnation of it, though they were really such, but by making use of general expressions, such as obtaining 'a full and fair representation of the people in Parliament' . . . terms the same in their expression, certainly the same in their import, as those, which were used in every act which passed in this country during the time of the Commonwealth . . . ; by these means and artifices they attempted to engage in their service the physical strength of men, who might not and did not discover the real nature of the plan. (Erskine 2.345–46)

This manner of speech act analysis pervaded the attorney general's entire strategy in the trial.[7] Assuming, albeit rightly, that the interpretation of a speech act requires knowledge of the appropriate context, the attorney general read certain phrases that appear merely to refer to reform as covert allusions to an esoteric Radical vocabulary held in common by Levellers, Jacobins, and Paineites. The prosecution assumed that the context was bifurcated, such that an utterance could be made against the background of one set of contextual items (e.g., the vocabulary of natural rights and French conventions), but interpreted, and uttered with the intention of its being interpreted, against a different background (e.g., the vocabulary of reforming rotten boroughs). An audience can be duped if it does not perceive the real background, and it is the critic's task to help that audience by identifying the appropriate context. This assumption often lent to the prosecution's discourse the appearance of a commentary, an alternation between quotation from the letters and speeches of members of the reform societies and description of or ironical allusion to contextual information. This procedure made the speech acts of the accused appear pervasively equivocal and thus turned equivocation into a premeditated and complex strategy of usurpation. At the same time, the procedure effected a usurpation itself, elevating the importance of the eavesdropper in interpretation, and it paradoxically impugned the sufficiency of the speaker's speech and of the hearer's understanding to make the speech act what it essentially (and legally) was.

Whether the attorney general is a sincere Lockean in his interpretive principles may be questioned, therefore, for as his introduction continued he betrayed more and more his strong concern with accusations made outside the courtroom (most notably by William Godwin) that the government intended to broadly construe the law and construct the reformers' activities into treason.[8] His assurances thus were motivated by a desire to dissociate his procedure from this accusation; but it is an accusation he did not entirely honor, for he ended up sneering at his opposition: "(what is asserted out of a court of justice no man pays much attention to)" (Erskine 2.325). He dutifully distinguished between the accusation of treason (compassing the death of the king) and overt acts which prove the accusation (such as conspiring to depose or imprison the king), and between these and acts which could only be constructed into treason (levying war against the king), since they do not necessarily imply compassing the death of the king. However, no sooner did he exculpate himself from indulging in the latter strategy than he betrayed a desire to reintroduce it: ". . . offences not so personal as those enumerated [under overt acts] fall within the same rule, as having a tendency to the same fatal end . . ." (Erskine 2.318–19). Thus he introduced an equivocation on the term "overt acts." For him, the reform societies' plan to call a "convention" to propose the reform of parliamentary representation resonated with reference to the French Convention and the subsequent deposition and execution of the king. By means of this strategy, he apparently kept within the strict meaning of "overt act," asserting that a convention called to depose the king is clearly an overt act that proves compassing the king's death. At the same time he gave the term great latitude, laboring to show that a convention called to reform really is a convention to depose, on grounds that to change the representation in Parliament from outside is to usurp Parliamentary authority—which in turn is to force the king into violent opposition to protect the constitution, a necessary act of opposition that might endanger his life (Erskine 2.320–21, 327–30).

The counsel for the defense, Thomas Erskine, rescued the accused traitors from the charge of conspiratorial equivocation by ridiculing the attorney general's supposed contextual readings:

> When the language of the letter, which is branded as ambiguous, thus stares them in the face as an undeniable answer to the charge, they then have recourse to the old refuge of *mala fides;* all this they say is but a cover for hidden treason. But I ask you, Gentlemen, in the name of God, and as fair and honest men, what reason upon earth there is to suppose, that the writers of this letter did not mean what they expressed? Are you to presume . . . that men write with duplicity in their most confidential correspondence, even to those with whom they are confederated? (Erskine 3.114)

The essential flaw in the prosecution's analysis—and the subject of ridicule by Erskine—is his supposing that the audience members were ignorant of the purport of the underlying speech act (indeed that there was an *underlying* speech act) and yet could act upon it—in short, that the writers chose language their hearers would not understand, in order to persuade them to perform acts they would reject. To Erskine this alternative is *prima facie* absurd (Erskine 3.114).

Erskine in effect maintained there is a difference between history and fiction, and that the attorney general's confusing the two constitutes an effort to introduce a new and unjust mode of interpretation. By means of his commentary and his dramatic sequencing of letters, the attorney general in a sense shifted the speech act, making it a figure for its real meaning, but (Erskine implied) the listeners could not perform a metaphor. Were the prosecution's representation of their speech act accurate, Erskine contended, the conspirators could not get the audience to perform precisely the act they envision: they would perform some other act. Between speaker and hearer the context of interpretation cannot differ.[9] Hence, his strategy called for reasserting the literal meanings of utterances, re-establishing the intended context, and interpreting the relevant law (25 Edward III) literally and narrowly. In the process, he effectually turned back upon the prosecution the accusation of fraud: by arranging letters, introducing innuendo, and giving an unwonted breadth to the law, they did a violence to the intentions of the accused and "constructed" a treason that was not there. He was successful in saving his clients from judicial condemnation, yet as Windham's phrase "acquitted felons" indicates, not from moral suspicion.[10] The legal system validated Erskine's presuppositions about language, but the assaults on those presuppositions did not cease.

The parliamentary debates in November and December 1795 on the Two Bills (the Treasonable Practices Bill and the Seditious Meetings Bill) dramatized the extent to which Erskine's victory *was* incomplete.[11] The accusation of fraud—and more especially the accusation of equivocation and abandoning customary modes of interpretation—was a commonplace in these debates. In the debate in the House of Lords on the Treasonable Practices Bill, the Earl of Lauderdale accused the bill's sponsors of shifting the meaning of treason and therefore of the constitution: "By the bill, a variety of new crimes and new treasons were introduced into the criminal code of the country; and by new framing the words and phrases to describe those crimes, the bill held out a dangerous innovation upon the constitution" (*PH,* 245–46).[12] Lauderdale invoked Locke's well-known hostility to unnecessary coinages as an obfuscating ploy to wrest from people their traditional rights. Lord Grenville attempted to free the bill from the accusation of subversive innovation by identifying it with precedent: "The bill . . . was in a great measure copied from the act in the reign of queen Elizabeth, and the act of Charles 2nd . . ." (*PH,* 245). In answer, the opposition contested the ministers' choice of precedent: the treason laws under Elizabeth and Charles II were excessive; that cannot be precedent which is out of line with the moderate main tradition flowing from 25 Edward III.

The accusation of excess in the bill implies the judgment that this bill is not the speech act it purports to be, and the ministers' indecision about what sort of bill to call it seems to corroborate suspicion of deception. At times they described it as if it were a "declaratory act"; at others they described it as a "temporary act." The opposition perceived that both terms, meant to palliate the severity of the bill, were being used vaguely and equivocally. Lord Grenville attempted to justify calling the act declaratory when he said: ". . . it having been found that difficulties sometimes arose in the construction of the acts now in force, it was intended by the variations from them in this bill, to ascertain precisely the meaning which was to be given to the whole of the treason laws" (*PH*, 248). The Earl of Lauderdale responded by impugning the Ministers' supposed intention merely to clarify, for the very reason that they introduced vague and unascertained language (*PH*, 251). The real intention, Lauderdale and his ally the Duke of Bedford insisted, derives from the government's failure in prosecuting Thomas Hardy, John Horne Tooke, and John Thelwall the previous year: they wanted to create new crimes so as to make it easier to prosecute the reform societies.

Nowhere is this suspicion more evident than in the anti-ministerial demand for proof of the connection between the activities of the reform societies and the attack on the king on the first day of Parliament 1795, the incident which grounded the ministers' entire case for the bill. Their demand for "a mass of evidence" and "a chain of reasoning" (*PH*, 249, 254) depended on the essential Lockean authorities of direct observation, credible witnesses and connected reasoning which must underpin all probable assertions.[13] They implied that a bill is a kind of speech act distinct from a law. It is not yet a performative of the kind exhibited in law, because its utterance cannot bring into effect what it utters.[14] It is rather a proposal to make such a performative. Before it can become a law, it must attain assent. The opposition contended that assent cannot rightly be given until the assertions which justify the bill are themselves justified by the conditions which usually support assertions, namely evidence. Apparently both sides subscribed to the criterion that truth must somehow be the foundation of legislative acts. Lord Grenville answered the demand, not by denying the need for facts but by claiming the facts were "notorious" (*PH*, 247–48). However, the opposition branded this hearsay, insufficient to constitute proof, in the absence of which the bill should not pass. They go further: ". . . not only is there this absence of proof, which should preclude us from taking any steps on the subject; in the conduct of ministers there are positive circumstances which give room for suspicion that they do not believe their own assertion" (*PH*, 259) and therefore are proceeding fraudulently.

It will be observed in these interchanges that both sides recurred to Lockean standards, invoking clarity and customary usage in their judgments. But despite their coinciding with the opposition in referring to Lockean standards of evaluation, it is clear that the ministerial party would at times have liked to substitute, in fact did substitute, other standards which co-existed very fretfully with Lockean ones.[15] Instead of providing evidence, they offered a variety of other sorts of proof, more traditional or Aristotelian in character. Samuel Horsley, for instance, used general plausible arguments showing that the people might be influenced by pamphlets and suggesting the similarity between this phenomenon and the influence of the Jacobins on the French people (*PH*, 269). In the debates in the House of Commons, Anstruther gave his speech an explicitly syllogistic structure (*PH*, 322–23).[16] William Grant's speech, applauded by all the ministerial side as a model of effective argument, depended heavily on the topical approach to invention (*PH*, 397–408). In his response, Fox too admired Grant's eloquence and ingenuity in finding topics, but pointed out that his argument was little to the purpose, sophistic, full of false dilemmas and pathetic appeals (*PH*, 407–16). When Hardinge in retort explicitly took issue with the demand for evidentiary proof, he attempted to distinguish juridical from legislative proof; the kinds of connections required by the opposition were simply not appropriate to the legislative requirement (*PH*, 427). The opposition, he hinted, were trying to introduce new criteria of argument. Sheridan responded that the criteria were customary, indeed had been met on former occasions, as in the debate on the suspension of the Habeas Corpus Act.[17]

In this contest there is a strong relation between each side's view of political speech acts and its view of authority. The ministers' confident reluctance to present evidence rested on something other than the presumed notoriety of facts, namely the belief that institutional authority is the real backing for their assertions. Hence, their satisfaction with Aristotelian argument, which merely demonstrates an existing relation of accepted truths, without discovering new ones. The relation between assertions backing a bill and facts is not the same as that between assertions in an inductive argument and facts. But to the opposition, this amounted to an assumption that a bill proposed by His Majesty's ministers was virtually a law. Ministers were conflating bill with law and thus forcing the country to take the one speech act for the other. The ministers' assumption explains why they wanted to rush the bill to committee; they felt substantive discussion was unnecessary and merely wanted to revise its terms into palatable form. Likewise, the opposition's assumption explains why Fox refused to participate in committee deliberations; he wanted the bill say what it essentially was and thus impart ministers' real intentions without disguise—in short to wear its "treason" on its face (*PH*, 383). The ultimate tendency of this proceeding, the opposition perceived, would be to transform monarchy into absolutism: conflating bill with law substitutes declaration for argument (*PH*, 373). Each kind of speech act has its specific conditions for successful performance, conditions which rest upon the customs and conventions of a people.[18] To change these is to enter into the political unconscious of speech acts and surgically alter it. There is simply a different set of givens for discourse in a free nation from that which obtains in an absolutist state.

There is still another way of looking at this situation but which leads to the same conclusion: as we have seen, the opposition believed that by means of new language the ministers introduced ambiguity into the concepts of sedition and treason. The result was that the people were unable to determine whether a given act was punishable or not or (alternatively) were forced to classify many innocuous acts as dangerous. This is precisely what Sheridan alleged when he criticized the terms of the Seditious Meetings Bill (*PH,* 315–16, 437). It would have required the local magistrate to disperse a meeting whenever it seemed, in his judgment, to verge on the seditious; to place such power in the hands of a single person, perhaps neither qualified nor inclined to understand the proceedings, certainly without a guarantee of uniformity of action among the various magistrates, would have destabilized the meaning of sedition. Such a situation of indeterminacy recollects the Hobbesian state of nature, in which one man's authority is as good as another's and from which escape can be effected only by an arbitrary consigning of authority into the hands of an absolute power. Thus, the re-introduction of indeterminacy of meaning into the conventions of communication sets up the conditions for, even if it does not actually constitute, absolutism.

The contest of authority became quite explicit toward the end of the debates. When it became evident that the bills would pass despite the weight of petitions sent against them, Fox deplored that Parliament should act against "the declared sense of a great majority of the nation" (*PH,* 383). In highly allusive language he announced his final judgment of the bills: ". . . if his opinion were asked by the people, as to their obedience, he should tell them, that it was no longer a question of moral obligation and duty, but of prudence" (*PH,* 383). Pitt immediately took up this phrasing, accusing Fox of "setting up his own arguments in opposition to the authority of the legislature" and matching Fox's innuendo with his own: "Happily for the country, this declaration of his principles is too clear to admit of a doubt" (*PH,* 384). Here, in a nutshell, is a replay of the Radical rhetoric and ministerial strategy from the 1794 treason trials: Fox's equivocal invocation of the right to resist fundamental assaults on the constitution was read by Pitt as a covert message to the public, inciting them to revolt. Conversely, Pitt's language too was capable of double meaning and contained a hidden threat: the country could see and avoid Fox's treason, or (alternatively) ministers could rightly interpret his allusions and prosecute if he uttered them outside of Parliament (*PH,* 384–85).

Though both sides equivocated, they agreed in condemning equivocation as an instrument to confuse observers and usurp power. The ministerial party accused the reform societies of criminal equivocation: using public meetings for the purpose of petitioning Parliament was a "pretext" for seditious acts (*PH*, 274). Pretext, rather than principle, and motivated by ambition, threatened Parliament's traditional, exclusive position as mediator with the king: "In fine, the sole object of the bill was, that the people should look to parliament, and to parliament alone, for the redress of such grievance as they might have to complain of . . ." (362). The opposition answered that the bill was proceeding on the flimsy "pretext" that the meetings of reform societies caused violence in order to pass laws protecting ministerial abuse of power (*PH*, 277). Pretext threatened the people's immemorial right to petition and usurped their authority concerning their own grievances. "The people are the proper judges of the grievances under which they labour," said Sheridan (*PH*, 315).

This was ultimately a difference about the nature and uses of history—especially in the form of precedent. To the ministerial party the constitution was static, but had to be protected by changing it. One part (rights to free speech) might have to be sacrificed for the good of the whole. What remained, however (free speech in Parliament), was still every bit as much the constitution, in a sense standing for the whole, and could hold its place until the missing part might be returned at the appropriate (safe) time. People act according to motives which are much the same whatever nation or period they occupy; conversely, laws are responses to present circumstances. Hence, they feel free to dig into the past for any examples that may be appropriate to the present exigencies. The opposition viewed the constitution, if not as constantly developing, as having made certain gains for freedom, particularly at the time of the 1688 revolution. These embodied rational principles of government, including the natural rights of man, which it is never safe to sacrifice. Each part lost destroys the delicate balance of king, lords, and commons. Moreover, each country has its characteristic history: the experience of France can never be substituted for the experience of England, and it is nonsense to expect that Englishmen will act as Frenchmen have. As a result, the past provides a certain inheritance which must be protected as the characteristic identity of the English.[19] To each side the use of "pretexts" and equivocations was an attack on the univocal meaning of the constitution—even though they conceived that meaning differently.

When Coleridge began his political lectures and pamphlet writing in 1795, he entered a highly charged field in which the participants were already rhetorically self-conscious: the accusation of fraud had become well-worked and ambiguous, and several speakers had already evolved a complex—if not always subtle—analysis of duplicity which had significant ramifications in the views of precedent and history that justified political action. In this contemporary polemic Coleridge found a language of analytical and allusive power with and within which to sound his "baby trumpet of sedition."[20] In the process, he responded creatively and ironically to the Lockean criteria of communication and inscribed on the debate a different relation between rhetoric and history.

The Plot Discovered is a revised and extended version of his Lecture on the Two Bills delivered in Bristol on 26 November 1795. At the time of its publication (probably by 6 December), the Treasonable Practices Bill and the Seditious Meetings Bill were about to be passed by Parliament. In consequence, the pamphlet never received very close attention from reviewers, and Coleridge was left to pursue his themes in the *Watchman* of 1796.[21] The pamphlet deserved (and deserves) more attention, both for the part it plays in the development of Coleridge's modes of argumentation and for its interpretation of the polemical scene he joined.

Coleridge used the same strategy that the antagonists in the Treason Trials and speakers in Parliament used, namely a subverting commentary on the words of their opponents. Following the hint by Fox, Coleridge proceeded phrase by phrase through the original version of the Two Bills in support of a paradoxical claim.[22] The original version can be read literally; that reading shows the bills to be a fraud, a conspiracy against the liberty of the people and, by identification, against the sovereignty of the king. The paradox arises from Coleridge's having to interpret a literal text at all and to "discover" the hidden "plot." If this is not a gross inconsistency in Coleridge's argument, the paradox points to the possibility that Coleridge was parodying his opponents, and indeed his procedure is very like the continuous ironic commentary of the attorney general in the 1794 treason trials. By using this method, by clearly recalling the strategy of the prosecution, Coleridge usurped the interpretive prerogative from the government and inscribed a Radical view on the claim to authoritative speech.

Coleridge joined the charge of the opposition in Parliament: that the Treason Bill's sponsors fraudulently used the attack on the king as pretext for the bill. In effect the ministers treated the assault on the king as an act which required cognizance of its real context in order to be interpreted—the supposed real context being the dissemination of seditious ideas at public meetings of reform societies, though they did not prove the connection with evidence. Like the opposition, Coleridge wrested interpretation of the speech act from the ministers by substituting what he deemed to be the real context: the ministers' war. "The dispersion therefore of seditious pamphlets was not the cause: *that* was the cause which gave to sedition the colouring of truth, and made disaffection the dictate of hunger, the present unjust, unnecessary and calamitous War—a War that brought dearth, and threatens slavery!" (*Lectures*, 287)

Ministers purported to read the action of the people literally, such a reading presupposing that there was a direct relation between the expression and the intention (it was a sincere act) as well as between the expression and

74

preparatory conditions such as context (they were contained by implication in the expression).[23] But, like the attorney general in the Treason Trials, by shifting the preparatory condition, they made the act a sign of a different intention. Coleridge's strategy of rescue, however, was somewhat different from Erskine's. To be sure, in a condensation of the common opposition arguments, Coleridge rescued the acts of the people from the imputed intention of treason (hunger, not treason, was their motive) and even from the imputed act of treason (an out-of-work spy was the only one who could have been so audacious as to throw the stone or fire the bullet). But in the process, Coleridge himself introduced an equivocation—one which did not at all rescue the supposed seditious pamphlets nor so neatly rescue the people. Ministers judged the pamphlets seditious by pointing to their effect, the attack on the king. The pamphlets might very well be seditious, Coleridge admitted; but if they provided the people with motives, it was only because they validated the people's own perceptions of government's neglect. There was *prima facie* guilt in the pamphlets, but they had to be connected with the people's actions as intentions in order to constitute actual guilt. That connection was provided by the ministers, who caused the circumstances that provided the connections between discrete entities; sedition and the people could never come together without the help of the ministers' war. This is a serious opposition argument, but Coleridge introduced complication into it by means of his equivocation: the pamphlets were seditious if the people acted upon *them,* but it is the ministers' war which made them appear true; without it the pamphlets were mere innocuous speculation—theoretical sedition, not real sedition. By this means, Coleridge enacted a form of "excuse" which, it became clear later, he believed was necessary to protect freedom of speech.

Coleridge wrought a similarly complex irony from an application of the Lockean criterion of clarity to speech act analysis. He depicted the ministers first as agents of obfuscation: "The existing laws of Treason were too clear, too unequivocal" (*Lectures,* 288). Like the opposition in Parliament, Coleridge believed the ministers devised the Treasonable Practices Bill in the wake of their failure in the 1794 trials, in order to make prosecution easier. *Univocal* language in the law, it appears here, insures justice, for it enables juries to perceive when "Judges might endeavour to transfer to these laws their own flexibility" (*Lectures,* 288). A little later, however, in an only apparent inconsistency, it is the possibility of *equivocation* which maintains the freedom of political speech. Here Coleridge fundamentally departed from the theoretical dependency upon Locke which both sides claimed.[24] He approved the existing treason laws because they admitted the possibility of a disjuncture between meanings and intentions. "By the existing treason laws a man so accused would plead, It is the privilege of an Englishman to entertain what speculative opinions he pleases, provided he stir up to no present action" (*Lectures,* 289).

75

It is the ministers' bill that proposed to draw a closer relationship between the two, for instance by erasing the element of *time:*

> It will be in vain to alledge, that such opinions were not wished to be realized, except as the result of progressive reformation and ameliorated manners; that the author or speaker never dreamed of *seeing* them realized; though he should expressly set forth, that they neither could be, nor would be, nor ought to be, realized in the present or the following reign; still he would be guilty of high Treason: for though he recommends not an attempt to depose his present majesty from the kingly name, yet he evidently recommends the denial of it to some one of his distant successors. All political controversy is at an end. (*Lectures,* 289)

In an interesting answer to the historical concerns of the Parliamentary debaters, gradual change was enabled by the gradually shifting meaning of the speech act. But whereas for them equivocation was a threat to stability and the maintenance of traditional rights or power relations, for Coleridge it enabled the preservation of the idea of new relations until shifts in power occurred by the gradual assimilation of conditions to the blueprint of language. Yet this model functions not by generating systems from a clear unequivocal text, but rather by means of an equivocal text gradually instantiating itself as conditions allow its covert meaning to emerge.

It seems that as a matter of necessity Coleridge evolved here an embryonic revolutionary/evolutionary rationale. Without some such opening in the interpretation of speech acts, writers and speakers would be forced into silence. Coleridge's invocation of the "spirits of Milton, Locke, Sidney, and Harrington! that still wander through your native country, giving wisdom and inspiring zeal!" (*Lectures,* 290–91) suggests a continuous tradition of utterances whose realization occurs after the time of their uttering, a kind of "reversionary treasure" (as Coleridge elsewhere says of words with ambiguous meaning which release their riches in the process of desynonymization).[25] Time sorts out the words of good influence from the mistakes: "Our ancestors were wisely cautious in framing the bill of treason; they would not admit words as sufficient evidence of intention. How often does the tongue utter what the moment after the heart disapproves!" (*Lectures,* 291). It requires time, if only a moment, to sift out genuine meanings, genuine intentions (those coming from the "heart"), ones which can enter the fructifying stream of tradition.

By means of a double move, the ministers attempted to introduce equivocality into utterances (they mean different things to hearer and eavesdropper) but insisted on univocality by extracting the legal, and punishable, interpretation. Coleridge feared that unless the law allowed to the people multivocal meaning, the opportunity to change their minds, the ability to mean one thing one time, another thing later, to have an "excuse," they would be trapped by their utterances. Further, the government would take advantage of the fact that all words really are susceptible of multiple meanings in order to confine them to the meaning of the government's choice. Through practiced manipulations of language—"from loss of memory to equivocation, and from equivocation to perjury" (*Lectures*, 292)—the ministers' hireling-witnesses were able to discount the possibly benevolent meanings and retain the malignant ones. Through charges to the jury and like "commentaries," judges too could operate upon the plethora of meanings to confine them to the one damning signification.[26] Thus, the law must be univocal, clear and restricted in what it punishes, so that it may be multivocal, show latitude in what it allows. If its scope is broad, it will be multivocal, inclusive in what it restricts, and univocal in what it allows.

The bills, then, clearly announced their intention to restrict freedom via their broad and equivocal language. By restricting freedom, they prevented gradual change, amelioration—history itself. Coleridge no doubt was able to perceive the diachronic dimension of the ministers' plot against language and rewrite the opposition's scheme of history into something more explicitly progressive, by means of his Priestleian bias, in which God not only works out his plan for humankind in history, but has built into the historical system a natural tendency toward gradual improvement. Evil, if such a thing exists in the necessitarian system, in which everything contributes to ultimate good— evil could only be an attempt to thwart the natural process of amelioration.[27] "Now if these ministers believe this, namely, that the Constitution as it at present exists is the best possible, they must likewise believe either that there is no God, or if there be a God, that he is not all-powerful or not benevolent" (*Lectures*, 295).

Perhaps this conception of history explains why, as I hinted on an earlier page, Coleridge's rescue of the people from imputations of guilty association with the revolutionary societies, and of the pamphlets from the stigma of seditious effects, is incomplete. A similar move can be seen in his treatment of John Thelwall, when he comes to consider the Seditious Practices Bill. He was not speaking entirely facetiously when he said the "import" of the bill "is briefly this—first that the people of England should possess no unrestrained right of consulting in common on common grievances: and secondly, that Mr. Thelwall should no longer give political lectures" (*Lectures*, 296). It had already been suggested in Parliament that Thelwall was the primary target of the bill.[28] Coleridge turned this suggestion to theoretical value, describing Thelwall in ambiguous terms, which we can now see as placing him precisely in history:[29] "Nothing could make him of importance but that he speaks the feelings of multitudes" (*Lectures*, 297). "The feelings of men," Coleridge went on, "are always founded in truth. The modes of expressing them may be blended with error, and the feelings themselves may lead to the most abhorred excesses. Yet still they are originally right: they teach man that something is wanting, something which he ought to have" (*Lectures*, 297). His analysis of

Thelwall's significance is very much in keeping with Coleridge's Hartleian-Priestleian philosophy: the feelings of individuals are an implanted mode of signifying to them when they are doing morally well or ill; pain is a means of prompting them to rectify their behavior or the conditions which dictate that behavior.[30] Coleridge called Thelwall "the voice of ten thousands," insofar as he spoke their feelings and attempted to pinpoint present imperfections; like Sidney and Harrington, he offered a language which might be related to the genuine, ultimate "heart" language, even if blended with error and excess.

Coleridge's treatment of the term "constitution" in a clause of the bill later removed in committee, however, suggests a more static view of language. The words of the clause would have given justices of the peace "unlimited and arbitrary power of dispersing" assemblies. "If this clause had passed," said Coleridge, "the word 'constitution' ought to have been erased," because it would have "erased" the referent for "constitution." Moreover, logically, the bill could not then have been called "law," would not have been consistent with the constitution, thus would not be "entitled to moral obedience." His reasoning: ". . . Parliament cannot [legally] annul the Constitution." If it does so, society is no longer in a state obliging obedience, but in a state of war. Thus, immediately the bill becomes law, the word "law" becomes meaningless. It is merely an "*Edict*" (*Lectures,* 300–1). It is evident that Coleridge here recurred to the static Lockean conception of clarity and steady adherence to customary meaning—and perhaps went further, toward a kind of idealism. What this not entirely ironic argument presupposes is that words have meanings which equivocal usage cannot change:[31] ". . . a Constitution, if it mean any thing, signifies certain known Laws, which limit the expectations of the people and the discretionary powers of the legislature" (*Lectures,* 300). The minister (William Pitt) wanted to submerge the meaning of "constitution" in the meaning of "government," with which it is not really identical. Keeping them separate was vital to the maintenance of freedom.

How does this view consist with Coleridge's argument that history depends upon equivocation? After all, what seems implied in the above argument is an almost Platonic conception of language: verbal truth is obtained not only by consistent usage, but by reference to some rational form. The Priestleian view of history, however, would admit that human beings cannot in fact judge mundane acts because what appears a divagation from truth may later turn out to be an important force for progress. Coleridge says this himself in his "Religious Musings," written around this time.[32] And the view appears as an argument for toleration in *The Plot Discovered;* hence, we find him in a footnote defending John Reeves' right to speech and deploring the opposition's gleeful prosecution of him in Parliament (*Lectures,* 304–5). But to say this is to place the equivocations of the people on the same level as the equivocations of the ministers. Both are equally dangerous—or equally innocuous.

Coleridge needed to place some limit on use of equivocation; otherwise, he would warrant a complete relativism or indeterminacy of language, which, as we have seen, threatens to return society to a Hobbesian state of nature that will end in absolutism. Hence, he appropriated the Christian conception of a pre-existing plan, one which the people's feelings draw them toward and cause them to instantiate. Linguistic change can thus be viewed as the usage of words righting themselves as users appropriate words to their true meanings and maintain behavior in steady relation to those meanings. The equivocation Coleridge would allow is a mode of avoiding violence to individuals, and of eliciting the possible meanings among which will eventually be found the true ones. It is also therefore a means of bringing about the realization of what has always existed potentially in God's plan. Hence, Coleridge had a way of discerning between salutary and dangerous equivocations after all. He criticized the equivocation of the ministers' Two Bills because, assuming perfection exists already, they would prevent the movement of history.

> Now the Constitution and Government are defective and corrupt, or they are not. If the former, the Bills are iniquitous, since they would *kill off* all who promulge truths necessary to the progression of human happiness: if the latter (that is, if the Constitution and Government are perfect) the Bills are still iniquitous, for they destroy the sole boundary which divides that Government from Despotism, and *change* that Constitution, from whose present perfectness they derive their only possible justification. (*Lectures,* 306)

Moreover, they would actually have destroyed a salutary equivocation, namely the classification of the British system as government "with the people." In Coleridge's three-fold classification of governments "*by* the people" (not confined to democracy), "*over* the people" (despotism), and "*with* the people," the third is really a category of movement from the first form to the second. In it the people do not have a perfect representation and ability to instruct the government, but neither do they lack all effective influence; rather, as in the late nineteenth-century British system, in which there was a free press and a right to petition (and thus "overawe") Parliament, the people could materially affect the laws that are made. Once the Two Bills had been passed, however, they would no longer be able to do so, and in consequence they would no longer be able to move that government toward the complete responsibility to the good of the people which constitutes the first form of government. The present British government could be called free by an equivocation, but the future British government will be univocally despotic (*Lectures,* 306–313).

This is also the theme of the parodic petition from the Danish subjects to their king—for whose "*anglicized*" actions Coleridge ironically apologizes (*Lectures,* 315). In the "petition" the Danes plead with their king to abandon the "forms" of freedom and reassume the "forms" of absolute power. In effect, then, absolutism would become freedom—as the king's voice truly would have become the voice of the people. Is this an argument for direct democracy or for absolute monarchy? A commonplace of late eighteenth-century argument is that democratic principles can lead to democratic tyranny. Coleridge's argument changed the valence of that observation: monarchical sovereignty is really democratic freedom when those terms realize their meanings. This is itself an equivocal argument—and a demonstration of what Coleridge meant by equivocation.[33] Coleridge depicted a moment of indeterminacy, of becoming, of change in relation and valence, and thereby captured the move of history itself. This fruitful indeterminacy allows the co-existence of many diverse voices, and hence encourages tolerance as a *modus vivendi.*

NOTES

1. I have found helpful J. G. A. Pocock's three-fold definition of "ideology": "(1) thought considered as rhetoric or speech in action; (2) thought determined and constrained by, and at times in tension with, the forms of speech available for its expression; and (3) a view of the world determined by the various factors that may be held to have determined it (there being no single preconceived theory as to what these may have been)"; see *Virtue, Commerce, and History* (Cambridge: Cambridge University Press, 1985), p. 216n.

2. The general theoretical underpinning for this intertextual and contextual study is M. M. Bakhtin's "Discourse in the Novel," in *The Dialogic Imagination,* ed. Michael Holquist and trans. Caryl Emerson and Michael Holquist (Austin: University of Texas Press, 1981), pp. 259–422. See especially pp. 276–82.

3. Jon Klancher offers an important perspective on the struggle for control over interpretation in *The Making of English Reading Audiences, 1790–1832* (Madison: University of Wisconsin Press, 1987). See for example pp. 5–6.

4. Albert Goodwin, *The Friends of Liberty: The English Democratic Movement in the Age of the French Revolution* (Cambridge, Mass.: Harvard University Press, 1979), pp. 270–71 and 238–39. Also see J. E. Cookson, *The Friends of Peace: Anti-war Liberalism in England, 1793–1815* (Cambridge: Cambridge University Press, 1982), pp. 92 and 100, demonstrating the tenacity of the liberal press.

5. Quotations from the introductory speeches of both Erskine and Scott in the 1794 treason trial of Thomas Hardy are taken from Thomas Erskine, *The Speeches of the Right Honourable Lord Erskine,* 3d ed., 4 vols., collected and ed. by James Ridgway (London: James Ridgway, n.d.) and are cited in text as Erskine, followed by volume and page number.

6. John Locke, *An Essay concerning Human Understanding,* ed. Peter H. Nidditch (Oxford: Clarendon Press, 1975). References to the *Essay* are cited by book, chapter, and section of this edition.

7. See John R. Searle, *Expression and Meaning: Studies in the Theory of Speech Acts* (Cambridge: Cambridge University Press, 1979), pp. 47–48.

8. See William Godwin, *Cursory Strictures on the Charge Delivered by Lord Chief Justice Eyre to the Grand Jury, October 2, 1794* in *Uncollected Writings (1785–*

1822), facsimile with introductions by Jack W. Marken and Burton R. Pollin (Gaines-ville, Fla.: Scholars' Facsimiles and Reprints, 1968), pp. 145–75.

9. Yet no doubt we can see that they do sometimes differ and that Erskine is attempting to maintain a naive view of interpretation that will stabilize it, rescue it from complete indeterminacy. John Searle presents a suggestive example in *Speech Acts: An Essay in the Philosophy of Language* (Cambridge: Cambridge University Press, 1969), pp. 44–45.

10. A phrase quoted by Coleridge in *The Plot Discovered,* in *Lectures 1795 on Politics and Religion,* Vol. 1 of *The Collected Works of Samuel Taylor Coleridge,* ed. Lewis Patton and Peter Mann (Princeton: Princeton University Press, 1971), p. 288. The editors cite the *Parliamentary Register,* Vol. 40, col. 39. References to this volume of Coleridge's *Collected Works* are hereafter cited in the text as *Lectures,* followed by the page number.

11. The Treasonable Practices Bill defined as treason printing or public speaking which advised or imagined the deposition of the king or his heirs from the power and name of monarch. The Seditious Meetings Bill prohibited any meeting of more than fifty persons (unless called by a magistrate) for the purpose or "pretext" of petitioning Parliament to change "matters established in church and state."

12. *The Parliamentary History of England,* Vol. 32 (London: printed by T. C. Hansard for Longman, et al., 1818). Cited in the text as *PH,* followed by the column numbers.

13. See *Essay* 4.15–17.

14. See J. L. Austin, *How to Do Things with Words,* ed. J. O. Urmson and Marina Sbisa (Cambridge, Mass.: Harvard University Press, 1975), pp. 45–54.

15. These disagreements over the kinds of proofs appropriate to this question could be evidence of a fundamental conflict in rhetorical and logical training. See Wilbur Samuel Howell, *Eighteenth-century British Logic and Rhetoric* (Princeton: Princeton University Press, 1971), pp. 42ff., 99–102, 112–13, 122–24, 261–62, 491–96, 515, and 548ff.

16. This could be due to his training in Scottish law. The use of the syllogistic structure in Scottish indictments came to the fore in Parliamentary debate in March 1794 on the trial of Thomas Muir of the previous year. See *The Parliamentary History of England,* vol. 30 (London: printed by T. C. Hansard for Longman, et al., 1818), cols. 1522–23.

17. See Goodwin, pp. 332–34.

18. Searle, *Speech Acts,* pp. 54–71, provides the background here.

19. This is, of course, an oversimplification, conflating the diverse views of persons each of whom has a complex relation to the available ideologies. But see *PH,* pp. 251–53, 260–64, 279–83, 298, 308–9, 311–19, 321–23, 337–41, 347–49, 356, 365–66, 370–71, 394–96, 399–400.

20. In a letter to his brother George, written around 10 March 1798, Coleridge disavows his early Radicalism, saying he has "snapped his baby trumpet of sedition." See Earl Leslie Griggs, ed., *Collected Letters of Samuel Taylor Coleridge,* Vol. 1 (1956; reprint Oxford: Clarendon Press, 1966), p. 397.

21. *Lectures,* pp. xlvi–xlvii, 278–79. P. Kitson offers a correction of the date of publication in "Coleridge's *The Plot Discovered:* A New Date," *Notes and Queries* (March 1984): 57–58.

22. See *PH,* p. 382. Coleridge consciously adopts the language of the Parliamentary debates throughout *The Plot Discovered.* See in particular *PH,* p. 480, and *PH,* p. 279.

23. Searle, *Speech Acts,* p. 65.

24. Or, rather, he penetrates to Locke's own relativism, which was neglected by the antagonists in the treason trials and by the Parliamentary debaters. See *Essay* 3.9.4–8 and 3.10.14–22. Also see Searle, *Speech Acts,* pp. 42–50, for some suggestive remarks on the relation between meanings and intentions.

25. See Michael Kent Havens, "Coleridge on the Evolution of Language," *Studies in Romanticism* 20 (1981): 163–84.

26. Coleridge has in mind the comments of Chief Justice Braxfield in the 1793 state trials in Scotland. See Philip Anthony Brown, *The French Revolution in English History* (London: Frank Cass and Co., 1965), pp. 106–7.

27. See Coleridge's *Lectures on Revealed Religion,* especially Lecture 1, in *Lectures,* pp. 109–10 and the sources cited in the notes. Also see Joseph Priestley's millenarian works, *Institutes of Natural and Revealed Religion* (1772–1774), in *The Theological and Miscellaneous Works of Joseph Priestley,* ed. J. T. Rutt, Vol. 2 (1817; reprint New York: Kraus Reprint Co., 1972), and *Sermon on Repeal of the Corporation and Test Acts* (November 1789), his *Fast Sermon* (1793), and *Fast Sermon* (1794) in *The Theological and Miscellaneous Works,* Vol. 15.

28. See *PH,* pp. 280 and 326, where Thelwall is named, and where it is revealed that the Seditious Meetings Bill is partly targeted against speakers who receive fees for their political lectures.

29. Coleridge's ambivalent attitude toward Thelwall is discussed in *Lectures,* pp. lv–lvi, lxxvii–lxxviii, and 297n. For a different view, see Nicholas Roe, *Wordsworth and Coleridge: The Radical Years* (Oxford: Oxford University Press, 1988), pp. 149–50.

30. Coleridge presents this view more explicitly in his *Lectures on Revealed Religion* in *Lectures,* pp. 105–6.

31. A good, though brief, analysis of Coleridge's linguistic views at this time is provided by James C. McKusick, *Coleridge's Philosophy of Language* (New Haven and London: Yale University Press, 1986), pp. 18–21.

32. Lines 192ff. in *The Complete Poetical Works of Samuel Taylor Coleridge,* ed. Ernest Hartley Coleridge, Vol. 1 (1912; reprint Oxford: Clarendon Press, 1968), p. 116. See also the note to line 192.

33. For an excellent biographical perspective on Coleridge's attraction to equivocation, see Donald Reiman, "Coleridge and the Art of Equivocation," *Studies in Romanticism* 25 (1986): 325–50.

British Women Poets and the Reverberations of Radicalism in the 1790s

Stephen C. Behrendt

The volume of the *Biographical Dictionary of Modern British Radicals* encompassing the Romantic period lists 214 figures representing various occupations and interests. Of these only four—Mary Hays, Catherine Macaulay, Helen Maria Williams, and Mary Wollstonecraft—are women, and Macaulay had died in 1791 and Wollstonecraft in 1797.[1] These numbers come from census takers who have been careless in their count of figures identified as or associated with Radicals, inconsistent in their criteria, and possessed of considerable gender bias to boot. Mary Darby Robinson, whose works often disclose Radical sentiments, is absent, for instance, while Robert Merry, the leader of the Della Cruscan circle with which she was for some time associated, is counted among the Radicals. Omissions and misrepresentations of this sort betray the modern resistance to seeing women who were associated with Radical circles and principles in the political terms in which they—and many of their contemporaries—saw and responded to them. Robinson had, after all, replied immediately and enthusiastically to Merry's *The Laurel of Liberty* (1790) with *Ainsi va le Monde* (1790). Her subsequent affiliation with the *Morning Post* (especially during Daniel Stuart's tenure as manager and editor), which brought her into contact with Coleridge and Southey, not only involved her with a liberal paper but also lent her access to an audience receptive to many aspects of the progressive agenda she encoded in her poems for that paper. For a vastly popular poet who had already as early as 1793 been publicly touted as not just "the *first Poet* now living" but indeed "the *first Poet*,"[2] this was of course an immediate advantage, even though her oppositional stance was less direct and conspicuous than that which we associate with Radical male contemporaries like Thomas Spence or John Thelwall. Although one hesitates to call her a Radical in the usual sense, Charlotte Smith enjoyed ready access to an interested readership by virtue of her very considerable reputation as author of the *Elegiac Sonnets,* which saw numerous editions. Moreover, both women increased their readerships significantly through their widely known novels which, like Smith's *Desmond* (1792) and *The Young Philosopher* (1798), could score political points no less than a poem like *The Emigrants* (1793).

When we look at the poetry (especially) actually published by some women of the Romantic period—whether they identified themselves actively and explicitly with the Radical agenda or whether their association was more implicit—we discover in the works of surpising numbers of them a remarkably consistent strain of social and political Radicalism. The predictably larger numbers of conventional and reactionary poems by other women notwithstanding, the existence of these nevertheless comparatively numerous expressions of Radical thought require more attention than they have historically received. The *vehicle*—poetry—may be unconventional for Radical women writers, and its activating *agent*—which is usually sentiment—may be routinely disparaged by critical opinion that seeks either "loftier" or more aggressive expression in "an official literary language" grounded in the discourse of the sublime whose figurations were for the most part forbidden to women by virtue of "gender- and class-inflected strictures" governing propriety and publication.[3] Nevertheless, there is no mistaking the elements of Radicalism that drive this counter-establishment poetry. We frequently find there, for instance, resistance to monarchy's impingement upon individual prerogative, expressed at times in opposition to war and at others in protest against the economic tyranny maintained by the aristocratic establishment over the population at large and over their ordinary commercial interests. And we see the consequences for the family unit in particular—whether it be the elemental nuclear family or the expanded national "family"—of the disruption of "natural" companionate relationships. Sometimes the poems articulate their Radicalism explicitly, as in Mary Darby Robinson's "January 1795," Elizabeth Moody's 1798 "Thoughts on War and Peace," or the 1795 "Lines Written by a Female Citizen!" attributed to the unidentified "F. A. C." Sometimes they take a slightly more indirect approach, as in Moody's "Anna's Complaint; Or the Miseries of War" (1795), Amelia Alderson Opie's "Ode on the Present Times" (1795), or the ambivalently militaristic "The Spanish Mother" (1809), attributed to "A Young Lady." But the consistency remains. This poetry deliberately resists and even renounces the hierarchical social and political structures of the embedded dominant patriarchy and substitutes for them a more egalitarian, companionate community, whose leading values are respect, tolerance, affection, and shared experience.

Much of Radical rhetoric, especially in the 1790s, turns on appeals to precedent and to the tradition of the "Norman yoke": the belief fed by Radicals like Richard Price, Joseph Priestley, and Major John Cartwright in the benefits to be derived from a reversion to that ancient and supposedly purer form of democratic government understood to have been particularly nurtured by Alfred the Great.[4] While this image was in fact largely a myth, it nevertheless offered a popular view of an originary British constitution that was associated in the popular mind with the politics of that distant period. In this respect the Radical movement, like the Glorious Revolution of a century earlier, aimed to demolish the prevailing order not to institute something entirely new (even the innovations of the Owenites were not entirely forward-looking), but rather to restore what had been eroded and ultimately lost in the takeover of power by an unsanctioned power elite that governed without consent. It is precisely because of the inherent *nostalgia* of this reversion to an idealized golden age and its associated governmental structure that Romantic Radicalism initially appealed so much to working-class citizens. For it was these people who felt most profoundly that they had been left out of the transition to the industrialized, capitalistic modern world. Lacking effective spokespersons or access to economic and political power, they naturally indulged in the "good old days" discourse that is the familiar recourse of those who feel most disenfranchised and excluded by a society—and its institutions—that appears to be passing them by without sufficient regard.

In this light it is especially striking that so little critical attention has been paid until very recently to the presence and the function of women within the Radical culture. For if any portion of the populace was excluded from the scene, they were. And yet for them there could be little solace in the Radical yearning for a return to the Anglo-Saxon ideal that had no more place for them than the contemporary socio-political structure seemed to have. Governed without their consent they surely were, but for them the mythic past offered no golden age during which they had possessed greater prerogative. Claims for women's rights, as James Epstein observes, were "problematically situated within popular radical discourse" of the period because the historical fact of women's exclusion meant that their claims could not easily be legitimated by the sort of appeal to England's past mounted by the Radical movement on behalf of men.[5] Their best hope for empowerment and enfranchisement appeared to lie with the improved socio-political and cultural situation foreseen by melioristic eighteenth-century thinkers like the feminist historiographer Catheraine Macaulay and the political philosopher William Godwin, a fundamentally egalitarian arrangement in which men and women were not competitors but partners. According to this paradigm, bettering the lot of "man" must inevitably improve matters for both sexes: a more enlightened (male) establishment would be far more likely to extend to women what had historically been denied them.[6]

This is one reason why education is accorded such a central place in the plans of feminists like Mary Wollstonecraft and Mary Hays, as it had been in those of Macaulay before them; education seemed to offer one viable avenue into the political and cultural prerogatives routinely available to men. One of the rare women publicly admitted to the male-oriented intellectual scene, Macaulay read in the history of England the record of the loss of the rights of man and the emerging indications, in her own times, of actual progress toward reattaining those rights "in a more perfect state."[7] Not all women writers adopted the largely millenial view of socio-political redirection exhibited in Macaulay's writings, of course, even given the climate of millenarian excitement that chararacterized the 1790s. But her reversion to that venerable Anglo-Saxon paradigm is instructive in its reflection of the ways in which women writers were constrained in their writing, to a significant extent, by a masculinist historiography *and rhetoric* which they had to adapt to their own often oppositional purposes. For if women's experiences and perspectives are themselves inherently bound and misshapen, *a priori,* by the nature of the male-centered language which female authors are forced to employ to communicate them, as is claimed by some modern feminist theory, then another obstacle enters the picture.

British women involved in the Radical movement had in any case to negotiate a complicated passage whereby they might participate in—and reap the rewards of—a movement designed to redress institutionalized social, political, and economic inequities, while at the same time resisting the masculinist paradigm implicit in the nostalgic *beau ideal* that was the putative objective of contemporary Radical politics. There *were* no "good old days" for them; any good days lay in the future. In fact, even what we usually think of as Radicalism, grounded as it was in "artisanal culture," was largely closed to women, as Donna Landry has argued.[8] Certainly women's very different circumstances meant that the ground for which, and over which, they struggled was not precisely the same ground with which their male counterparts were principally concerned. Not even E. P. Thompson, in his monumental *Making of the English Working Class,* fully appreciated the extent to which both his tale and his manner of telling it were overwhelmingly masculinist. As Caroline Steedman remarks, in that work "class was constructed as a masculine identity in both its origin and expression, even when not all the actors were male."[9] In this sense socio-economic class may be seen at once to reflect the literary communities to which various authors belonged and to underscore the conventions that governed both what was published and who published it—as well as who read it. This makes doubly important the sort of research published in recent years by scholars like Landry, Terry Lovell, and Cheryl Turner on the economic conditions under which women authors worked and their implications for class-oriented valuations of their works.[10] And it lends credence to Eleanor Ty's important observation that while Romantic women writers frequently contested, rebelled against, or repudiated them, they nevertheless often "inadvertently participated in the perpetuation of existing cultural, social, and linguistic categories of women and assignments of gender."[11] Although she has in mind novelists of the 1790s, Ty's comment is no less relevant to the work of female poets.

Tracing the Radicalism of women authors of the Romantic period, particularly when one chooses to focus on poetry rather than prose—fiction or otherwise—can involve a circuitous journey, for the texts in question are not always where the modern inquirer might expect to find them. Vivien Jones offers a representative example when she observes that a poem on the fall of the Bastille ("The Bastille: A Vision") intrudes conspicuously into the sentimental environment of Helen Maria Williams's novel, *Julia* (1790). There the Radical feminist socio-sexual ethic embedded in the narrative culminates in a dramatic "reconciliation" that mediates and resolves the tension that has been building in the novel between "illicit" sexual desire and the chastening influence of woman's inherent ingenuous nature. Interestingly, this dramatic crisis coincides textually with the appearance of that poem whose subject is the renovatory purpose of revolutionary violence. Jones remarks that "this conjunction of sentimental sexual narrative with historical event" suggests one way in which Williams was able to liberate herself from the role of "acceptably decorous female poet and novelist" which the contemporary reader *expected* to encounter in a work whose author was known to be a woman.[12] Mixing genres in this fashion (which anticipates the historical novel) enables authors to thematize Radical arguments in terms of historical events. This tactic at once insulates the author (because the historical event is "real" and therefore part of the common cultural currency) and underscores the philosophical or political point being made (for the very same reason). In short, it enables the author to convey ideologically Radical ideas without seeming to do so. In a politically dangerous time—which the last decade of the eighteenth century surely was—this is a reasonable enough subterfuge. But was anyone fooled?

Richard Polwhele was not, for one, nor were those anti-Jacobin contemporaries who nodded approvingly over their copies of *The Unsex'd Females,* published in 1798, or over the pages of its lengthier predecessor, Thomas James Mathias's *Pursuits of Literature,* from which Polwhele borrowed his title.[13] Polwhele had complained in print a decade earlier about the "contempt of the domestic duties" that he regarded as "the prevailing vice of our modern women," who "prefer an intercourse with those who have little concern for her happiness, to the conversation of her family and friends, who must be necessarily interested in her welfare."[14] The latter phrase identifies the source of Polwhele's outrage: the spirit of personal and social independence that was prompting women to venture outside the tight domestic circle in which their role and activities were severely constrained by culturally enforced expectations about their domestic duties. It is not just that Polwhele was by 1798 worried about some women's admiration for French republican principles (and hence their interest in politics) and "their sexually liberated notions."[15] More to the point, he worried that their public endeavors—whether in politics or in print (and they were in fact often one and the same)—threatened the traditional patriarchal family, which he regarded as the foundation of all comfortable societal stability. Ironically, perversely even for a clergyman, Polwhele seemed blind to the argument advanced by so many Radical women writers that the prevailing establishment's appetite for international and domestic domination (including the domination in the private home that Polwhele took for granted)—like the warmaking that was the inevitable consequence of that appetite—posed an even more immediate physical threat to the family unit.

Nor were some women less concerned, as we learn for instance from Anne Grant's caustic remarks on Helen Maria Williams's efforts in poetry and prose alike to teach the lessons of "Equality's new-fangled doctrines" from the very midst of the "murder and sacrilege" that Grant held responsible for "Seine's blood-crimsoned water." "Inebriate" from quaffing liberty's draft, Grant continued, "the glories of old father Thames she decried."[16] The gendering of the Thames—and hence of the English political and intellectual entity—in male terms reminds us of the reactionary tendency to cast women's opposition in terms of unnatural (because anti-authoritarian) independence. Over and over, attacks on the *politics* of Radical women writers were couched in post-Burkean tut-tutting about the shocking violations of *decorum* constituted by their writings, which are treated as intrusions into a discourse that historically excluded their voices. This helps explain Sarah Spence's pious and thoroughly gendered iteration of men's and women's roles in a 1793 pamphlet commenting on the impending war: "As a Woman, I would seek Peace and domestic felicity; relying on the Judgement of my Husband in all political affairs; conscious that it is not the province of my sex to investigate the various sources from which political information may be derived."[17]

Reactionary readers recognized the inherent potential for trouble anytime Radical principles are smuggled into works intended for popular readerships. Like the Gothic novel and the Gothic drama, with which it shared many features, the early Romantic sentimental novel held great potential for subversion, and not just because Radical poems could be buried there or because their characters could be spokespersons for politically Radical views—as happens in Charlotte Smith's *Desmond* (1792)—or for socially and culturally Radical ones more specifically relating to sexual relations—as in Mary Wollstonecraft's *Mary, A Fiction* (1788), Eliza Fenwick's *Secresy* (1795), or Mary Hays's *The Victim of Prejudice* (1799). More importantly, such works typically embrace the intellectual and aesthetic agenda of sentimental fiction, one of whose chief objectives is the generation of feelings of "sympathy" in the sense in which David Hume and others had understood it: as that distinctly moral force by means of which "we enter into the sentiments of the rich and poor, and partake of their pleasures and uneasiness." When we sympathize with "the passions and sentiments of others," Hume writes, those passions and sentiments first manifest themselves in our own minds "as mere ideas" which are "conceiv'd to belong to another person." But on further contemplation the distance between stimulus and responding mind lessens: the resemblance and proximity of those external passions and sentiments to others of which we are ourselves the authors leads us to convert those essentially neutral "ideas" into emotionally and intellectually charged "impressions," so much so that at length "we are convinc'd of the reality of the passion."[18] It is in this intellectual *and emotional* space, in which that separation is dramatically reduced, that the danger to established institutions was seen most especially to lie.

Poetry's great strength, historically and actually, has to do with its power to move and evoke, to manipulate how the reader responds to its subject matter. The most effective poetry appeals to the reader's instinctive desire to participate with the author in the "making" of the work, a process that reduces the separation between author (and the author's characters or personae and what they say) and reader in a manner analogous to the reduction of distance of which Hume speaks. Polwhele and his like worry that readers will so fully *sympathize* with what is conveyed in the text's words that they will be unable—or unwilling—to distinguish their own ideas from those which the author has embedded in the text. The logical consequence is that such readers will then come to regard the words—and the Radical ideas—contained in the text as ideas and impressions which they, rather than the author, have produced. The reader will in this scenario find in the text reinforcement for impressions—and convictions—which that reader will be seduced into believing are her or his own; they will seem to come from within the reader rather than from without. The text becomes verification, not suggestion, casting the reader rather than the author in the role of sower of Radical seed. It is against just this sort of rhetorical seduction that the establishment and its spokespersons direct their fire.

As well they should. One may reasonably enough read in poems like "January, 1795" or "The Birth-day" Mary Robinson's deliberate attempts to destabilize the system by dramatizing for her readers the suffering of the excluded under an established system of callous privilege:

Pavement slippery, people sneezing,
Lords in ermine, beggars freezing;
Titled gluttons dainties carving,
Genius is a garret starving.

Lofty mansions, warm and spacious;
Courtiers cringing and voracious;

Misers scarce the wretched heeding;
Gallant soldiers fighting, bleeding.
("January, 1795," 1–8)

But Robinson's poem is no simple exercise in the dialectical dualisms of the "haves" and the "have-nots," for the poem reminds the reader of the subtle gradations within both the positive and the negative categories itemized there, even as it implies (as it continues to do for today's readers) the essential timelessness, the inevitable universality, of the terrible state of affairs it starkly and unblinkingly depicts. This stark representation of "what is" as a way of highlighting the more pressing issue of "what is *not*," typifies Romantic Radical discourse, from early authors and publishers like Paine and Spence and Eaton to later ones like Hone and Wooler, in all of whose works it is immediately apparent. This sort of discourse occurs also in the works of agrarian and working-class poets, as well as in those of women.

The rhetorical ploy of the negative definition is evident within both the texts *and the titles* of Jacobin novels like Robert Bage's *Man As He Is* (1792) and *Hermsprong; or, Man As He Is Not* (1796) or William Godwin's *Things As They Are* (subtitled *Caleb Williams;* 1794). That it is there as well in the writings of Williams, Robinson, Smith, Anna Letitia Barbauld, and a host of other women tends to come as something of a surprise to those whose experience with Romantic writing has been shaped by ideological assumptions that have for most of this century governed ideas about Romantic readers, writers, texts, and responses. By the later eighteenth century, as Stuart Curran writes, poetry had been "sealed off as a male, upper-class fiefdom, requiring for its license not simply birth and breeding, but a common education and exclusive standards of shared taste."[19] This is one reason why, as Curran and others have demonstrated, when women engaged in politically committed writing, their efforts were typically branded as inappropriate for a woman's pen (and mind), even when the sentiments were no more (or less) Radical than those of their male contemporaries. Indeed, as I have already mentioned, their critics often adopted the convenient ploy of criticizing their writing as "unnatural," as Mathias and Polwhele did, as a sort of "monstrosity" unbecoming of a woman. This diversionary rhetorical tactic enabled them to avoid engaging the Radical content of the writing. That being so, we might expect to find in the writings of enterprising women a different approach to their task.

As indeed we do. Anne Janowitz helpfully reminds us that one such traditionally excluded category of writing involves those poems "which attempt to *intervene in* rather than *represent*" political and social movements.[20] It is in relation to this category that poems like "January, 1795" and "The Birthday," together with a host of others like Opie's "Ode on the Present Times" (1795), may most fruitfully be examined. This interventional impulse governs the eighth line of Robinson's "January, 1795," for example: "Gallant soldiers fighting, bleeding." The pathos evoked by a conventional line of this sort is predictable enough. But we need to contextualize the line, forgetting for a moment the extent to which our continual exposure via the modern media to omnipresent and seemingly universal violence has largely anesthetized us to that violence and to its effects. A generation that dined for a decade with televised images of carnage in Vietnam, for instance, or another that daily faces appalling domestic gang violence, may have some trouble fully sympathizing (to use Hume's word and his sense) with the actual lived reality that informed the experiences of, especially, women who composed such lines in the 1790s and afterward and women who read and understood them.

Again and again in poems that can be attributed with some confidence to women, there emerges in passages about war and the death of "gallant soldiers" a mixture of anger, helplessness, and inevitability, laced with authentic pathos. Elizabeth Moody's ballad is typical:

Ah, William, wherefore didst thou go
To foreign lands to meet the foe?
Why, won by war's deceitful charms,
Didst thou forsake thy Anna's arms?[21]

Note how Moody enhances the universality of the speaker's experience by rendering it in conventionally domesticized, gendered fashion through the traditional Christian names, the trope on seduction, and the apparently innocent pun on "arms" in the stanza's final line. Poems of this sort—and there are many of them—are very much a part of the Radical agenda. The argument they mount against war—that it is actively and inevitably destructive to that most basic of human objectives (Rousseau's *Second Discourse* notwithstanding), interpersonal community—is inherently also an argument against the contemporary government and the values that undergird it. That establishment engages in war at the expense of countless victims whose numbers include not just the wounded or killed men but also the multitude of emotionally and economically mangled "survivors"—the families for whose welfare that same government responsible for their mutilation cares not one whit. In this light it is not surprising that Moody's poem, which first appeared in 1795, was subjoined in 1796 to a remarkable sixty-four-page pamphlet by "Humanitas" (George Miller) called *War a System of Madness and Irreligion.*[22]

Images of the home, of the family, of the hearth and the domestic circle—all of which regularly stand in for implied figurations of the nation—constitute a large and powerful presence within the Romantic ethos in the 1790s. This presence shares much with the "feminine Romanticism" that Anne Mellor has suggested advocated a *progressive* change in the political and social order, a change grounded on "the trope of the family-politic," or the concept of "a nation-state that evolves gradually and rationally under the mutual care and guidance of both mother and father."[23] War is merely the most dramatic and dangerous threat to this shared care-giving. In poetry written by women—as well as in many poems written by men which assume rhetorical personae of women—these images of the domestic and the national community are jeopardized by the looming, predatory shadows of warfare. A poem called "The Dying Soldier," whose unknown author may be male or female but which was published, significantly, in 1798 in the *Lady's Magazine,* reverts to this theme in the voice of the soldier, who ruefully wonders

> Why did I wander from my native vale,
> And leave my cottage, where Contentment smil'd?
> Where all was happiness and peace. —Ah! why
> Did I e'er mingle in the strife of kings,
> And change the sickle for the gleaming sword,
> The low-fenc'd garden for th' embattled plain,
> Deep-ting'd with blood?
>
> (ll. 2–8)[24]

The speaker in Opie's "Ode on the Present Times," composed and published in the wake of Kosciuszko's defeat in 1794, likewise invokes the image of omnivorous death that levels all distinctions of nation, party, and ideology in universal and indiscriminate destruction. Who are those, the speaker asks of Freedom,

> . . . that madly bear
> Against thy sons the venal spear?
> Are they not men? —then say, what power
> Can bid my bosom mourn no more;
> O where's the fiend-delighting ban
> Forbidding MAN to weep for SLAUGHTERED MAN!
>
> (ll. 43–38)[25]

It is not a matter of French, British, Russian, or Polish; it is simply men killing men, brothers slaying brothers. In this orgy of senseless mutual slaughter, the female voice attempts to intervene.

Women's particular, gendered role in the domestic sphere of course lends a moral and ethical legitimacy to the concerns they express in their own writing. Speaking as wives, mothers, sisters, and "guardians of family and community values,"[26] they can articulate elements of the Radical agenda in ways that at least partially insulate them from the sort of criticism that could be levelled against the more explicit Radical discourse of the men. What is especially distinctive about Radical poems in this mode is their tendency to identify the government (and far less frequently the nation) as one of the threats. As is the case with the Radical agenda generally, the established government is figured as a threat equally to the domestic circle—the family—and to the national family that is often emblematized in the caricature print under the female figure of Britannia, the "mother" country, beset by companies of males whose garb identifies them with the traditional institutions of power. Interestingly, by the end of the Regency, under the very different circumstances of post-Waterloo Radical/reform agitation, much of this familiar iconography came to bear startlingly altered signification. George Cruikshank's astonishing and sexually charged *Death or Liberty!* (1 December 1819), for instance, melds this familiar image with the iconography of the rape of Lucretia (as for instance in Titian's version); here Britannia is sexually assaulted not by representatives of Government (domestic or foreign) but rather by the skeletal figure of death, from behind whose neck flares in the wind a cape bearing the words "RADICAL REFORM."[27]

Of particular interest are the poems of the unidentified "F. A. C." As Michael Scrivener notes, her poems are among "the most uncompromisingly militant" of the Radical and Reform press.[28] Like much of Radical rhetoric, they contrast the sacrifices of "the brave revolutionaries of the seventeenth century" to the unprincipled cowardliness of the citizens of the contemporary world. Her poem, "Lines Written by a Female Citizen!" which Thelwall published in the *Tribune*,[29] presses several characteristic keys. The poem opens with the poet asking her muse why she is asleep at such a desperate moment, when many a "weeping peasant" beholds "his harvest trampl'd, and his hopes forlorn, / His kindred slain, and his once happy cot, / . . . Wrapt in devouring flames, or prostrate laid / By frantic glory's desolating trade" (ll. 7–14). The ravages of war ("frantic glory's desolating trade") are apparently continental (since they are reported as having already occurred). But the description hints with foreboding at the consequences should the conflict spread to English soil, as was fully expected.

Turning from this sad spectacle, the poet assesses the situation in Britain:

> Here as I turn with sympathy oppress'd,
> With indignation rising in my breast,
> My injur'd country's woes demand my care.
> Detested scrowls [scrolls] her ripening fate declare:
> Britannia's children droop in galling chains,
> And lawless Pow'r her boasted annals stains;
> With strides gigantic shakes the trembling land,
> And lifts aloft oppression's iron hand!
>
> (ll. 15–22)

Notice the immediate appeal to "sympathy" as the narrator's response to the effects of war in France; the circumstances are stripped of nationalistic signifiers by virtue of their universal pathos: it is not *Frenchmen* who are victimized but undifferentiated "peasants," who are simply *people,* whatever their nationality. This responsive "sympathy," which the poem presents in strongly maternalistic, nurturant terms, is the source of the two corresponding emotions delineated in the remainder of the poem: indignation and protectiveness. The latter is what makes "my injur'd country's woes" "*demand*" (rather than merely excite) the speaker's care, and the demand is that of the child upon the mother: it is Britannia's *children* who concern the speaker. Moreover, the choice of Britannia, the female emblem of England, further underscores the "femaleness" of the poem's frame of reference. It is "power"—specifically the "lawless" power that a governing establishment has arrogated to itself in defiance of the historical "laws" of individual and societal rights—that oppresses the nation and stains the "boasted annals" of British liberty. The result is the erosion and finally the death of "each lov'd right and privilege" (figurative children) as "Freedom from her native seat retire[s]" (ll. 51–52). While the poem implicitly contrasts the nation's current crisis with that of the revolutionary seventeenth century, the final lines hearken back to the myth of the Anglo-Saxon golden age, and to

> Those sires who dar'd with tyranny contend,
> A peoples' dearest interests to defend,
> Anxious their *charter'd liberties* to save . . . .
>> (ll. 57–59; my emphases)

Coming in the poem's penultimate line, the politically and culturally overcoded reference to "charter'd liberties" serves a powerful rhetorical purpose.

The combination of rhetorical and thematic forces marshalled in this poem reminds us of those we encounter repeatedly in Jacobin fiction of the period, in which "political radicalism, concern for the poor, and effusive emotionalism" are merged, as they are in the fiction of authors like Wollstonecraft and Thomas Holcroft.[30] Power is linked in F. A. C.'s writing with "titl'd Pomp" and "fell Injustice" in the "sinking state, / Where thousands perish for the proud and great" (ll. 24–28). Interestingly, F. A. C. explicitly defines that fallacious "greatness"—using the familiar reverse definition—in contrast to "worth and virtue" (l. 29), which become by definition and by default alike the attributes of oppressed citizens:

> Virtue must shrink from man's inveterate foe;
> From those who honest industry despoil,
> Fed by the tradesman's and the peasant's toil—
> Their toil who labour for their scanty meal,
> Constrain'd the woes of indigence to feel,
> While the best produce of their daily gains,
> The drones of vice and luxury maintains.
>> (ll. 30–36)

94

This passage is remarkable in its anticipation of later poems like Percy Bysshe Shelley's "Song to the Men of England" which take up both the bee-figure of the "drone" (drawn in particular from Mandeville's *Fable of the Bees* [1714]) and the notion of a privileged class that feeds, in defiance of all natural laws, off the labor of an oppressed class whose subjugation has grown so habitual that its unnaturalness is no longer even questioned. Notice, too, that F. A. C. introduces tradesmen here, joining their cause to that of the peasant. Given England's growing reputation as a "nation of shopkeepers," and given the still-current identification of peasantry more with continental than British rural life, we may read in this passage another fusion of mutual interest across lines of both class and nationality. This is of course a central strategy of 1790s Radicalism, an internationalizing of the issues so that the contenders in the drama are not England and France but rather the oppressors and the oppressed, whose respective interests (on both sides of the channel) establish solidarities along ideological lines rather than geographical or strictly nationalistic ones. Radical writers draw these ideological lines in terms of fidelity to *principle* (reason, liberty, community) rather than to nation, so that a writer like Richard "Citizen" Lee, a member of the London Corresponding Society, could argue in 1795 in favor of a "cosmopolitan" view that disdained the narrow distinctions drawn by nationalistic jingoism as "disorderly passions" that disrupt or demolish the preferred "diffusive spirit of universal affection."[31]

Here is where the female voice of a poet like F. A. C. carries special force, for the sympathetic response (for which "affection" is the ubiquitous token especially in early Romantic writing) that provides much of the motivating force in this poem (and others like it) is closely related to the tradition of sentiment. The historical association of sentiment with women's experience and women's writing had grown increasingly pronounced in the later eighteenth century with the emergence of the novel as predominantly a woman's literary form. Throughout poems like "Lines Written by a Female Citizen" the supposedly "natural" or "instinctive" nurturant response of woman informs the concern with—and the indignation at—aggressively male manifestations of "lawless Pow'r" like the "strides gigantic" and the "iron hand" that shake "the trembling land" (ll. 21–22). It is worth considering the pointed ambiguity of "the trembling land." Perhaps the land trembles from the repercussions of that gigantic power-figure's strides. But perhaps the land, the nation (historically associated with the female in the gendered rhetoric of political discourse), trembles with the fear of the often-abused spouse. Or perhaps the land trembles, just as the speaker does, with indignation and an impending explosion of revolution. There can be no question that F. A. C. artfully plants all these implications in this powerful poem; the use in the title of the blatantly inflammatory double identifier, "a Female Citizen," anticipates and underscores the several varieties of solidarity among the oppressed that the poem goes on to explore.

95

The *Tribune,* operated by John Thelwall after his acquittal in the notorious Treason Trials of 1794, was a major, albeit short-lived, player on the Radical scene. So was the *Moral and Political Magazine,* which, like Thelwall's *Tribune,* had its roots in the London Corresponding Society and which likewise lasted less than a year.[32] It is not surprising, therefore, to find F. A. C.'s work there as well. Her "Invocation to the Genius of Britain"[33] again opens with a lament over slumber at this perilous moment. But instead of the poet's muse being asleep, as in the other poem, it is now "the Genius of Britain," "brave spirit of a free born race!" that slumbers even "when shame, when ruin, and disgrace, / Are dealt unsparing from the hand of pow'r" (ll. 1–4). As happens regularly in the millenarian verse of the 1790s with which Radical poetry shares so much thematically, rhetorically, and stylistically, and as happens too in the poetry composed during the later and much altered Radical insurgency of the Regency, the poet implores this "brave spirit":

> Spirit awake! awake! once more inspire,
> With glowing energy each Briton's soul,
> Teach him to emulate each god-like sire,
> And scorn to stoop beneath a base controul.
> (ll. 21–24)

The call to wake and rise echoes again and again in Radical writings throughout the Romantic period, as writer after writer implores her or his readers and auditors to shake off the repressions which established powers have gradually imposed upon the populace and which that populace has come, out of sustained habit, to regard not as an imposition but rather as the unfortunate but inevitable—and even natural—state of affairs.

F. A. C. recycles material we have already seen in the "Lines Written by a Female Citizen," including the figure of "oppression's giant form," which again paces "the trembling land" "While abject slav'ry with submissive mien / Stoops low to kiss the terror dealing hand" (ll. 25–28). Here we see again the skill with which F. A. C. combines multivalent references, connecting the volatile issue of slavery with a psychologically astute observation about the tendency of victims of ongoing abuse to defer to—even to become romantically attracted to—their abusers. Furthermore, her delight in loaded language is obvious in her command to the "brave Spirit," in the especially visible context of the poem's final four lines:

> . . . with a strong and powerful arm
> *Arrest* the dreaded tyrant on his way,
> Nor, yielding to the *terror* of *alarm,*
> The mandates of despotic pow'r obey.
> (ll. 33–36; my emphases)

96

"Arrest" again suggests not just the action of physically bringing to a halt but also, more significantly, the unlawful nature of the authority by which power controls the situation and the lawful remedy to that usurpation. Likewise, the caution not to be swayed by "the terror of alarm" is easily transposed into a warning not to be so overwrought at the alarm over the terror (in France) or at the possibility of an invasion (in England) as to be seduced into supporting the dictates of the unlawful domestic power as a supposedly preferable alternative.

The sheer rhetoricality of much of Radical writing suggests the extent to which authors sought to emulate, if they could not actually practice, the dynamics of spoken discourse. Less an affectation than an attempt to suggest actual verbal inflection, the abundance of exclamation points underscores this auditory aspect of Radical verse. David Worrall has written that the ultra-Radicals preferred speech to writing because "the oral mode of textuality was less susceptible to scrutiny by the Government's surveillance system."[34] While this is of course true, we must nevertheless credit the poets with a strong sense of the effects upon a reader—especially a reader who is "sympathetic" in the sense in which I have been using the word here—of the powerful orality of their verse. This point applies to verse forms no less than to rhetorical features, for that matter. The effectiveness of popular forms like the four-line ballad stanza or verse explicitly designated as song (generally with the tune to which it is to be sung noted at the head of the poem) in propagating the Radical agenda cannot be underestimated. Nor should it be forgotten that these particular poetic *forms,* which were resurrected in 1765 in Bishop Percy's *Reliques of Ancient Poetry* and popularized thereafter in the work of writers of all stripes, were associated by Percy and others with the tradition of the "Saxon bard," whose utterances to the people in these simple poetic forms, in a language and rhetoric they could easily understand, were understood to possess "powerful political and moral force."[35] That Canning and Frere (to name the principals) opted in the *Anti-Jacobin* (November 1797 to July 1798) to adopt these models to satirize reform-minded poets who used such forms tells us much about both their wide currency and their effectiveness as vehicles for ideological argument.[36]

Women's presence on the Radical scene is further indicated by the appearance in the 15 January 1798 *Anti-Jacobin* of "Lines, written at the Close of the Year 1797" and attributed to "An Englishwoman."[37] Given the *Anti-Jacobin*'s practice of pointedly responding to actual publications by authors whom the editors regarded as dangerous Jacobins, we must assume that this poem is meant to respond to one or more female authors. This smugly nationalistic poem answers the sort of rhetoric we see in F. A. C.'s poetry by reverting to the same ostensible historical heritage invoked by the Radicals:

Yes! unsupported *Treason's* standard falls,
Sedition vainly on her children calls,

While cities, cottages, and camps contend,
The King, their Laws, their Country to defend.

(ll. 23–26)

These are not the ancient authorities sacred to the Radical ideology, but rather those represented specifically by Pitt and contemporary Toryism. That the rest of the poem entrusts British welfare—and indeed the welfare of the entire world—to "Heav'n" from which "the flame of British courage burns" and to "HIM" "At whose 'great bidding' empires rise and fall" (ll. 35–39) reflects that strain of eighteenth-century nationalism by which England had designated itself the new Israel and its citizens the chosen people. Within this schema it was the current possessors of power whose interests were best served by the secular deification implied in this new Israel, not the disenfranchised and the unenfranchised whom the Radicals sought to remind of the putative status and authority (in)vested in them (rather than in a set of rulers) under the ancient Anglo-Saxon *beau ideal.*

Of course, not everyone subscribed to that gilded image of an English promised land, and the price of dissent was often considerable, especially for women. I want to close not with another poem from the 1790s but rather with one published more than a decade later. The reception accorded Anna Letitia Barbauld's *Eighteen Hundred and Eleven* is instructive, for Barbauld (who in 1793 had published an interventional prose treatise on the state of affairs in England[38]) possessed a considerable reputation in her lifetime. Remarkably, the opening of this powerful poem picks up the themes—and even the language—of F. A. C.'s poems of some fifteen years earlier, itemizing the ways in which "Colossal Power with overwhelming force / Bears down each fort of Freedom in its course" so that

... where the Soldier gleans the scant supply,
The helpless Peasant but retires to die;
No laws his hut from licensed outrage shield,
And war's least horror is the ensanguined field.

(ll. 7–22)[39]

Even granting that the thrust of Barbauld's poem is far different from that of most Radical poetry of the 1790s in its Volneyesque vision of a future in which liberty thrives not in the Old World but rather in the New, in the Americas, the poem shares with them the conviction of British error, British guilt. Indeed, it envisions a future that seems to bear out the predictions of her old acquaintance, Coleridge, who had in his "Ode to the Departing Year" (1796) declared "O Albion! thy predestin'd ruins rise" (l. 146). Just as Coleridge chastised his country's errors and misplaced priorities in poems like the ode and "Fears in Solitude" (1798), and much as Wordsworth had followed suit in the political sonnets of 1802 and then publicly regretted his "unfilial fears" (l. 8) later in the year, in a sonnet like "When I have borne in memory," so too does Barbauld assert to and about Britain that "Thou who hast shared the guilt [for the protracted war] must share the woe" (l. 46). Interestingly, in its assessment of the poem which it recognized as possessing considerable literary merit, the *Eclectic Review* reverted back to the very word that Coleridge and Wordsworth had used in their poems, remarking of the poem's tone that it is "in a most extraordinary degree unkindly and unpatriotic—we had almost said unfilial."[40] It echoes, too, the sentiments of Opie in poems like the "Ode, Written on the Opening of the Last Campaign" (1795) and "Ode on the Present Times," in which latter poem she laments the misfortune of "FAMINE" (l. 67) about to descend on England ("O Britain! ill-starred land"; l. 55) as a result of the nation's orgy of warmaking.[41] As in poems I have cited earlier, Opie's message, like Barbauld's, has less to do with nationalistic thinking than it does with the universal effects of war upon both contending parties—and most especially upon its most innocent victims.

My point here is simply that like Radicals and liberals alike during the entire period of the Gallic Wars, Barbauld (whom one must hesitate to call a Radical, even in the immediate context of *Eighteen Hundred and Eleven,* given her normally characteristic "balanced, sensible, moderately reformist" writing[42]) takes to task a national military policy that reflects the socio-economic forces working throughout the period to the disadvantage of those with most to lose—their lives—from the protracted war. Naturally most of the printed response to Barbauld attacked her for her apparently subversive intent, particularly since the terms on which the Radical assault on power and privilege in England was mounted had changed significantly after the collapse of the Peace of Amiens, the shameful (self-)coronation of Napoleon, and the prosecution of the blatantly imperialist Peninsular Wars. The staunch Tory reviewer John Wilson Croker excoriated Barbauld with particularly mean-spritied sarcasm in the *Quarterly Review* for her decision "to dash down her shagreen spectacles and her knitting needles, and to sally forth . . . in the magnanimous resolution of saving a sinking state."[43] Little had changed, it appears, for the Radical woman writer—or even the usually moderate re-fomer—who essayed the interventional mode. Like her sisters two decades earlier, Barbauld is faulted specifically and explicitly for her indecorous and short-sighted (thus the specatcles) rejection of the emblems of her gender (her knitting needles) and her intrusion into the male arena of political discourse. What Sarah Spence had written about the mutually exclusive, gendered purviews of men and women seemed still to hold firm within the mainstream culture as a whole in 1812, when Barbauld's poem appeared. That the strains of Radical thought visible in women's poetry of the 1790s modulate into something else—something seemingly far more determinedly "domestic"—in the inhospitable climate of the Regency should not surprise us. For the conclusion of the Napoleonic Wars in 1815 removed one of the principal themes of that variety of Radical discourse which women poets had made, in a special way, their own.

NOTES

1. *Biographical Dictionary of Modern British Radicals,* Vol. 1: 1770–1830, ed. Joseph O. Baylen and Norbert J. Grossman (Hassocks, Sussex: Harvester Press, 1979).

2. The first phrase is from *The True Briton.* The latter hyperbole reflects the thinking of the *Oracle* and the *Morning Post;* see Lucyle Werkmeister, *A Newspaper History of England, 1792–93* (Lincoln: University of Nebraska Press, 1967), pp. 311–12. To be sure, it was not a Radical poet to whom these accolades were directed, but to a Della Cruscan whose *Modern Manners* (1793) was an instant success and whose *Monody to the Memory of the Late Queen of France* (1793) was much admired by the British press generally.

3. Lucinda Cole and Richard G. Swartz, " 'Why Should I Wish for Words?' Literacy, Articulation, and the Borders of Literary Culture," in *At the Limits of Romanticism: Essays in Cultural Feminist and Materialist Criticism,* ed. Mary A. Favret and Nicola J. Watson (Bloomington: Indiana University Press, 1994), p. 162.

4. See for instance Albert Goodwin, *The Friends of Liberty: The English Democratic Movement in the Age of the French Revolution* (Cambridge, Mass.: Harvard University Press, 1979), pp. 33, 56–57.

5. James A. Epstein, *Radical Expression: Political Language, Ritual, and Symbol in England, 1790–1850* (New York: Oxford University Press, 1994), p. 23.

6. See for instance the arguments developed by Mary Wollstonecraft in her *Vindication of the Rights of Woman* (1792); the anonymous author of *Thoughts on the Condition of Women* (no date, but probably late 1790s and conjecturally attributed to Mary Darby Robinson); Mary Hays (also writing anonymously) in *An Appeal to Men of Great Britain in Behalf of Women* (1798); Mary Ann Radcliffe in *The Female Advocate* (1799); and, later, men like William Thompson in his *Appeal of One Half of the Human Race, Women, Against the Pretensions of the Other Half, Men, to Retain Them in Political, and Thence in Civil and Domestic Slavery* (1825).

7. Lynne E. Withey, "Catharine Macaulay and the Uses of History: Ancient Rights, Perfectionism, and Propaganda," *The Journal of British Studies* 16 (1976): 59.

8. Donna Landry, *The Muses of Resistance: Labouring Class Women's Poetry in Britain, 1739–1796* (Cambridge: Cambridge University Press, 1991), p. 268.

9. Carolyn Steedman, "The Price of Experience: Women and the Making of the English Working Class," *Radical History Review* 59 (1994): 109–19. Steedman points out that others have made this point before her, most notably Joan Wallach Scott, *Gender and the Politics of History* (New York: Columbia University Press, 1988).

10. See Landry; Terry Lovell, *Consuming Fiction* (London: Verso, 1987); Cheryl Turner, *Living by the Pen: Women Writers in the Eighteenth Century* (London: Routledge, 1992).

11. Eleanor Ty, *Unsex'd Revolutionaries: Five Women Novelists of the 1790s* (Toronto: University of Toronto Press, 1993), p. 14.

12. Vivien Jones, "Women Writing Revolution: Narratives of History and Sexuality in Wollstonecraft and Williams," in *Beyond Romanticism: New Approaches to*

Texts and Contexts, 1780–1832, ed. Stephen Copley and John Whale (London: Routledge, 1992), pp. 178–79.

13. Richard Polwhele, *The Unsex'd Females: A Poem* (London: Cadell and Davies, 1798). [Thomas James Mathias] *The Pursuits of Literature;* Part I appeared in 1794, Parts II and III in 1796, Part IV in 1797. Thereafter, the poem went through many editions. By 1812, the year of the sixteenth edition, it had grown to a large quarto volume of 542 pages, with copious notes, translations of passages, and a detailed index. Interestingly, after the initial publication of Parts I–III by Owen, publication was taken over by Becket, who was still involved in its publication in the 1812 sixteenth edition, where "Becket and Porter" are identified prominently on the title page as "Booksellers to the Prince Regent."

14. Rev. Richard Polwhele, *Discourses on Different Subjects,* 2 vols. (London: Cadell, Dilly, Wilkie, Rivington, Law, and Buckland, 1788), 2:90, "On the Dissipation of Fashionable Women."

15. Ty, p. 13.

16. Anne Grant, "A Familiar Epistle to a Friend," *The Highlanders, and Other Poems* (London: Longman, Hurst, Rees, and Orme, 1808), ll. 174–85.

17. Sarah Spence, "A Fragment Taken from a Piece written about 28 January 1793," and entitled, *Thoughts on the Impending War, Poems and Miscellaneous Pieces* (Bury St. Edmunds: Sarah Spence; London: J. Johnson, 1795), p. 91.

18. David Hume, *A Treatise of Human Nature,* ed. L. A. Selby-Bigge (Oxford: Clarendon Press, 1888), pp. 362, 319–20.

19. Stuart Curran, "Women Readers, Women Writers," in *The Cambridge Companion to British Romanticism,* ed. Stuart Curran (Cambridge: Cambridge University Press, 1993), p. 182.

20. Anne Janowitz, " 'A Voice from across the Sea': Communitarianism at the Limits of Romanticism," in *At the Limits of Romanticism,* p. 85.

21. Mrs. [Elizabeth] Moody, "Anna's Complaint; Or the Miseries of War; Written in the Isle of Thanet, 1794"; first published in the *Universal Magazine* 96 (March 1795); reproduced in Betty T. Bennett, ed., *British War Poetry in the Age of Romanticism: 1793–1815* (New York: Garland, 1976), pp. 149–50.

22. "Humanitas," in *War a System of Madness and Irreligion. to which is subjoined by way of a conclusion, The Dawn of Universal Peace. Wrote on the last Fast Day, 1796.* Although no publication information appears, a pencilled note on the title page of the British Library copy identifies the author as "George Miller of Dunbar." The title page of this presentation copy also bears this inscription: "Presented by the Author to the editor of the Philanthropist with best wishes that his efforts to put an end to the horrid and barbarous custom of War may be crowned with the most complete success." The editor was Daniel Isaac Eaton; *The Philanthropist* was the more economically and socially oriented successor to his *Politics for the People,* which ceased publication in March 1795, the month in which *The Philanthropist* began a run that lasted forty-three weeks, until early 1796.

23. Anne K. Mellor, *Romanticism and Gender* (New York: Routledge, 1993), p. 65.

24. The poem is reproduced in Bennett, *British War Poetry,* pp. 224–25.

25. Reproduced in Bennett, *British War Poetry,* pp. 140–42. The poem, which bears in the position of subtitle the date, "27th January 1795," originally appeared

in the Norwich press, in *The Cabinet* 2 (1795): 92–94, where it was attributed only to "N."

26. Epstein, *Radical Expression,* p. 23.

27. Reproduced in *Graphic Works of George Cruikshank,* ed. Richard A. Vogler (New York: Dover, 1979), p. 17.

28. Michael Scrivener, *Poetry and Reform: Periodical Verse from the English Democratic Press, 1792–1824* (Detroit: Wayne State University Press, 1992), p. 123.

29. *The Tribune* 3, no. 38 (1795): 105–06. The poem is reproduced in Scrivener, pp. 122–23.

30. William Stafford, *Socialism, Radicalism, and Nostalgia: Social Criticism in Britain, 1775–1830* (Cambridge: Cambridge University Press, 1987), p. 43.

31. Richard Lee, *A Summary of the Duties of Citizenship: Written Expressly for Members of the London Corresponding Societies* (London, 1795), pp. 19–28. Lee's comments are cited by Epstein in *Radical Expression,* p. 8.

32. The *Tribune* appeared in 1795–96; *The Moral and Political Magazine* ran from July 1795 to June 1796; Scrivener, pp. 108–9, 127.

33. Reproduced in Scrivener, pp. 129–30.

34. David Worrall, *Radical Culture: Discourse, Resistance, and Surveillance, 1790–1820* (New York: Harvester Wheatsheaf, 1992), p. 5.

35. Bennett, *British War Poetry,* p. 51.

36. See *Poetry of the Anti-Jacobin,* ed. L. Rice-Oxley (Oxford: Basil Blackwell, 1924).

37. The poem is reprinted in *Poetry of the Anti-Jacobin,* pp. 32–33.

38. "A Volunteer" [Anna Letitia Barbauld], *Sins of Government, Sins of the Nation; or, A Discourse for the Fast, Appointed on April 19, 1793* (London: J. Johnson, 1793).

39. The poem is reproduced in *The Poems of Anna Letitia Barbauld,* ed. William McCarthy and Elizabeth Kraft (Athens: University of Georgia Press, 1994), pp. 152–61.

40. The *Eclectic Review* 8 (1812): 474; cited in *Poems,* p. 310n.

41. The poems are reproduced in Bennett, *British War Poetry,* pp. 137–42. A native of Norwich, itself a center of Radical dissent, Opie (née Alderson) had many Radical friends, including both Wollstonecraft and Godwin.

42. William Keach, "A Regency Prophecy and the End of Anna Barbauld's Career," *Studies in Romanticism* 33 (1994): 577.

43. *Quarterly Review* 7 (1812): 309.

RHETORICAL MISSILES AND DOUBLE-TALK:

Napoleon, Wordsworth,
and
the Invasion Scare of 1804

BRENDA BANKS

As the French Revolution disintegrated into the Napoleonic Wars and Napoleon seemed poised to invade all of Europe, internal debates in Great Britain over governmental reform and social justice gave way to a largely univocal nationalistic rhetoric aimed at bolstering domestic solidarity and intimidating the enemy. Not all British weapons employed against Napoleon were fashioned from metal and loaded with gunpowder, however. A broad variety of anti-French rhetoric was launched from many sites. Consider, for instance, this rhetorical missile, an epigram published by Britain's *Morning Post* on 20 January 1804, under the nom de plum "PRENEZ GUARDE" and implicitly addressed to Napoleon:

> A HINT ACROSS THE CHANNEL
> You make such a pother
> From one month to t'other,
> Bout coming our Isle to subdue;
> That shou'd you delay
> Still the visit to pay,
> Our Armies shall—"wait upon you!"

As frequently happened, this witty epigram reduces the French Consul to an object of ridicule while shaping the reader's opinion of France and her associated Radical ideologies by appealing persuasively to a sense of patriotism in a national emergency. Wit turns the tables, allowing the British in their geographically defensive position to become verbal aggressors.

Though France would eventually succumb to defeat, for a number of months in 1803 and 1804 Napoleon's threat to invade Britain appeared very real indeed. The British administration's reaction to this threat was to bombard the people with alarmist propaganda that simultaneously urged readiness and prompted ridicule of the enemy.[1] The first generation of British Romantic poets has often been accused of embracing the administration's nationalistic rhetoric and discarding their Radical politics with embarrassing haste. This generation had not only experienced the French Revolution as impressionable youths, but had in many cases originally supported the revolutionaries enthusiastically. However, their recantation of this support around the turn of the century was a painfully slow and guilt-ridden affair, not the comfortable, self-centered apostasy suggested in the second generation of Romantic poets' revisionary tales about their predecessors. In an historical arena where open political discourse could lead to serious consequences, these poets' utterances were often more complicated, and more subversive, than they have at times been portrayed over some two centuries.

William Wordsworth had an especially close relationship to the Revolution and its various players, having traveled through France in 1790, 1791–92, 1802, and perhaps 1793 as well.[2] In the two years following his last visit, he attempted to account in verse for what appeared to him the Revolution's most disturbing product, Napoleon. When we recall that as Wordsworth composed many of his political sonnets and the French Books of *The Prelude* in 1804 Napoleon was preparing a much publicized invasion of Britain, the topical urgency of this poetry re-emerges, as does the pivotal nature of this year for both the poet and his nation. Indeed, understanding when and how Wordsworth's generation of intellectuals refashioned their ties to revolutionary France has become essential to understanding the politics of Romanticism.[3]

As I will demonstrate, in the political sonnets and the French Books, Wordsworth expresses a rare (and too rarely understood) opposition to the British administration's counterrevolutionary propaganda. That Wordsworth's Radicalism is commonly believed not to have survived into the nineteenth century is likely due to what Paul Magnuson has described as "a kind of double talk" into which agitators for change characteristically slip during particularly repressive periods, such as wartime.[4] With the passage of years, readers may lose the decoder mechanisms needed to break into such artfully disguised speech. Indeed, for many twentieth-century commentators, much Romantic poetry has assumed an opacity resembling quietism but which may, in fact, mask an entirely different quality.

Wordsworth was wise to retreat into double-talk at this time. Surely he could no longer engage as explicitly in public political discourse as he had, for example, in his unpublished "Letter to the Bishop of Llandaff" of 1793. In this, perhaps the young Wordsworth's most overtly Radical text, he tacitly approves the use of violence to achieve revolutionary objectives: "a people could not but at first make an abuse of that liberty which a legitimate republic supposes. The animal just released from its stall will exhaust the overflow of its spirits in a round of wanton vagaries, but it will soon return to itself and enjoy its freedom in moderate and regular delight."[5] He seems even to justify the elimination of the French monarchy, if not the execution of King Louis XVI:

> At a period big with the fate of the human race, I am sorry that you attach so much importance to the personal sufferings of the late royal martyr. . . . But there is a class of men who received the news of the late execution with much more heart-felt sorrow than that which you among such a multitude so officiously express. . . . They are sorry that the prejudice and weakness of mankind have made it necessary to force an individual into an unnatural situation, which requires more than human talents and human virtues, and at the same time precludes him from attaining even a moderate knowledge of common life and from feeling a particular share in the interests of mankind.[6]

Note that Wordsworth's chief objection to the monarchy is the "unnatural situation" into which it presses a fallible human being. An objection to too much power in the hands of a single individual will prove to be the common thread uniting Wordsworth's youthful and mature ideologies.[7]

Nevertheless, Wordsworth's brazen manifesto reflects a stance from which the young poet quickly withdrew. Witness his two well-known letters to William Matthews in the late spring of 1794: although he avows that "I am of that odious class of men called democrats, and of that class I shall for ever continue," he backs away from the sentiments of the "Letter" when he says, "the destruction of these institutions which I condemn appears to me to be hastening on too rapidly. I recoil from the bare idea of a revolution."[8] A decade later, as a husband and new father settled in the Lake District, Wordsworth had learned to express his views more carefully, as the times required. But it is too simple to label Wordsworth an apostate to the Revolution. To maintain the political stance of the "Letter" after the rise of Napoleon would have represented political suicide and perhaps the loss of one's physical freedom and well-being. It was an untenable position.

I. Rhetorical Missiles across the English Channel

By 1804 the brief peace of Amiens had fallen apart, the cross-channel travel by nostalgic ex-Radicals like Wordsworth that it engendered had ceased, and it had become unfashionable to praise the French Revolution, which seemed only to have created a monster, Napoleon Bonaparte. As the year opened, England anxiously awaited the expected invasion, Napoleon's forces having been gathering at Calais for months. Every shot heard along the Channel stirred fears that the invasion had begun. In early February, the firing of a lime kiln in Northumberland brought out the local volunteer regiment, fully prepared to engage Napoleon's forces. While the volunteers' overzealousness is laughable, Britons believed they had good reason to be alarmed. The administration and the press saw to that.

As the invasion scare took hold, the administration clamped down more tightly than ever on subversive activities and publications. A number of laws passed since the outbreak of the Revolution (many under the aegis of Pitt) gave the administration remarkable power to protect itself. In 1790 the Habeus Corpus Act was suspended; next came the Royal Proclamation against "sedition" that allowed the *in absentia* trial and conviction of Tom Paine on the charge of treason; additional Treason and Sedition Acts in 1795 and 1799 made political meetings and speeches illegal; in 1799 came the Acts against Combination, aimed at abolishing trade unionism, and other laws enforcing press censorship. The administration routinely squelched publication of oppositional political views by threatening publishers with imprisonment. Authors were no safer from the government's wrath: Wordsworth's contemporary, William Blake, was tried (but acquitted) on a charge of sedition in 1803.

Owing largely to such pressure, the British press began to present a surprisingly unified political front as it fanned the fire of invasion hysteria in early 1804. Whereas the eighteenth-century press had begun to exhibit a modern, dialogic interplay between establishment and opposition voices, for a short period during the Napoleonic Wars the infant Radical press in Britain was throttled.[9] For example, the *Monthly Review,* which had vigorously supported the Revolution at its outset, restrained its Radical views during the Napoleonic Wars, when founder Ralph Griffiths' son and associate, George, joined his local volunteer regiment and became a colonel.[10] And after its sale in 1803, the *Morning Post* quickly became a vehicle of the Addington ministry, later earning the epithet "The Fawning Post."[11] An exception to this trend is the *Edinburgh Review,* which, emerging from Scotland's tradition of dissent, remained quietly opposed to counterrevolutionary discourse. Elsewhere opposition, which had struggled since Britain declared war with France in 1793, was now virtually suppressed. The editors of the *London Times* commented upon this phenomenon:

> The present united and ardent spirit of the people; the general sense not only of the justice but the necessity of the war, and the universally-acknowledged attention of Government to the public security, throw difficulties in the way of Opposition which it cannot surmount. . . . [It is] left therefore, to the last resources of base and selfish minds, to calumny and falsehood.[12]

Such statements leave little room for debate. F. J. Maccun describes the English newspapers' function at this time as one of "ultra-writing," or propagandistic flagellation of their readers' already thriving hatred for the French, rather than reporting of "facts."[13] In dismissing such writing as worthless to scholars of the period, however, he misses an important point. The energetic

106

British propaganda industry of the Napoleonic Wars explains how even sympathetic Britons were induced to return to intense, anti-French rhetoric just over a decade after they had celebrated the dawn of "liberty" in their sister nation.

In January, for example, the *Morning Post* provided front-page coverage of the invasion threat nearly every day. On the 4th, the *Post* reported that the weather was now fair enough for the French army to put to sea; on the 5th, that British troops were ready all along the coast for the invasion, with Admiral Cornwallis waiting with his ships off Brest, several minor skirmishes with the French having taken place in the Channel in the past few days; on the 11th, that although many rumors of invasion had recently proven false, the invasion was still highly likely. Meanwhile, Napoleon's Boulogne flotilla continued preparations begun the summer before. He had ordered shipbuilding to proceed in ports throughout Europe and had brought the Grand Army to Calais. Clearly one of the most terrifying aspects of the growing flotilla would have been its sheer proximity to England, where, on a clear day, one can see across the Channel to the coast of France. Moreover, Napoleon's known tactical genius must have fed the uneasiness. The British learned, for instance, of his "eccentric prospect" of lining up enough flat-bottomed boats—about 1,200, he figured—to make a bridge from Boulogne to Dover across which to march his troops, rather than sailing them across in the conventional manner.[14]

The British papers countered with bravado. In fact, the *Post* editors claimed, "we court the combat" with Napoleon.[15] The *Post* boasted that Napoleon's "pigmy armadas" would be incapable of reaching England, because in order to succeed, the French forces would have to destroy every ship in the Channel big enough to carry a gun.[16] A charged word, "armada" is a calculated rhetorical weapon recalling for the British their much celebrated historical defeat of an invading continental host, and aiming at strengthening readers' nationalistic resolve.

For months, the newspapers' invasion coverage would vacillate between such swaggering and outright alarmism, but either way, the invasion scare would figure continually in readers' consciousnesses. The prospect of an avenging "Boney" was even used to frighten children into good behavior. The rising sense of alarm also seemed to increase the acerbity of attacks on Napoleon in the works of caricaturists like Gillray, Rowlandson, and Cruikshank, whose anti-Gallicism peaked in the years 1803–1805.[17] At the same time, the British press pummeled what was left of revolutionary sympathies among its readers. Representations of the French in the British papers, like representations of the invasion threat, were of one stripe in early 1804. In its efforts to galvanize British spirit, the press portrayed France as deprived of its civil freedoms under the iron hand of its dictator. Britain, in contrast, was represented as a land of liberty, with a pedigree of successful and bloodless "revolutions."

The British press's rhetorical weapons were often deadly effective. Representing the French character as foppish and irrational, though hardly a new tactic, now became uniformly pervasive. The papers often skewered the French with sarcasm, as in the titles of two "French" plays, the fictitious readings of which are announced in the *Morning Post* of 3 January 1804: "*Le Fou Raisonable,* a Comedy,*" and "*L'esprit de contradiction,* a comedy." Both titles suggest French befuddlement, opposing ideologies reduced to oxymoron in the former example, as opposed to unified English sensibility. Or take this wickedly tongue-in-cheek allusion: "Is there no *Southsayer* in France so charitable as to whisper to BONAPARTE, that an *Emperor's Crown* may excite many a Republican *Brutus* to consign him to the fate of JULIUS CAESAR?"[18] Descriptions of skirmishes in the English Channel commonly took on a sarcastic tone as well: "With their wonted candour . . . the enemy reduce the number of vessels taken [in the channel on Jan. 3] to three."[19] More effectively than anger or diatribe, such sarcasm urges readers to laugh derisively at an inside joke, while persuading them to find its subject ridiculous. As Marilyn Butler writes, "cleverness and wit are intimidating qualities, not comforting to the socially inexperienced reader, but demanding his respectful assent."[20] With witty sarcasm the press bolstered its already considerable power to shape readers' opinions.

The energy behind this sarcasm may have been rooted in Britain's defensive position at this point in the Napoleonic Wars. G. M. Trevelyan has called the years 1800–1804 "the four best years of [Napoleon's] life." He seemed unstoppable. When, in May of 1803, the disingenuously negotiated "Peace" of Amiens had fallen apart, with it disappeared a short-lived British sense of security that was not to return for another decade. The resumption of the war was inevitable because Napoleon had never meant to cease his push across the continent, intent upon isolating it from British trade. Holland, Belgium, the western bank of the Rhine, Switzerland, and most of the Italian Peninsula were now under his rule.

And so, early in 1804, it was far from certain that Britain would defeat Napoleon. Even though Britain had secured important naval victories at Texal (1797) and at Aboukir Bay (1798), the Second Coalition against Napoleon had dissolved in 1800–1801, leaving Britain the lone obstacle to French military ambitions. Not until later in 1804 would the Third Coalition form, and not until 1805 would Admiral Nelson secure the pivotal victory against Napoleon at Trafalgar that would destroy all French hopes of overcoming Britain's mastery of the seas. In 1804, Britain's future looked tenuous and would continue to look so for some time.[21]

Napoleon's encampment just across the English Channel had seriously dampened any remaining enthusiasm in Britain for the Revolution. Not surprisingly, the public recantation by even the most stalwart British Radical intellectuals of their former revolutionary enthusiasm can be assigned to the early years of the nineteenth century. Napoleon styled himself "heir of the Revolution," and former sympathizers could only abhor the Revolution and make an embarrassing public retreat from their original enthusiasm.

Indeed, the majority of British had come to agree with Edmund Burke that the Revolution had failed to create an improved social order.[22] As one editorial summed it up:

> The French Revolution seems now to have attained a kind of climax. The blood and massacre which have distinguished and disgraced France, the murder of its sovereign, the exile of its Princes, the humble state of the country, and the unsettled condition of Europe, combined to confer the title of Emperor on an upstart Corsican, who possesses an extent of power, and exercises a tyranny unknown to any of the long succession of the legitimate Sovereigns of that transformed and devoted country, which he rules with a rod of iron.[23]

It is shocking to see the *Times* suggesting that the "legitimate" Bourbon dynasty, which it seemed to forget had never been well-loved in England, would provide a desirable alternative to Napoleon's presumably illegitimate power. In fact, the restoration of the Bourbon monarchs became the aim of each of the European coalitions that fought France from the 1790s onward. Accordingly, the British press now commonly represented France as embracing what the formerly oppositional *Morning Post* termed a "career of murder . . . with all the horrible features by which the blood-stained reign of ROBESPIERRE was distinguished."[24] This conflation of Napoleon's France with that of the Terror was more than a party line; it was echoed in papers of widely differing political allegiances. By linking oppositional discourse with Radical ideology and with France as aggressor, the administration and the press largely silenced domestic opposition.[25]

The British considered France's current belligerence the natural result of its Radical experiments in governmental reform. As Conor Cruise O'Brien has written:

> Far from spreading liberty in the world, the French Revolutionary expansion strengthened reaction by ensuring that resistance to the French Revolution would be associated with nationalism in other countries, which were challenged by the violent strain of French nationalism released by the French Revolution. This was the response in England, Russia, Spain, as well as in the countries of early occupation. Thus French Revolutionary expansion, far from disseminating the ideas of the Enlightenment, actually hindered the progress of those ideas, by causing them to be associated with the belligerent chauvinism of one particular nation, calling itself *la Grande Nation*.[26]

This development signaled not only the Revolution's failure, but the counterrevolution's success. The struggle between revolutionary and counterrevolutionary ideologies further polarized British classes, encouraged nationalistic sentiment, increased the suffering of the poor, and restrained the enlightenment ideal of humanitarianism among the upper classes.[27] This hardening of both the English class structure and the political power structure under Pitt's administration had curtailed dialogue over the nature of the ideal political state: the administration now spoke a largely unified discourse of power that could not easily be contradicted.

Whether acting as mouthpieces of the administration, or whipped into sincere nationalistic frenzy, British newspaper editors continued to reinforce this discourse of power. On 5 May 1804, for example, having read the latest *Moniteur,* the official publication of Revolutionary France, the *Morning Post* editor mocked its common association of France with the Roman Republic: "The article from Boulogne is exceedingly ridiculous . . . it exhultingly compares the French gunboats to the gallies of the antient Romans, as if similar gallies, in the present state of nautical tactics, would be of any consideration." Indeed, the smokescreen of Roman associations created by Napoleon's own propaganda arsenal was a formidable rhetorical force. In 1802, Napoleon had declared himself "First Consul" of France; in May of 1804, he asked the French Assembly to declare him "Emperor of the French." This line of continuity from the ancient Roman Empire to the post-Revolutionary French Empire was integral to Napoleon's justification of his rule over France. But the *Morning Post* editor destroys this connection in the passage above, reducing inflated metaphor to its literal equivalent. Readers are urged to laugh at France's self-representations, torpedoed by understated British wit.

The deadliest rhetorical missiles were reserved for Napoleon himself. And what little discourse dared to represent Napoleon sympathetically was vigorously attacked. One reviewer described a booklet entitled The *Life of Bonaparte* as a "mischievous little publication" designed to "raise the character of Bonapart in the estimation of the people of this country. . . . It is clearly the work of a Jacobin faction, who have pushed it through seven editions, and who, we know, have taken incredible pains to circulate it among the peasantry, particularly in Kent."[28]

Kent, of course, in southeast England, was seen as the most likely site of an invasion; thus, it was the most dangerous area in which to allow subversive ideas to take hold. Such oppositional discourse, when circulated among the "peasantry" in Kent or elsewhere, threatened Britain's socio-economic status quo, as did the suggestion that the lower classes might learn to admire Napoleon. Even the *Critical Review,* considered fairly liberal at the time, styled Napoleon as "a conspicuous performer in the most disgraceful excesses of . . . terrorists and assassins"—presumably alluding to earlier revolutionaries.[29] And it observed that another recent publication, *The Life of Napoleon, as it Should Be Handed Down to Posterity,* by J. Mudford, told a tale that was "not the real life of Bonaparte . . . [who] is a much greater rogue than [Mudford] paints him."[30]

Not surprisingly, the *Anti-Jacobin Review,* created in the 1790s expressly to battle the Revolution, attacked with particular viciousness. Among its claims were charges that Napoleon often ordered seriously wounded soldiers marked to be buried alive with the dead, that he had once slaughtered a pot dog who ate his dinner, and that he had killed a girl he had impregnated by giving her arsenic pills to induce a miscarriage. In fact, the *Anti-Jacobin Review* charged that Napoleon had committed more crimes in six months than all the Bourbon princes did in six centuries. He was, simply, "that base-born upstart, the Corsican Usurper."[31]

Clearly, liberal publications shared with their more conservative counterparts a personal antipathy to Napoleon. Indeed, consumed with Napoleon, British discourse seemed by 1804 largely to have forgotten the revolutionary idealism of the early 1790s, revealing a kind of selective amnesia of the national consciousness. In this climate, to have been a partisan of a nation that now threatened the sovereignty of one's own country was a fact best forgotten. The British press of 1804 helped suppress such memories by saturating its readers' minds with diatribes against Napoleon, that metonymical representation of France. By 1804, few of her citizens seemed to have noticed how Britain was backsliding.

II. DOUBLE-TALK AS DEFENSE MECHANISM

Now consider Wordsworth, who had supposedly "retired" from politics and other worldly concerns, when he moved to the Lake District several years earlier. Once an ardent apologist for the French Revolution, Wordsworth had by 1804 grown to despise Napoleon and lament the aggression in which France had engaged under his rule. Critics have sought recently to pinpoint the moment when Wordsworth presumably rejected his youthful Radicalism, with many arguing that this transformation happened early and abruptly. But Wordsworth did not simply awaken one morning a Tory. As I have argued elsewhere, the French Books of *The Prelude,* in particular, reveal a coping distinction that he began to make when he looked back upon the Revolution between early "innocent," "Girondin" revolutionary idealism and later "violent," "Jacobin" ruthlessness.[32] The distinction is a fictional one, first fabricated by the Girondins and Jacobins themselves, but it permitted Wordsworth and his contemporaries to mitigate whatever guilt or anger they may have felt over being forced to abandon their Radical discourse. That is, if the Revolution could be said to have betrayed itself with the ascendance of the "violent" Jacobins and Napoleon, then former British Radicals could be pardoned for once supporting the Revolution, as well as for eventually abandoning France's cause. They could, in fact, escape the charges they seemed to court of hypocrisy and apostasy.

Wordsworth's interpretation of the Revolution was ahead of its time. Later scholars, beginning with de Tocqueville several decades after Wordsworth, have similarly viewed Napoleon's rise to power as the outcome not of the Revolution's reforms, but of the political power vacuum created in France first by the emasculation of the nobility under Louis XIV, and then by the fall of Louis XVI.[33] Certainly, upon assuming power, Napoleon quickly dismantled revolutionary reforms and increased the centralization of the French government under the executive branch, much as Louis XIV had done. Although Napoleon's Civil Code, ratified in 1804 but largely ignored by the British press, retained equality of all citizens before the law, it also reinstituted a husband's legal authority over his wife and ownership of her property, as well as giving him increased authority as head of the family to divide property among his heirs—a reversal of the Girondins' effort to abolish the abuses of primogeniture. In addition, the Code restored the primary legal assumption of a defendant's guilt that revolutionary legislators had overturned.

Napoleon, moreover, violated the Declaration of the Rights of Man's promise of freedom of expression, reducing the number of papers published in Paris from seventy-three to thirteen (mostly his mouthpieces) and censoring the theatre. Not unlike his British counterparts, he violated France's constitutional rule against holding suspects arbitrarily and without charge, for example moving against the emigrés in Germany in the spring of 1804. On the basis of flimsy evidence that the exiled Bourbon Duc d'Enghien was plotting his assassination, Napoleon invaded neutral Baden, then had the Duc arrested, tried, and executed as a warning to his enemies.

In 1802 Napoleon sent an expeditionary force to Haiti to renew the institution of slavery, which had been abolished by the revolutionaries. He regulated the French economy to respond to the needs of the war instead of continuing the free-trade policies of the Girondins. In 1802 he abolished existing schools, replacing them with *lycées* under more direct government supervision and featuring a more patriotic curriculum and military-style discipline. And perhaps most symbolically, the Consulate of 1799 overturned the doctrine of popular sovereignty that the Declaration of the Rights of Man had promulgated. Although the male citizens of France retained their right to vote, henceforth this vote meant less because members of the assemblies were now appointed, not elected.[34] In the last analysis, Napoleon was more a creature of reaction than one of revolution.

Wordsworth seems to have appreciated that Napoleon felt little affinity for the Revolution's ideals, but in wartime, rather than speak unpopular political views directly by re-articulating those ideals, Wordsworth opted for a type of double-talk. This Janus-faced discourse is complicated for many by the fact that Wordsworth's political sonnets of 1802 to 1804 often echo the press's anti-French rhetoric and invasion hysteria. When some of these political sonnets appeared in the *Morning Post* amid its daily invasion scare propaganda, Wordsworth, like his friend Coleridge in the outwardly conciliatory "France, an Ode," seemed to have publicly recanted his former Radical sympathies.

Returning from his most recent visit to France, Wordsworth composed a number of sonnets vigorously challenging England to defend its shores from the "Usurper," Napoleon. For instance, "To the Men of Kent, October, 1803" exhorts these men staunchly to resist the imminent invasion, against which they would provide the first line of defense. The sonnet ends,

> No parlaying now! In Britain is one breath;
> We all are with you now from shore to shore:—
> Ye men of Kent, 'tis victory or death!

Similarly, in "Lines on the Expected Invasion 1803," Wordsworth echoes the press's call for a unified front against the enemy:

> Come ye—whate'er your creed—O waken all,
> Whate'er your temper, at your Country's call;
> Resolving (this a free-born Nation can)
> To have one Soul, and perish to a man,
> Or save this honoured Land from every Lord
> But British reason and the British sword.

Such ideological solidarity, Wordsworth asserts, is necessary while Britain is jeopardized: but he represents a comparable ideological unity in Napoleon's France as a lamentable phenomenon. In "October 1803" ('These times'), he writes,

> How piteous then that there should be [in France] such dearth
> Of knowledge; that whole myriads should unite
> To work against themselves such fell despite:
> Should come in phrensy and in drunken mirth,
> Impatient to put out the only light
> Of Liberty that yet remains on earth!

Wordsworth's distinction is that this unity, in contrast to Britain's, emerges not from rational resolution, but from irrational "phrensy," thus apparently echoing the charge that the French are irrational.

Of Napoleon, Wordsworth composes epithets as bitter as any in the press. In the sonnet, "I grieved for Buonaparte" of 1802, he wonders, "The tenderest mood / Of that Man's mind—what can it be? what food / Fed his first hopes? what knowledge could *he* gain?" Again, in "October, 1803" ('When, looking'), he writes,

> I see one man, of men the meanest too!
> Raised up to sway the world, to do, undo,
> With mighty Nations for his underlings. . . .

113

In "Anticipation. October, 1803," Wordsworth goes further; he celebrates the inevitable deaths that resistance to Napoleon's invasion would incur:

> And even the prospect of our brethren slain,
> Hath something in it which the heart enjoys:—
> In glory will they sleep and endless sanctity.

Not surprisingly, these political sonnets have contributed to the perception that Wordsworth had reversed his political views in the decade following the Revolution. However, as Alan Liu and Stephen Behrendt have demonstrated, these superficially patriotic poems are not as ideologically one-dimensional as they first appear.[35] The very two-part form of the Petrarchan sonnet that Wordsworth employed urges opposition, and in these political sonnets, Wordsworth subtly wavers between chauvinistic cheering and stern criticism of Britain. Alongside the sonnets previously mentioned stands the "Milton!" sonnet, in which Wordsworth charges that "England . . . is a fen / Of stagnant waters" and "We are selfish men." And in "England!" he concludes

> Therefore the wise pray for thee, though the freight
> Of thy offenses be a heavy weight:
> Oh grief! that Earth's best hopes rest all with Thee!

As Liu argues,

> even as we read the mounting patriotism of the sonnets, we must realize that Wordsworth's saber rattling is finally as complicated as Hamlet's in the long interregnum between his first resolve and his bloody fifth act. If Wordsworth's sonnets were a soliloquy, they would begin, "To be or not to be English." Thus while his framing argument is indeed aligned with the English public, it contains within itself a divisive counterargument dedicated to *reforming* the public.[36]

But reforming the public and its institutions had gone out of fashion along with the Revolution itself. Wordsworth's continued efforts at reform, though cloaked in diatribe against Napoleon, nevertheless represented a daring enterprise.

Befitting their more expansive form, the French Books of *The Prelude* offer a wide-ranging revisionary view of the Revolution, which the poet at one point again disguised by invoking popular anti-Napoleon rhetoric. Wordsworth's opposition in the French Books to the counterrevolutionary vein of public discourse is more daring than it is in the sonnets. He not only criticizes England, but celebrates the original ideals of the French Revolution, distinguishing them from Napoleon's violent aggression. While the French Books were written scarcely a year later than many of the political sonnets, however, *The Prelude* would not be published until 1850.[37] Thus, their complex oppositional ideologies have often been obscured by the poem's late appearance on the stage of Wordsworth's career. But in the French Books, Wordsworth defends the Revolution from both Britain and Napoleon, resisting the administration's overpowering discourse even as he appears to attack Napoleon in the very style of that discourse.[38] Wordsworth refers to Napoleon only once in the *Prelude,* and even then implicitly, but what he says reveals a great deal about where the evolution of his political sympathies stood in 1804. In Book Ten, Wordsworth openly deplores Napoleon's December coronation:

> finally to close
> And rivet up the gains of France, a Pope
> Is summoned in to crown an Emperor—
> This last opprobrium, when we see the dog
> Returning to his vomit, when the sun
> That rose in splendour, was alive, and moved
> In exultation among living clouds,
> Hath put his function and his glory off,
> And, turned into a gewgaw, a machine,
> Sets like an opera phantom.[39]

To some extent, Wordsworth echoes the press's counterrevolutionary discourse here in representing the coronation as unnatural—leaving France to set like a "gewgaw, a machine." But he also claims that Napoleon has negated the "gains" of France, that he has killed a natural process, a "sun / that rose in splendour." The politically incorrect implication is that the Revolution had followed a natural, "living" process, a process now subverted by an unnatural empire.

Let us delve more deeply into the implications of this passage. It has been noted that it characterizes France's embrace of Napoleon by echoing Corinthians 2:22, where Paul warns about the perniciousness of "false prophets":[40]

> For when they speak great swelling *words* of vanity, they allure through the lusts of the flesh, *through much* wantonness, those that were clean escaped from them who live in error. . . . For it had been better for them not to have known the way of righteousness, than, after they have known *it,* to turn from the holy commandment delivered unto them. But it is happened unto them according to the true proverb, the dog *is* turned to his own vomit again; and, the sow that was washed to her wallowing in the mire. (2:18, 21–22)

By alluding to this biblical passage in his description of Napoleon's coronation, Wordsworth suggests that the dog—France—has relinquished its quest for liberty and regressed to the despotic rule of a single, powerful man, a form of rule that the revolutionaries had endeavored to abolish. Rather than contrast Napoleon unfavorably to the French kings he supplanted, as the press had done, Wordsworth stresses the similarities between kings and emperors. Much

115

like the monarch Wordsworth had described in the "Letter to the Bishop of Llandaff," Napoleon has attained an "unnatural situation" of power and is consequently removed from sympathy with his subjects.

Wordsworth's subtle biblical reference equates revolutionary ideals with knowledge of God and with righteous living, a daring connection to draw in 1804. It is daring as well to imply that Napoleon represents a return to a despotic past. Seen in this light, Wordsworth's appropriation of Paul's warning against *false* promises of liberty reveals not an anti-revolutionary, but rather an anti-empire, subtext. Wordsworth judges Napoleon's power unnatural not because he is "that base-born upstart, the Corsican Usurper," as the *Anti-Jacobin Review* styled him. It is rather his ideological descent from the unnaturally powerful Bourbon kings overthrown by the revolutionaries to which Wordsworth objects.

In sum, amid a flurry of rhetorical missiles aimed scattershot at Napoleon and the revolutionaries who preceded him, Wordsworth stands more firmly than is generally appreciated, voicing a quiet but potentially subversive distinction. This subversiveness is cloaked, as wartime circumstances required, in the double-talk of imaginative literature. Repositioning Wordsworth in the context of the public political discourse of the year 1804 reveals a man coming to grips with the failure of his revolutionary ideals to improve the world. His courageous struggle to reclaim the ideological high ground highlights the cowardice of the fawning press in thrall to the British administration. Moreover, a re-examination of this struggle undermines subsequent critics' faulty assessment of Wordsworth as anti-ideological apostate of the Revolution.

NOTES

1. It is perhaps to be expected that the delayed confrontation with France on the shores of England would become displaced by a battle of words. The fast growing readership of Britain in the Revolutionary and post-Revolutionary eras gave rise to an explosion of periodical literature: seventy-six newspapers and periodicals were published in England and Wales in 1781, but by the first decade of the nineteenth century, about forty new newspapers and periodicals were started each year, the number rising by 1832 to 250. See Ivon Asquith, "The Structure, Ownership and Control of the Press, 1789–1855," *Newspaper History from the Seventeenth Century to the Present Day,* ed. George Boyce, James Curran, and Pauline Wingate (London: Constable and Co. Ltd., 1978), p. 99.

2. Regarding the mysterious possibility of Wordsworth's 1793 visit, see Mark L. Reed, *Wordsworth: The Chronology of the Middle Years, 1800–1815* (Cambridge, Mass.: Harvard University Press, 1975), p. 147, and Stephen Gill, *William Wordsworth: A Life* (Oxford: Oxford University Press, 1990), pp. 77–78.

3. The debate about Wordsworth's political development continues to rage, as it has done since Hazlitt's famous comments in *The Spirit of the Age,* through contemporary reviews of *The Prelude* when it was published in 1850, and intensifying in the last several decades with critics such as Geoffrey Hartman, M. H. Abrams, James K.

Chandler, and Marilyn Butler perpetuating the myth of Wordsworth as turncoat. Nor has the perception that Wordsworth hastily repudiated politics disappeared from recent scholarship. For example, Laurence Lerner ends a recent essay with this remark: "Politics is an important presence behind much of Wordsworth's poetry, but is either laid aside by the poem, or needs to be laid aside by us"; see "Wordsworth's Refusal of Politics," *Studies in English Literature, 1500–1900* 31 (1991): 673–91. Others see an accommodation of political realities rather than withdrawal from political engagement in Wordsworth's post-revolutionary writings, notably Marjorie Levinson, Paul Magnuson, Reeve Parker, and Nicholas Roe. Most recently, Roe has argued for recognition of the evolving *Prelude* of 1799, 1805, and 1850 as a single text-in-process that retains Wordsworth's belief in the "radical equality of humankind"; see "Revising the Revolution," *Romantic Revisions,* ed. Robert Brinkley and Keith Hanley (Cambridge: Cambridge University Press, 1992). Evan Radcliffe has asserted that the value of "universal benevolence" in *The Prelude,* when considered in historical context, suggests Radical connotations. See "Saving Ideals: Revolution and Benevolence in *The Prelude,*" *Journal of English and Germanic Philology* 93 (1994): 534–60. And James A. W. Heffernan has demonstrated how in *The Prelude,* Wordsworth "does not simply show how his past self gradually discovered what his present self knows; he reveals a present self profoundly shaped by the past, a self that keeps alive the 'dread vibration' of sympathies with power that he felt at the most violent stage of the Revolution"; see "History and Autobiography: The French Revolution in Wordsworth's Prelude," *Representing the French Revolution: Literature, Historiography, and Art,* ed. James A. W. Heffernan (Hanover, N.H.: University Press of New England, 1992), p. 58.

    4. See "The Politics of 'Frost at Midnight'," in *Romantic Poetry: Recent Revisionary Criticism,* ed. K. Kroeber and G. Ruoff (New Brunswick, N.J.: Rutgers University Press, 1993): 189–203.

    5. *The Prose Works of William Wordsworth,* ed. W. J. B. Owen and Jane Worthington Smyser, 3 vols. (Oxford: Clarendon Press, 1974), 1:38.

    6. *Prose Works,* 1:32–33.

    7. For a sophisticated discussion of what "natural" and "unnatural" might have meant to Wordsworth, see James K. Chandler, *Wordsworth's Second Nature: A Study of the Poetry and the Politics* (Chicago: University of Chicago Press, 1984).

    8. To William Matthews, 23 May 1794 and 8 June 1794, letters 4 and 5 of *The Letters of William Wordsworth,* ed. Alan G. Hill (Oxford: Oxford University Press, 1984), pp. 12, 15.

    9. See John O. Hayden, *The Romantic Reviewers* (Chicago: University of Chicago Press, 1969), p. 252; James Curran, "The Press as an Agency of Social Control: An Historical Perspective," Boyce, p. 64; and Asquith, p. 111.

    10. Derek Roper, "The Politics of the *Critical Review,* 1756–1817," *Durham University Journal,* n.s., 22 (1961): 117–22.

    11. Wilfrid Hindle, *The Morning Post, 1772–1937: Portrait of a Newspaper* (London: George Routledge & Sons Ltd., 1937), p. 105.

    12. *London Times,* January 11.

    13. See *The Contemporary English View of Napoleon* (London: G. Bell & Sons, Ltd., 1914).

    14. *Morning Post,* February 4.

    15. *Morning Post,* March 20.

16. *Morning Post,* January 7.

17. Maccun, pp. 69–72.

18. *Morning Post,* May 10.

19. *Morning Post,* January 21.

20. Marilyn Butler, ed., *Burke, Paine, Godwin, and the Revolution Controversy* (Cambridge: Cambridge University Press, 1984), p. 215.

21. See G. M. Trevelyan, *A Shortened History of England* (1942; London: Penguin Books, 1987), Book 5, Chapter 3.

22. See David Erdman, "Wordsworth as Heartsworth; or Was Regicide the Prophetic Ground of Those 'Moral Questions'?" *The Evidence of the Imagination,* ed. Donald H. Reiman, Michael C. Jaye, and Betty T. Bennett (New York: New York University Press, 1978), pp. 12–41.

23. *London Times,* May 15.

24. *Morning Post,* April 11.

25. Alan Liu links the emergence of univocalism in the British Press to a single disturbing event, Napoleon's execution of the emigre Duc d'Enghien: "Immediately after news of d'Enghien's death [in February 1804] reached England, popular opinion followed a bipartisan, strikingly convergent strategy of defaming Napoleon"; *Wordsworth: The Sense of History* (Stanford: Stanford University Press, 1989), p. 437.

26. "The Decline and Fall of the French Revolution," *New York Review of Books* (15 February 1990): 48.

27. See E. P. Thompson, *The Making of the English Working Class* (New York: Vintage, 1963).

28. *Anti-Jacobin Review* 17 (1804): 190–91.

29. *Critical Review,* ser. 3, 2 (1804): 383.

30. *Critical Review,* ser. 3, 2 (1804): 346.

31. The *Anti-Jacobin Review* 17 (1804): 192, 296, and 299. As an enterprise of Pitt's ministry, the *Anti-Jacobin Review* worked openly to discredit any remnants of revolutionary ideals in British intellectual life. Although its title suggests opposition, the *Anti-Jacobin Review* sought not to engage Radical ideologies in debate, but to thoroughly shut them out of public discourse.

32. See Brenda Banks, " 'Vaudracour and Julia': Wordsworth's Melodrama of Protest," *Nineteenth Century Literature* 47 (December 1992): 275–302.

33. See François Furet, *Interpreting the French Revolution,* trans. Elborg Forster (Cambridge: Cambridge University Press, 1981).

34. See Charles Breunig, *The Age of Revolution and Reaction* (New York: W. W. Norton & Company, 1977) chapter 2, *passim.*

35. Liu; Stephen C. Behrendt, "Placing the Places in Wordsworth's 1802 Sonnets," *Studies in English Literature 1500–1900* 35 (1995): 641–67.

36. See Liu, pp. 428–36. I cannot agree, however, with Liu's ultimate thesis regarding Wordsworth's "denial" of history in *The Prelude.* By focusing on the Simplon Pass and Mount Snowden episodes to arrive at this thesis, Liu simply offers a sophisticated retelling of Geoffrey Hartman's Wordsworth story.

37. In 1804–1805, as he completed the thirteen-book *Prelude,* Wordsworth expected to complete and publish in the near future the epic that Coleridge so desired him to write, *The Recluse,* prefaced by *The Prelude.* In fact, it was not until 1839 that he relinquished the idea of ever completing *The Recluse,* which he had viewed as the

only justification for publishing "the poem to Coleridge," as he thought of *The Prelude.* Thus, although it was not to be so, Wordsworth originally intended that *The Prelude* would be read by his contemporaries. It is intriguing to ponder what early publication of *The Prelude* might have done to Wordsworth's political reputation as a turncoat.

38. My 1992 article in *Nineteenth Century Literature* discusses other resistances to the administration's official reading of the Revolution found in the French Books. Nor should it be forgotten that some of *The Prelude*'s 1850 reviewers found the poem Radical, despite the fact that it was written by the author of *The Excursion.* For a quick overview, see Roe, pp. 87–88.

39. William Wordsworth, *The Prelude, 1799. 1805. 1850,* ed. Jonathan Wordsworth, M. H. Abrams, and Stephen Gill (New York: W. W. Norton and Company, Ltd., 1979) 10:931–40.

40. Wordsworth, Abrams, and Gill, eds., the 1805 *Prelude,* p. 410, n. 4.

John Thelwall

and

the Press

Michael Scrivener

"The liberty of the press is like the air we breathe.
When we have it not—we die."[1]

John Thelwall's intellectual activities were many and various: the most
prominent Radical lecturer in the 1790s was acquitted for treason in
1794; became later an extremely successful speech therapist and teacher
of elocution, as well as a medical scholar specializing in speech disorders;
and was a prolific man of letters who corresponded with Coleridge, Wordsworth, and Godwin, and who published numerous books of fiction, poetry,
and essays. He also published widely and extensively in periodicals over the
span of four decades. Altogether he edited five different periodicals. From
1789 to 1792 he earned fifty pounds a year editing the *Biographical Imperial
Magazine,* a mostly apolitical journal.[2] After being acquitted for treason he
edited the *Tribune* for about a year, until the Gagging Acts of 1795 made first
the lectures and then the journal impossible. In 1818, during the revival of
the reform movement, he purchased the mildly reformist weekly paper the
Champion, became editor, and turned it into a Radical reform newspaper.
After the *Champion* folded in 1822, Thelwall's next editorial venture was the
Monthly Magazine, which he edited from December 1824 to the end of 1825,
when the magazine's new owners fired him because of his Radical politics.
His very last stint as editor came the following year, when he edited his own
but very short-lived journal (January to June 1826), the *Panoramic Miscellany.*[3] Upon the demise of this last periodical it seems that Thelwall, now in
his sixties, retired for good from political journalism.[4]

120

Of the five periodicals Thelwall edited, he had complete control over three: the *Tribune,* the *Champion,* and the *Panoramic Miscellany.* The *Tribune* was the most successful because in 1795 he had a large and attentive audience of London Radicals and liberals. Were it not for government repression, the *Tribune* would have continued longer. We know least about the *Panoramic Miscellany;* I have not been able to locate any copies of this periodical. The *Champion,* however, was successful: Thelwall ran the weekly newspaper to promote Radical reform for three years (December 1818 to December 1821), and he and his newspaper actively participated in London Reform politics. Although the *Tribune* and the *Champion* are superficially similar, the *Tribune* is actually more like Cobbett's later *Political Register,* a vehicle for the political ideas of the editor, whereas the *Champion* conformed to the ordinary requirements of a London weekly newspaper, with topical news, crime reports, advertisements, and so on.

With the *Biographical Imperial Magazine* and the *Monthly Magazine,* Thelwall edited periodicals he did not own. As a young writer without a reputation, he had least control and influence over the *Biographical Imperial Magazine.* Although Thelwall inserted much of his own poetry under various pseudonyms into the verse columns of the *Biographical Imperial Magazine,* he had clearly limited discretion with the magazine as a whole, whose format and outlook were for the most part predetermined as a source of politically unthreatening middle-class entertainment and information. Its claim on the middle-class reading public was its emphasis on biographical information. By the time Richard Phillips chose Thelwall to be editor of the *Monthly Magazine* in 1824, both the magazine and the new editor were well-established, so that although Thelwall had to answer to both Phillips and the readers who expected continuity with the previous incarnations of the magazine, he in fact had considerable latitude as editor that he indeed exploited. He and Phillips had known one another for almost thirty years, so each knew what to expect from the other.

An editorial situation involves the following: the editor and his own agenda; external pressures from the government and the market; and the formal logic of each periodical in terms of the reader's expectations. Because Thelwall had so little control over the *Biographical Imperial Magazine* and because I have never seen a copy of the *Panoramic Miscellany,* I will concentrate my focus on the *Tribune,* the *Champion,* and the *Monthly Magazine.* As the *Champion* has been unaccountably ignored by political and literary historians, I will deal with it the most extensively. Some of the issues I will examine in light of these very different editorial situations are the following: Thelwall's complex negotiations with his readers, especially in terms of his self-definition as a writer and editor; the several ways in which he framed the connections between imaginative literature and politics; and finally, the various revisions and utilizations of journalistic conventions.

121

* * *

The *Tribune*'s primary purpose was to publicize more widely Thelwall's already well-attended lectures (around 500 people—sometimes as many as 700—paid six pence to attend each Wednesday and Friday night) and to provide as well a written transcript of Thelwall's biweekly lectures so that he could protect himself legally against the kind of government misrepresentation of his words that actually occurred at his treason trial.[5] Prosecution witnesses, paid informers some of them, characterized Thelwall's speeches as more violent and incendiary than they apparently were, but as there was no transcript of the speeches, he could assert only that his own memory was more accurate and his character more credible than that of his accusers. When he started his lecture series in London in February 1795, he hired someone to transcribe his speeches. He could have printed, of course, the written text he actually read from at his lectures, but so worried was he about possible prosecution that he used a stenographer. The *Tribune*'s subtitle reads as follows: "Taken in short-hand by W. Ramsey, and Revised by the Lecturer." What motivated the notice of revisions by the lecturer, as such revisions suggest an after-the-fact tampering with the oral language? Perhaps the "revisions" were to correct any errors Ramsey might have introduced accidentally. The journal's motto, published every week at the top of the front page, is from the poet William Hayley: "To paint the voice, and fix the fleeting sound." Thelwall's precautions to provide a reliable record of his spoken words cannot entirely remove uncertainties that a hostile prosecuting attorney could have exploited in a trial. If called upon to explain the "revisions," Thelwall would have been in the same position as in 1794, asserting the reliability of his own testimony as more truthful than that of his accusers. Even without the notice of "revisions," a zealous attorney general could have merely impugned the accuracy of Ramsey the transcriber. Nevertheless, his precautions were effective up to a point because he was not prosecuted for any of his lectures or issues of the *Tribune*. Instead, the government eventually banned political lecturing outright, and it was obvious to everyone at the time that the primary target for the repressive legislation was Thelwall's very popular series of lectures. When he adjusted his lectures to meet the letter of the new laws, restricting his comments to the politics of classical antiquity, he was several times almost kidnapped and murdered by violent anti-Jacobins, with the obvious connivance of the government, until he was forced to retire from politics altogether in 1797.[6]

The *Tribune* lectures treat extensively the issues and anxieties of representation. The anxiety about linguistic representation and the fear of prosecution are present in every issue, as written language seems to be a not entirely secure means of representing speech. The lectures themselves are on representation, as Thelwall defends Radical reform—universal male suffrage and annual parliaments—and defends himself as a "tribune" whose words represent the interests of the disenfranchised. Just as writing is prone to error as it attempts to represent speech, so too are political representatives and tribunes. Thelwall goes to some lengths justifying himself as a tribune, explaining his credentials as a democratic representative, and alerting his audience to the dangers of mediation and leaders of any kind. Thelwall declares his selflessness, as he sacrifices both money and fame for delivering the lectures to "the oppressed and industrious orders of society" (1: vii). The most compelling proof of his "character" and "principles," of course, was the recent treason trial, to which he returns and upon which he comments continually in his lectures. None of the other treason trial defendants assumed such a prominent political role after the trials, indicating, as E. P. Thompson suggests, a remarkable degree of courage on Thelwall's part.[7] In providing a normative definition of how government ought to but does not work, Thelwall also provides a description and justification of the tribune who plays the role of government's good conscience: an individual with "superior knowledge and leisure for reflection" has the opportunity to "discover the proper remedies" for social evils and "to direct the popular attention to the means of counteracting their effects" (1: 7). The only morally defensible reason for the power and privilege enjoyed by government officials is to provide public service. Thelwall rejects explicitly a direct democracy because this political form is appropriate only for a small state (2: 210). Representative democracy is not perfect, but it is the most desirable political system for Britain. Nevertheless, representation is a vexed issue. Thelwall must refute those on the right who find adequate the already existing form of representation and those on the left who are impatient with any kind of mediation.

One of the recurrent metaphors Thelwall uses is the traditional one of the body politic; also, he presents himself as a "political physician" who will administer to the body's diseases. The physician metaphor for political tribune emphasizes the organic wholeness and self-sufficiency of a society that requires only temporary but sometimes intrusive intervention to stimulate the body's own healing. The political physician is like a surgeon who removes dead tissue. One must attack prejudice aggressively, according to Thelwall: "to cut up wide and deep rooted prejudices" (1: 149). Thelwall is somewhat anxious about the authoritarian implications of the metaphor of the political physician, as he criticizes Robespierre (1: 149) and insists upon moderation: "All amelioration must be gradual; no society ever reached at once from absolute tyranny to perfect freedom; no person ever rose from raging disease to floral health in an instant" (1: 162). The ambiguity of the diseased body/ political physician metaphor can be inflected to emphasize the need for external assistance from the physician or the self-maintaining organicism of the body. The metaphor records Thelwall's own ambivalence over his role as tribune.

Godwin challenged Thelwall's lectures as dangerous and irresponsible, implying that despite himself Thelwall was becoming another Robespierre.[8] Although Thelwall concedes that political will-formation must be the consequence of individual reflection, not passions created in a crowd, he nevertheless defends his role as educator and suggests that thinkers also need to meet and discuss issues with "different classes of society" (2: 184). In another defense of the plebeian public sphere, Thelwall insists that his own education was achieved during activities within political associations and debating clubs (3: 246–47). In one of his last lectures he links his own Radical lecturing with Athenian democracy, insisting that the health of the ancient democracy depended on a lively theatre. Contrasting London's small number of theatres—two—with the more robust Athenian and Shakespearian theatrical cultures, Thelwall connects democracy and dramatic literature (3: 302–03).

Thelwall defended his lecturing, but the full implications of those lectures troubled him. For one thing, his audience was socially mixed. It included laborers not nearly as educated as he was, middle-class professionals just as well educated as he, and often a small group of government partisans and spies who heckled, hissed, booed, and otherwise tried to disrupt his speeches. The plebeian/middle-class split in his audience was underscored by the two different editions of the *Tribune* that he published, one almost twice as expensive as the other. There may have been informal question-and-answer sessions after the lectures, but neither the *Tribune* nor any other written record suggests that the lectures offered anything but the single voice of Thelwall. As he was an extraordinarily effective lecturer and an experienced participant in public debates, one cannot doubt that even these seemingly monological lectures were in fact marked by all kinds of intersubjective and dialogical forces that Thelwall experienced as a matter of course. Although the *Tribune* has an intimate tone and contains some of the best political prose written in the 1790s, the uncertainty of the implied reader also characterizes the journal. The persona Thelwall constructs in his lectures is most often the tribune who is the physician to the body, that is, the audience. At other times the persona is that of a fellow-plebeian who has had the same experiences and sources of knowledge as those in the audience. Thelwall seems ambivalent about the poor people who follow his lectures; he knows that the government is more likely to prosecute him if his audience includes what it considers a potentially violent mob. Indeed, in one issue he broadcasts that more "middling" class than "common" people are now attending his lectures than previously (2: 349).

Overall, the *Tribune* is a remarkable literary achievement, possibly his best work as a political writer. In the lectures printed in this periodical, Thelwall walks a fine line between Enlightenment rationalism and French Revolutionary insurgency, educational lectures and revolutionary oratory. The *Tribune* is marked everywhere by a sense of crisis, fear of government prosecution, and hope of democratic insurgency. The government judged its effectiveness to be serious enough to silence it.

When several decades later Thelwall purchased and edited the *Champion,* both he and the reform movement had changed since the 1790s. He was now a successful speech therapist and teacher of elocution, a secure member of London's middle class, a veteran of reformist politics who had survived with his commitment to Radical reform fully intact. While his former friends Wordsworth and Coleridge had become Tories, he continued to promote Radical reform. The *Tribune* addressed a mostly artisanal and lower-middle-class audience. The *Champion,* however, was unquestionably middle class: the weekly newspaper cost ten pence a copy (compared to three pence and six pence respectively for the *Tribune*'s inexpensive and deluxe editions) and provided business news, stock prices, and theatre reviews. Thelwall justified addressing an exclusively middle-class readership by saying that the laboring classes already supported Radical reform; the important educational work was with the middle class, which supported at best a moderate reform far short of universal male suffrage. The main difference between the *Champion* before and after Thelwall took it over was its political perspective. Leaving the format essentially the same, Thelwall dramatically changed the content and overall direction of the periodical. Under the editorship of John Scott it was politically to the right of Hunt's *Examiner* and resembled the *Examiner* in its cultural politics, even drawing upon the same group of London literati for reviews and articles.[9] Under Thelwall, the *Champion* was to the left of the *Examiner* in national and economic politics but resembling it otherwise, especially in its cultural and literary perspective. Unlike the *Examiner* or the *Champion* under Scott, Thelwall's *Champion* was a movement publication, a vehicle for political information and exhortation in an activist context. Thelwall did not just edit the paper and write essays. He was a major force in Radical Westminster politics. He spoke at public meetings, organized protests, composed proclamations, and plotted strategy in one of the most politically volatile periods in British history, 1819–1821. The uniqueness of Thelwall's *Champion* was that it combined Radical reform activism with uncompromisingly high intellectual standards in terms of both literary culture and political philosophy. I believe it was the only periodical at the time with a primarily middle-class readership that promoted Radical reform—universal male suffrage and annual parliaments. As in the 1790s, Thelwall experienced repression; he was arrested in May 1821 for seditious libel. The repression seems to have been effective in driving Thelwall from the *Champion,* for he had little direct involvement with the periodical during its last six months of existence in 1822.[10]

In the 1790s Thelwall was London's most prominent political lecturer and journalist with a large plebeian audience. In the post-Waterloo period, however, William Cobbett, the Spencean socialists, and Henry "Orator" Hunt replaced him in that position. In print and in public speeches Thelwall criticized pointedly and often what he believed were the inconsistencies and demagoguery of Cobbett, Hunt, and the Spenceans; his post-Waterloo politics, although Radical, were not as Radical as they once were. Thelwall's new emphasis was unity on the left, forging a coalition with the reformist Whigs, the Burdettites, and the extraparliamentary Radicals to effect meaningful change. He criticized whatever he felt weakened overall reformist unity, blaming especially the timid Whigs for ceding, by their inactivity, leadership to demagogues like Henry Hunt and Cobbett.

For over three years Thelwall's Radical reform periodical was a not insignificant participant in London reformist politics. Indeed, I do not believe historians, including E. P. Thompson, have given Thelwall his due as a reform politician at this time, nor have literary and cultural historians fully appreciated the extraordinarily high quality of journalism that Thelwall produced week after week for three years. His critical intelligence is evident everywhere, from lead articles on politics—usually formal epistles to public figures like prominent Whig leaders or government ministers—to the more personal essay form of his "Mirror of the Week," in which he tried to capture some salient aspect of the recent past. He also wrote almost all of the theatre and literary reviews. Thelwall would not allow anyone else to summarize parliamentary debates. He accomplished all of this while also attending regularly various meetings promoting reform or protesting repression. Only occasionally did he draw upon other talent. From September to December 1821, he gave someone else, probably Francis Place (a former fellow "citizen" in the London Corresponding Society), prominent room for essays on political economy. Thomas N. Talfourd reviewed extensively the work of Charles Lamb and Charles Lloyd. Thomas Hardy, his friend from the London Corresponding Society and a fellow victim of the 1794 treason trials, contributed numerous pieces. Nevertheless, the *Champion* was otherwise all Thelwall, including numerous poems by him in the poetry columns.

It is difficult to summarize the overall political thrust of Thelwall's *Champion,* although he maintained certain consistent focuses. Countering the xenophobic and nationalist prejudices that were a part of the reform culture, Thelwall insisted that the current political conflict was a world-wide one between revolutionary democracies and counter-revolutionary despotisms. He pleaded with Whigs who were liberal and reformist to take an activist role, especially after Peterloo, to provide leadership for a coalition of unified reform forces; at the same time he drew relentless attention to the failures of the Whigs, past and present. He stressed unity on the left, tactical compromise, principle over personalities. He criticized fellow reformists ruthlessly if he felt they harmed overall unity or promoted violence, but as soon as a reformist became an object of government repression, Thelwall suspended criticism and provided political support. Toward Henry Hunt, arrested after Peterloo, and the Spencean socialists, who were executed after the Cato Street conspiracy was broken up, the *Champion* was very sympathetic, despite their political disagreements. Thelwall not only protested vigorously acts of repression, repressive legislation, and the institutions of repression, he also provided philosophical and political justification for a free press and other civil liberties. His political journalism consistently tried to use topical issues and momentary passions to illustrate more philosophically abstract issues.

Out of the many different topics—political, literary, economic, and philosophical—one might choose to investigate, I will focus on a very small area: Thelwall's responses to Byron and Scott. Further, I will examine some of the ways Thelwall negotiated the issue of repression, including the enigmatic manner in which he left the *Champion.*

Thelwall regarded Byron as a great poet, probably the age's greatest, but he viewed Byron's work as flawed by immorality. According to Donald Reiman, the *Champion* was second only to the *Examiner* in being the most important reviewing newspaper at the time.[11] John Scott's *Champion* had favored the Leigh Hunt circle and literary Romanticism in general. Thelwall too was a literary Romantic, but he was extremely critical of Byron. Whereas Byron came to Pope's defense and attacked Bowles, Thelwall, the more consistent Romantic, favored Bowles. According to Thelwall, Pope was at the highest levels of the second tier of great poets—below the first tier of Shakespeare, Milton, and Sophocles. With more art than nature, more wit than imagination, Pope "could not look into the great store-house—the secret womb of Nature, and comprehend her incipient probabilities; or draw from thence the materials of a world of his own—which, tho unreal, should have all the consonance of reality" (5 May 1821: 285).

In terms of politics, Thelwall should have been predisposed to favor Byron, as Thelwall knew well and occasionally collaborated with Byron's friend Hobhouse. However, Thelwall seems to have almost hated Byron. It is interesting that Thelwall could enjoy the ironic self-reflexiveness of Sterne and even practice a form of Radical irony in his 1793 experimental novel the *Peripatetic.* His entire literary oeuvre is marked by a variety of guises and personas, from Sylvanus Theophrastus to Wentworth Chatterton;[12] one of his literary master themes is sexual seduction. Nevertheless, Thelwall found Byron's self-reflexiveness, irony, self-referencing, and sexual preoccupations offensive. If his reaction to Byron is more than a negative self-identification, it may have something to do with the way Byron's poetry provoked Thelwall's hatred of the aristocracy and his defensiveness about his social situation.

In the *Champion's* reviews of Byron's *Mazeppa* and first two cantos of *Don Juan,* the recurrent theme is the immorality of Byron's verse. Echoing ultraconservative objections to Byron's poetry, Thelwall says of *Mazeppa:* "Adultery, Adultery, Adultery is the Cuckoo strain from beginning to end, of which massacre and assassination are the only reliefs" (25 July 1819: 471).

Thelwall is even more severe with *Don Juan*, which he finds not only immoral but ultimately demoralizing, as Byron scoffs at any and all traces of idealism. Unlike most of Byron's conservative reviewers, Thelwall concedes that parts of the poem are truly great: the "Ode to Venice" and parts of *Don Juan*, like the Haidee episode in the second canto. He admits that Byron is a powerful poet but condemns unequivocally the overall moral tendency of his poetry (1 August 1819: 488–500).

Thelwall in fact was neither prudish nor especially moralistic in his literary criticism, but the way Byron represents women, sex, and consciousness in his poetry evokes for Thelwall an aristocratic power and privilege he had spoken and written against his entire life. In Thelwall's early poetry, seduction and abandonment of women is a recurrent theme allegorizing the immorality of aristocratic power. In his second novel, the villain is a sexually predatory aristocrat. Thelwall consistently portrays sexual exploitation as an aristocratic violation of social morality. He typically represents women and the poor as victims of aristocracy. Byron's emphasis on female sexuality and the overall anarchic power of sexuality in general undermines the sentimental narrative of female victimization Thelwall takes for granted as an allegory of the aristocracy's abuse of power.[13] He reads Byron as defending aristocracy and its privileges. Similarly, Byron's subversion of all kinds of dualism, especially of mind and body, Thelwall reads as social allegory. Thelwall narrativizes upward social mobility as spirit overcoming matter, mind over body. In his own life he salvaged with much difficulty leisure hours for reading and "self-improvement" from all the other hours devoted to necessary labor as an apprentice. The various ways in which Byron's poetry makes fun of idealistic exertions of the will against materialistic pressures strike Thelwall as social mockery of people like himself. Even the imaginative freedom of *Don Juan*, its self-mockery and self-dramatization, its linguistic playfulness, all seem to Thelwall to be signs of aristocratic privilege: Byron can get away with almost anything because of his social position, whereas Thelwall's social status depends entirely on the words he produces and how they are received. Thelwall's allegorical reading—or misreading—of Byron's poetry is perhaps itself an allegory of his middle-class position, how he achieved it, and the anxieties it generated.

Thelwall finds a clever way to poke fun at Byron while at the same time using his aristocratic connections against the government: by publishing "Extract from the Third Canto of Don Juan, which Mr. Murray is said to have lately returned to Lord Byron for Revisal" (22 July 1820: 478). The four stanzas of ottava rima are strongly satirical of George the Fourth, but Thelwall protects them from being a pretext for government prosecution by ridiculing the hypocrisy of leaving alone a Tory publisher who prints material that otherwise would be libelous. Indeed, when *Don Juan* was published by John Hunt, the publisher was not prosecuted.

In Thelwall's review of *Ivanhoe,* he focuses on Scott's Tory allegiance and his service as one of the writers for the *Quarterly Review.* He finds the novel highly critical of what the *Quarterly* reviewer typically praises, namely, aristocratic feudal culture: "the labours of the *Novelist* may atone for those of the Reviewer" (15 Jan. 1820: 43). In Thelwall's judgment, *Ivanhoe* is a critique of feudalism, including the Norman conquest and its "military Feudalism," along with the "pestiferous doctrines now in fashion" and especially current in the *Quarterly Review.* He sees Scott as self-divided between the Radical insights of the novelist and the conservative commitments of the reviewer, adumbrating Lawrence's distinction between teller and tale. Thelwall applies the strong criticism of religious bigotry in the novel to contemporary circumstances, thinking obviously of the persecution of Richard Carlile that the *Champion* protested on numerous occasions: "then the Jew, it is now the deist" (43). The novel is not perfect in form or content, Thelwall asserts, for its episodic style impedes overall structure and epic meaning, and the novel fails to develop the positive aspects of Saxon culture, especially its democratic institutions.

If there is something we might call Radical literary criticism in the Romantic period, Thelwall's *Ivanhoe* review surely has to be a specimen. The various distancing frames which Scott places on the critique of feudalism Thelwall erases completely, presenting instead a political allegory. Thelwall entirely ignores the symbolic representation of compromise, mixing, and national unity in order to stress the ways in which Scott's Tory values are undermined by his own novel. Quoting an especially anticlerical speech in the novel, Thelwall notes wryly that he finds the passage reminiscent of Richard Carlile—then in Dorchester jail for religious blasphemy—illustrating effectively the government's hypocrisy in prosecuting only certain kinds of religious heresy while leaving others unpunished. He not only seizes as unambiguous the novel's protests against antisemitism but expands the theme to one of religious bigotry, a recurrent emphasis in the *Champion,* Thelwall insisted that one's religious views enjoyed absolute freedom that could never be impinged upon by government. That a novel may possess meanings the novelist might not fully accept or endorse is a critical commonplace now, but when Thelwall applied the idea to Scott it was hardly commonsensical.

For the *Champion,* the way literature fits into political ideology is different from the way it operates for the *Tribune.* In the *Tribune* the few pieces of poetry are political songs circulated at London Corresponding Society meetings in the open air and at taverns and coffee houses. These songs are a continuation of politics in a different literary form. Literature in the *Champion* has more autonomy; politics is generally kept separate from various forms of "entertainment," from the theatre to poetry and novels. Conceivably one could read the *Champion* for its non-political articles, its items of business news, its entertainment columns. Indeed, to satisfy himself and many of his readers,

Thelwall developed a special literary section called "The Renovator" and promised to publish the literary pieces in a separate volume.[14] It is inconceivable that one could read the *Tribune* as anything other than Radical politics from cover to cover. As the Byron and *Ivanhoe* reviews indicate, the esthetic realm was relatively independent of politics: the artist's own politics did not necessarily transfer unchanged in the artwork; the political allegory of the artwork did not necessarily coincide with the artist's own politics. Clearly, however, political meanings of some kind determined literature, whatever the degree of esthetic autonomy.

On the relation of politics and art Thelwall struck a middle position between an entirely political esthetic (or rejection of art altogether as hopelessly entangled with aristocratic culture) and complete esthetic autonomy: "We are no patriots of the School of Hebert. Every thing that is connected with the refinement and real elegancies of social civilization, is dear to our imagination; and the interests of taste and genius are only not as dear as the general interests of man. They constitute a delightful part only: the others embrace the whole" (25 March 1820: 197–98). This passage, while clearly rejecting a puritanical or revolutionary esthetic iconoclasm, or an estheticist repudiation of politics, still implies two utterly separate realms that in most of Thelwall's other writing have more dialectical interactions. Thelwall's own practices as a political writer and as a literary critic exceeded his ability to reflect abstractly on art and politics.

Not so subtle, however, was the government repression. When Thelwall returned to political activism and journalism in late 1818, there had already been several years of post-Waterloo reformist agitation and repression. In 1817, according to E. P. Thompson, there were "twenty-six prosecutions for seditious and blasphemous libel and sixteen ex officio informations filed by the law officers of the Crown," but on balance the reformists seem to have won in court.[15] The government lost many of its important cases, especially the William Hone trials. Hone's acquittals for libel seemed to indicate a new degree of press liberty. Thelwall was hardly naive, as his experiences in the 1790s were educational enough, and he was indeed prepared to suffer the consequences. In one speech at a Westminster meeting, in fact, he addressed the repression issue directly, recommending caution but firmness, expecting the reform movement to produce its share of martyrs and victims of repression, but declaring that one must not panic but instead orient one's self to the perspective of an idealized posterity (3 June 1820: 355–56). After Peterloo and the agitation over Queen Caroline, it was only a matter of time before someone as prominent in the reform movement as Thelwall would have to return to Old Bailey. The *Champion*'s readership enjoyed a huge boost after Peterloo: Thelwall reported on 12 February 1820 that his circulation was up by a third. Thelwall was a prominent speaker at Westminster reform meetings, behind only Burdett and Hobhouse in importance. In early 1820 Stoddart's

New Times was calling for the suppression of the *Champion,* but apparently no action was taken then. Renewed calls for the suppression of the *Champion* came in early 1821, this time from Daniel Stuart's *Courier,* and the result was Thelwall's arrest in May. He was imprisoned overnight before his bail hearing the next day. The *Champion* took on the Constitutional Association (the "Bridge-Street Gang") in numerous consecutive issues in May and June. The specific charge was a "libelous" "Mirror of the Week" essay in the 25 February 1821 issue—an utterly arbitrary charge, for Thelwall's comments on Burdett's prosecution and Peterloo were entirely unexceptional; indeed, he had written far stronger things on other issues. The one most vulnerable to prosecution was probably the 26 February 1820 issue, in which he discussed the recent Duke of Berri's assassination as symptomatic of overall injustice; he did not endorse the violence but traced its real cause to continued tyranny—only to find out, just as the essay was being read, that the Spencean socialists had been arrested for an attempted *coup d'état* shortly thereafter. He courageously maintained the same line of argument with the Spenceans, who were later executed. Thelwall's jury was picked in June (9 June 1821: 363), but the trial did not take place until December, when it was delayed again upon the discovery that Constitutional Association members were included in the jury pool for the cases brought by the same Association. Thelwall declared in court that he was so anxious for his case to be tried that having the case over his head from session to session was worse than being convicted, that he was willing to go ahead with his trial, even if the jury had Constitutional Association members in it. After consulting with his lawyer, he withdrew his request for a trial, and the case was held over until next session (15 December 1821: 797–98). Apparently there never was a trial. At the time Thelwall was fifty-seven years old.

Perhaps the Constitutional Association simply dropped its prosecution once it learned that Thelwall was leaving the *Champion* anyway. Perhaps the very purpose of the prosecution was not to imprison Thelwall but to silence the *Champion.* One would need of course more documentary evidence to know for certain, but the inference seems inescapable: Thelwall was driven from the *Champion* by repression. Without Thelwall the *Champion* survived only another six, rather lackluster, months. Compared with his treason trial acquittal, the suppression of the *Tribune* and his lectures, and the anti-Jacobin violence against him in 1796–1797, the demise of the *Champion* was anticlimactic. Thelwall seems to have been preparing himself for a prison sentence; for one thing, he started republishing his poems written in 1794 from the Tower in the poetry columns of the *Champion* starting in August 1821. The sentences being handed out to reformists in 1820–1821 were not especially long—from three to twelve months—but the fines, and especially the security money for further "good behavior," could ruin a publishing operation. The

131

Champion folded, then, not because it lost readership, but because of political repression.[16]

The final journal that Thelwall edited to be discussed here is the *Monthly Magazine,* a periodical that first emerged in 1796 as a creative response to the Gagging Acts that suppressed Thelwall's *Tribune.*[17] The *Monthly Magazine* was politically Radical but also very discrete. It concentrated almost exclusively on cultural and philosophical issues, sustaining an Enlightenment project at a time when the Enlightenment was associated with revolution, and upholding what was called at the time Rational Dissent—a religious perspective associated with political rebellion. In its early years, when the *Monthly Magazine* was the middle class's most innovative and courageous periodical, Thelwall published a number of his poems and essays in it. By December 1824, however, when Thelwall took over as editor, a great deal had changed. The Rational Dissent movement had become a far more cautious and smaller Unitarian sect, and the middle class in general was more conservative. The liberal middle class had moved on to the *Edinburgh Review* and, later, the aggressively utilitarian *Westminster Review.* The middle class in general was almost as unnerved by the insurgent laboring class below it as it was resentful of the aristocracy above it. In short, the *Monthly Magazine* under Thelwall's editorship was old-fashioned in its format and outlook. For the most part Thelwall kept the format as it had been since the beginning, reflecting undiluted Enlightenment values as readers contributed and responded to essays. The magazine tried to achieve encyclopedic coverage of every area of human knowledge, from foreign languages and geography to techniques of land drainage. It tried to note, if not review, every single book that was published and place it in an appropriate category. After Thelwall was fired by the new owners of the *Monthly Magazine* at the end of 1825, the new version of the magazine scuttled most of its Enlightenment features and attempted to capture the prosperous but ideologically conservative middle class.

Thelwall's *Monthly Magazine* is distinctive for a number of reasons. When Thelwall tried to alter the format slightly, the loyal readership apparently rebelled, forcing him to retreat. His minor innovation was to reserve for the editor, namely himself, the lead article. Since 1796 the lead article in this periodical had always been a substantial essay by one of its reader-contributors. Thelwall also greatly expanded what had been a slight column at the end of each issue, the "Notices to Correspondents." Under his editorship the "Notices" took up an entire page of print and became a kind of free-wheeling dialogue with contributors. He also added a "Topic of the Month," a long essay in each issue on a variety of topics. The early *Monthly Magazine* had no such editorial intrusions, for when the original editor John Aikin contributed an essay, he did so unobtrusively and never in the form of an attention-getting "Topic of the Month." Ironically enough, Thelwall's innovations were all in the direction of Romantic journalism, emphasizing the personality and control of the editor or small group of writers.

As the "Topic of the Month" essay was his most provocative innovation, I want to look at one such essay briefly. The essay for January 1825 is remarkably assured of its audience and its expectations, as Thelwall fairly casually ponders the arbitrariness of choosing a single topic in a month during which so many things occurred. How does one decide what is important? He touches upon a recent scandalous trial of Colonel Berkeley and the Miss Foote he seduced and abandoned as something everyone would know about, but as it is a low, gossipy topic, it cannot be the main focus of the essay. Nevertheless, in a footnote, he provides his morally outraged commentary. He then moves to another well-known episode of the month, the scaring of a horse and the subsequent injuring of its rider by an especially loud Punch and Judy show. Some members of Parliament had called for the banning of puppet shows in London's streets. Thelwall indignantly defends the Punch and Judy shows, tracing them to their ancient origins in sacred medieval drama and protesting the class bias of banning entertainments enjoyed by the poor. By the end of the essay he finally settles upon the new prevalence and power of joint-stock companies for an appropriate subject and strongly condemns these irresponsibly speculative attempts at monopoly control. (Later "Topic of the Month" essays would be devoted to analyzing critically the new stock companies.)

Notable here, I think, is Thelwall's ambivalence: he is clearly interested in the "low" subjects of the seduction trial and the Punch and Judy show, but his Enlightenment scruples force him to drive those subjects to the periphery. He uses a Romantic genre, the personal essay, to provide an Enlightenment critique of financial speculation, but before doing so he digresses in a Romantic manner—after Charles Lamb or Byron—about the curiosities of London life. This ambivalence shows up elsewhere. He scorns gossipy books about Lord Byron, but laments the suppression of Byron's autobiography. He identifies the two greatest writers of the age as Lord Byron and Maria Edgeworth, using utterly incompatible criteria in praising each one. He condemns various suppressions of liberties since the 1790s, but sees overall progress because of the "diffusion" of knowledge through the middle and lower classes, thanks to the freedom of the press. Although nostalgic for Enlightenment values that are clearly eroding, he nevertheless affirms the reality of progress.

The ambivalences and perhaps even contradictions that one finds in Thelwall's *Monthly Magazine* show that his stance toward middle-class culture and politics is not easy to characterize. His firing as editor brought to an end a particular Enlightenment style of cultural work. The new Enlightenment style of the *Westminster Review* was very different, professionalized and consumer-oriented; another strand of the Enlightenment was picked up and developed by the *Retrospective Review,* which combined antiquarianism with an academic style. The exclusively working-class newspaper, the *Trades Newspaper,* emerged the same year Thelwall edited his very last journal, and it continued yet another strand of Enlightenment thinking, one that he had contributed to so significantly in the 1790s. Thelwall, however, was always also a literary Romantic. He sided with Bowles and against Pope's defenders in the famous controversy, as in reviews he placed "imagination" above the lower "fancy" and valued the "power" of Byron despite the moral failings he loathed. He was one of the very few intellectuals of his time who served significantly in both the plebeian and middle-class public spheres. Thelwall's long journalistic and editorial career is proof, if any were needed, of the central importance of the periodical press to the public sphere in shaping both the political and cultural issues of the time. Thelwall was able to exploit the possibilities for contributing usefully to three very different periodicals: an activist, nearly revolutionary journal in the 1790s that cultivated an artisanal public sphere, a middle-class weekly newspaper that was both activist and culturally sophisticated, and a middle-class magazine without any activist dimension that carried out the Radical Enlightenment assumptions of rational dissent.

NOTES

1. Quotation from John Horne Tooke, one of Thelwall's early mentors in the Radical movement, and whose treason trial in 1794 directly preceded Thelwall's. The quotation served as Thelwall's motto for the *Champion* after the Six Acts were passed.

2. Mrs. [Cecil] Thelwall, *The Life of John Thelwall* (London: John Macrone, 1837), p. 34. For a summary of Thelwall's career, see my "The Rhetoric and Context of John Thelwall's 'Memoir,' " in G. A. Rosso and Daniel P. Watkins, eds., *Spirits of Fire: English Romantic Writers and Contemporary Historical Methods* (London and Toronto: Associated University Presses, 1990), pp. 112–30.

3. On the *Panoramic Miscellany,* see Warren E. Gibbs, "John Thelwall and the *Panoramic Miscellany,*" *Notes and Queries* 155 (1928): 386. See also Mary Thale, ed., *Selections from the Papers of the London Corresponding Society* (Cambridge: Cambridge University Press, 1983): "In 1826 his friends raised £1000 for a magazine he wanted to start," p. 387 n. 4.

4. In his four decades of work in the press he contributed many essays and poems to periodicals he did not edit. In the 1790s he contributed to the *Universal Magazine,* the two London Corresponding Society journals (*Politician* [1794–1795] and the *Moral and Political Magazine* [1796–1797]), and the *Monthly Magazine,* to which he continued to contribute in the many years prior to his assuming editorship in 1824. Of the new periodicals he was especially fond of the *Retrospective Review* (1820–1826), perhaps the first truly academic-specialist periodical, for which he wrote at least one article, on the eighteenth-century orator, Henley (14 [1826]: 206–25). He declined to write for the *Westminster Review* because it would not promise to accept his essay until it was refereed by the editors; he felt his reputation and accomplishments were such that the refereeing process was insulting. See his letter of 22 May 1824 to Francis Place, who did indeed write for the *Westminster Review;* British Library Add. MS.

37949, f. 143. Further research will no doubt reveal more Thelwall contributions to the periodical literature of the Romantic period.

5. *Tribune,* 3 vols. (1795–1796). A good selection of *Tribune* articles is now readily accessible in Gregory Claeys' *The Politics of English Jacobinism: Writings of John Thelwall* (University Park: Pennsylvania State University Press, 1995), pp. 65–327.

6. The fullest, most recent treatment of the violent attacks on Thelwall in 1796–1797 is by E. P. Thompson, "Hunting the Jacobin Fox," *Past and Present* 142 (1994): 94–140. Thelwall himself wrote about the experiences extensively, both at the time they happened and later; *An Appeal to Popular Opinion Against Kidnapping and Murder, Including a Narrative of the Late Atrocious Proceedings at Yarmouth; 2nd edition,* (London: J. S. Jordan, 1796). In the *Champion* 24 Oct. 1819: 670–71, Thelwall describes a hitherto unrecorded episode of violence against himself at Stockport in 1797.

7. E. P. Thompson, *The Making of the English Working Class* (New York: Vintage, 1963), 157–66. See also Thompson's other work on Thelwall, "Disenchantment or Default? A Lay Sermon," in Conor Cruise O'Brien and William Dean Vanech, eds., *Power and Consciousness* (London and New York: University of London Press and New York University Press, 1969), pp. 149–81; and "Hunting the Jacobin Fox," *Past and Present* 142 (1994): 94–140.

8. See Godwin's essay, *Considerations On Lord Grenville's and Mr. Pitt's Bills, Concerning Treasonable and Seditious Practices, And Unlawful Assemblies* (London: Joseph Johnson, 1795), and their exchange of letters in relation to the parliamentary deliberations that would result in the repressive Two Acts or Gagging Acts, in Charles Cestre, *John Thelwall, A Pioneer of Democracy and Social Reform in England During the French Revolution* (London: Swan Sonnenschein, 1906), pp. 203–4, and in the *Tribune* the whole preface to volumes 2 and 3: 101–5. On this controversy see the interesting exchange between Isaac Kramnick and John P. Clark in the *American Political Science Review* 66 (March 1972): 114–28; 69 (March 1975): 162–70. Thelwall and Godwin eventually reconciled.

9. See Winifred F. Courtney's essay on the *Champion* in Alvin Sullivan, ed., *British Literary Magazines: The Romantic Age, 1789–1836* (Westport, Conn.: Greenwood Press, 1983), pp. 98–104.

10. Beginning in January 1822, the *Champion* has a new publisher, Thomas Wood, and the only certain Thelwall materials are several poems inserted in a few issues. The last six months of the *Champion* illustrate how talented Thelwall was, because in his absence the periodical becomes insufferably dull.

11. Donald H. Reiman, ed., *The Romantics Reviewed,* Part B (New York: Garland Publishing, 1978) 2:519.

12. Sylvanus Theophrastus is the Thelwallian narrator of *The Peripatetic* and Wentworth Chatterton is Thelwall's favorite *nom de plume* taking responsibility for his poems inserted in the *Biographical and Imperial Magazine.*

13. In his review Thelwall approves of *Don Juan's* satire on the bluestockings, asserting that "the happiness of domestic life requires an obvious superiority of intellect and attainment on the husband's part" (25 July 1819: 472). Thelwall is perhaps forgetting his own feminist heroine, Seraphina, in *The Daughter of Adoption* (London: Richard Phillips, 1801).

14. The "Renovator" began 1 July 1820. Thelwall published in 1822 a collection of *Champion* literary essays and poetry as a separate book.

15. Thompson, *The Making of the English Working Class,* p. 720.

16. I disagree, therefore, with Courtney's conclusion that the *Champion* declined from the heights achieved by John Scott because of Thelwall's editorship. She neglects entirely the Constitutional Association's prosecution of Thelwall in 1821. See Sullivan, ed., *British Literary Magazines: The Romantic Age,* pp. 98–104.

17. On the *Monthly Magazine* see my *Poetry and Reform: Periodical Verse from the English Democratic Press 1792–1824* (Detroit: Wayne State University Press, 1992), p. 131; Sullivan, ed., *British Literary Magazines: The Romantic Age,* pp. 314–19; Jon Klancher, *The Making of the English Reading Audiences, 1790–1832* (Madison: University of Wisconsin Press, 1987), pp. 39–41.

MAB AND MOB:

The Radical Press Community in Regency England

DAVID WORRALL

I n December 1792, six months after the Royal Proclamation against sedition, an informer wrote to the Association for Preserving Liberty and Property Against Republicans and Levellers (APLAP) to tell them about "the Conduct of a Man [who] keeps a little Pamphlet Stall the Top of Chancery Lane. The Songs [and] libells are the Most Seditious & Inflamatory I ever read." The correspondent went on to describe how:

> I went the next Morning to buy the Same Songs but he told Me he has sold them all—(his price is a penny apiece) I asked him where I could buy them—he Said he was the only person that Sold them and a Man Came & left them with him—he says I have something in My pockett (this he Spoke very Softly) pulling out a Small Pamphlet which was the plan of a Society in Holborn for the reform of Parliament—writ in the Most Seditious Language.

In this report—very much a minor incident in the government's increasingly systematic surveillance—are present in embryonic form all the makings of the fugitive print culture of English Radicalism in the years 1790–1830: the particular identification of the publisher or bookseller; the sale, dispersal and discussion of "Songs [and] libells" in public places; the low price; the vendor's evasive and noncommittal information about sources of supply; the surreptitious introduction (and availability) of more politically extreme literature; the Radical agenda of the publication's contents. Finally, last but not least, there is the act of information-giving itself, in this case to the loyalist extraparliamentary APLAP.[1]

This essay will show that the post-war Radical press in England was innovative, assertive and mutually supportive of its distinctive political culture. In tracking the lives of printers, publishers, vendors, readers and authors, it will demonstrate that the Radical press functioned as an identifiable community which can be located by analyzing place, time and family.

Throughout the period 1790–1830 there were pervasive pressures on the publication and dissemination of the Radical press. Government surveillance increased during the 1790s, while prosecutions for seditious utterance only reached their height after 1820. The role of the APLAP in the early 1790s was largely subsumed in the morally improving drive of the Cheap Repository Tracts movement from 1795 and then, after the war, by campaigns of prosecution instigated by the Society for the Suppression of Vice. During that time, due in no small measure to the lasting repercussions of Tom Paine's *Age of Reason* (1794), the targets of loyalist persecution veered away from the political to the religious content of the Radical press.

Of course, print was not the primary medium of Radical activism. The spoken word, at least in London, held the tantalizing potential of precipitating an immediate uprising and insurrection.[2] To Radicalism's rhetorical modes must be added non-verbal forms of communication. Symbolic clothing, such as the white hat, was closely related to other rhetorics and should be considered as integral with linguistic communication. In 1819 the impoverished Spencean hairdresser, musician, Cato Street activist and poet Edward James Blandford wore his white hat proudly when he came before the lord mayor of London's magistracy (at the same sessions as *Republican* editor Richard Carlile), charged with possessing weapons and seditious placards. Two weeks after Peterloo, when the *Manchester Mercury* picked up the story from the London newspapers, it carefully retained this detail. For Blandford, as for others, the white hat held a symbolic content every bit as intentional as his pro-Queen Caroline broadsides or poetic contributions to Thomas Davison's short-lived journal, *Medusa.*[3] In Radicalism's incessant traversing of the available rhetorics in its culture, the white hat spawned its own eponymous periodical, which, in turn, used its platform to applaud Radical speech-making and deplore its poor reporting in conservative newspapers.[4] It is important to remember that the Radical press always had this complex interaction with its disenfranchised artisan culture—a culture which represented itself in more ways than simply by the written or spoken word.

Nevertheless, print had the flexibility to play a part in even the most localized debates in which these symbolic languages contested. When the Manchester and Salford Committee of Sunday Schools was beset by children arriving for lessons wearing "*white* or *drab Hats,* and *other badges* or *appendages* now used by persons whose political conduct and opinions are subversive of the Religion, and hostile to the Constitution and Government, of the Country," the committee empowered itself to send the children home and employed a local printer to produce a handbill announcing their decision.[5] The parents of the Sunday School children are unrepresented agents in this minute social interaction but, implicitly, the politics of symbolism must have been discussed, and suitable rhetorical strategies decided upon, in the domestic household between wife and husband, parent and child. This oscillation between print and non-print expression finds vivid exemplification in a threatening note hand-written by a London mechanic to "your bloody Highness" in the summer of 1819 ("if you dont adopt some measure to procure some relief for the poor your bloody head shall come off and some other person Elected more fit to Govern the Country Not Such a Gouty Old bugger as you"). Despite the extremity of this communication (signed by "One of the bloody Gang"), the correspondent demanded "to have your proposals printed and pasted up in Every Street throughout the metropolis or there will be a bloody Massacre."[6] This intricate network of mixed-media rhetoric and counter-rhetoric is typical of the context within which the Radical press was situated. Printed journals were only a small part of Radicalism's symbolic economy.

The (brief) existence of the *White Hat* journal, as well as the politicized millinery it denoted, implies the presence of a politically active populace. Fortunately, the very level of government surveillance designed to monitor the situation left many records of the audience for the Radical press. At the Mulberry Tree, Moorfields, London, on Sunday evenings in 1817 a spy reported how "they read Cobbett, Wooller, Sherwin, . . . the Room will hold at least 100 with ease, it is crowded to Suffocation evry Debate night."[7] The reading aloud of the latest Radical publications in taverns and coffee houses amongst the populace in the places they frequented was common. On another day at the Mulberry Tree, with twenty-eight persons present, the assembly read aloud the "Newspaper call[ed] the Constitution . . . and a Part of the Poem of Watt Tyler."[8] The Radical press's circulation was not confined to the capital. Although it is not remarkable to find *Cobbett's Weekly Political Register,* T. J. Wooler's *Black Dwarf* and *Sherwin's Political Register* available in Moorfields, it is more unexpected to find that at rooms in Kings Arms Court, Nottingham, Radicals "recommended with great warmth" the London-printed "Theological Comet, Republican, Medusa, Cap of Liberty, Black Dwarf and other seditious & Blasphemous publications."[9] The *Black Dwarf* and Richard Carlile's *Republican* were long-lived journals, but Robert Shorter's *Theological Comet,* Davison's *Medusa* and James Griffin's *Cap of Liberty* were published for only a few months, mostly in late 1819.[10] In another northern England industrial town, one informer claimed that "the printer . . . sells 500 or 600 of the Black Dwarf Weekly the circulation of them has a most mischevious effect in that populous neighbourhood."[11] And yet this penetration of the provinces by the London press was not without its own local interventions and innovations.

During the Queen Caroline affair, an enterprising printer in Penzance, Cornwall, travelled up to London to purchase a pro-queen ode published by

John Fairburn before pirating it back in Penzance under his own imprint, much to the annoyance of the local authorities.[12] In early 1817 authorities in Kendal, Westmoreland, found a seventy-three-year-old "Itinerant unlicensed" "Vagabond" selling a Manchester printing of Cobbett's *To the Journeymen And Labourers of England, Wales, Scotland, and Ireland* (1816) in the local village of Broughton-in-Furness. With a caution perhaps born of the 1790s, the old man "doubtless had many Copies but he never produced more than one at once."[13] Radicalism's transmission methods, designedly, were too casual to admit of easy control. Around the same time, a vagrant weaver was imprisoned in Wisbech, Cambridgeshire, for selling a Norwich printing of London pressman William Benbow's "inflammatory Paper" (a poster), entitled *Proposal to Murder the Queen.* He carried "a Quantity" of them "to vend for the purpose of enabling him to reach Nottingham."[14] Whether Radical pamphlets travelled overseas by equally provisional routes, it is difficult to judge. The black orator Robert Wedderburn's claim in an 1817 issue of his *Axe Laid to the Root* that Jamaican slaves were "singing all day at work about Thomas Spence, and the two Evans' in Horsemonger Lane prison, and . . . The free Mulattoes are reading Cobbett's Register" might be taken with a pinch of salt—except that three years later the informer John Brittain reported how Wedderburn's friends "reccomend that small Pamphlets should be prepared, to be sent out to India to those suffering Blacks to open their eyes, that they might strike for their long lost liberty."[15] If these examples of the circulation and penetration of the London-based press hint at metropolitan dominance, an examination of the English provinces reveals a robust press supported by local activists with their own agendas.

In the Midlands town of Dudley, the first issue of the Radical journal the *Patriot* (motto: "God armeth the Patriot") in late 1819 was forwarded to the authorities by an informer who found it "suspended on a Gibbet and the market Cross," whence it appears to have been left by its supporters rather than its detractors.[16] Not far away, the editor of the *Lichfield Mercury,* J. Amphlett, hoaxed the authorities by self-addressing a printed handbill *To the Editor of the Lichfield Mercury* and signing it "A Magistrate" in order to condemn the flogging of four men in nearby Stafford.[17] More remarkably, in Gosport, Hampshire, someone printed a playbill strikingly appropriating an otherwise innocuous text:

Under the Patronage of Col. Brown,
and the Officers of the 28th Regt..
For the benefit of Mr. Miller.
Gosport theatre,
On Friday, October the 25th, 1816,
Will be presented (never performed here) the celebrated Play
called,

140

The *VOICE OF NATURE*

. . .

The

Judgement of King Solomon,

Has furnished the Dramatics of this piece . . . with an assurance, that however cruelty,
aided by power, may for a time oppress by its strength, the supplicating hand of
helpless innocence, or blight by its influence the fostering kindness that would protect
it, yet the hour must arrive, when justice will assert its right, and demand redress. . . .

It presents a most striking

LESSON TO KINGS,

Shewing them, . . . by having laws with an even balance,

distribute alike to

THE RICH AND POOR.

Whether this was an impishly Radical actor or a disaffected military man (of whom there were plenty after the war), the playbill makes an innovative materialist or deistic seizure of the play's title, hoaxing the local authorities sufficiently for them to forward it to the Home Office.[18]

In Newcastle in 1819, a self-improvement group called "The Union Society of Political Protestants" printed their *Declaration and Rules* and organized themselves on a seminar principle, spelling out "what papers and books shall be purchased" in their classes: "The works recommended, are Cartwright's Bill of Rights, which ought to be had in all Classes—also the Black Book—Bentham's Reform Catechism, and other works—Ensor's Works—Cobbett's Papers against Gold, and his Weekly Register also the publications of Wooler, Sherwin, &c."[19] The reading recommended by the Political Protestants shows a revealing combination of civil economics and accessible political theory.[20] Such political reading groups were important in promoting communal political identity as well as providing an audience for the Radical press.

Artisans sometimes first encountered Radical literature via complicated developments in their programs of reading. One *Republican* correspondent, the Castleton, Yorkshire, dyer and threadmaker Amariah Batty, declared that he first became a religious skeptic after reading, of all things, Richard Watson's famous anti–*Age of Reason* tract, *An Apology for the Bible* (1796). Unpredictably, Batty's reading of Watson's pious book had "opened the way for doubt, and as I went on to examine it fairly those doubts were strengthened, and I became anxious to possess Thomas Paine's 'Age of Reason.' " After Batty read Paine in the summer of 1821, he went on to read other skeptical materialist authors, such as Mirabaud (pseud. d'Holbach), Volney and Voltaire.[21] Another *Republican* correspondent, T. R. Bayley Potts of Brick Lane, Whitechapel, followed a similarly convoluted route to skepticism. After joining the Cateaton Street Free-Thinking Christians, Potts found that their library included skeptics and deists such as Gibbon, Priestley, Locke and Paley but not the Voltaire, Mirabaud, Volney, Paine and Eliu Palmer he longed for.[22] The publication of these semiautobiographical letters demonstrates that an important function of the Radical press lay in providing opportunities for individuals to share Radical opinions in ways potentially enabling to other free-thinking or reformist organizations.

It is possible that provincial artisan reading groups, such as the Newcastle Political Protestants, were better provisioned with Radical reading than their London counterparts like the Freethinking-Christians, perhaps because they were less fearful of surveillance. In the capital, the crippled teacher and poet Thomas Hazard, imprisoned on suspicion of treason after allowing his school-rooms to be used by the Cato Street conspirators in February 1820, claimed that his premises had only been used "an hour on Monday evenings to read the Manchester Observer in." As he wrote indignantly in a manuscript poem appended to his letter, "this is call'd freedom."[23] The veteran Spencean campaigner Thomas Evans, Sr., after his release from a second term of imprisonment under a Suspension of Habeas Corpus, had only to affix to the windows of a house in Long Alley, Moorfields, a notice declaring that "This Shop will be opened in a few days as a Patriotic Coffee House" and that "the patriotic Newspapers & political Registers, so succinctly calculated to enlighten the public Mind will be taken in" for a visit to be made by a spy who carefully noted not only Evans's undiminished activism but also that the premises were "nearly opposite Batchelers printing & Bookshop where many of Hone's or Woollers Papers are sold."[24]

Eighteen months later, Batcheler's name was still being forwarded on a list of "Printers & Book Vendors selling . . . Seditious Publication[s] and Notices last night," nine days after Peterloo, when the metropolitan Radicals were backing the Manchester martyrs.[25]

By the time of Peterloo, a self-sufficient, provincial press existed in Manchester which actively exchanged ideas and personnel with colleagues in London. In theory the *Manchester Observer* could call on a distribution system which included *Republican* editor Richard Carlile's shop in Fleet Street, *Medusa* editor Thomas Davison's premises in Duke Street, Smithfield, as well as that of the Wardour Street, Soho, pressman Thomas Dolby. In addition to these London agents, the *Manchester Observer* also had outlets in Birmingham, Liverpool, Leeds and Rochdale. The *Manchester Observer* eventually came to be linked with the most ultra-Radical strand of London politics when the Spencean Thomas John Evans, Jr., took over its editorship from James Wroe in early 1820. It is worth looking at Evans, Jr.'s, background in order to assess the type of experience he brought to the *Observer*.

Evans, Jr., was a fairly cosmopolitan Radical by this time. During the armistice year of 1814 he had travelled at his Spencean father's behest on an ideological mission to United English exiles in Paris ("I consider you the agent of mankind that no oppertunities are to be lost of propogating the true

Philosophy of Nature").[26] Evans, Jr.'s, inside knowledge of ultra-Radical physical force elements in London must have promised a good chance for a north-south dialogue informed by someone with an exceptional activist commitment. The London ultras, especially in late 1819, were acutely aware of the strategic importance of finding support in the northern industrial towns which they sensed to be lacking in the more diffuse, unpredictable and constantly watched capital. Evans, Jr., announced his goal in an *Observer* "Prospectus" to be that of "rendering the Radical Reformers of the Metropolis, and of the North more thoroughly acquainted with the steps taken by each in furtherance of their common purpose."[27] A few months later, the country then awash with speculation about the fate of Queen Caroline, Evans, Jr., signified this objective ideologically by printing in the *Manchester Observer* a "National Prayer" which was a pure extraction of Spencean agrarianism: "The hand of oppression, O LORD!, still presseth heavily upon us. Thou gavest to man the earth for his inheritance, and all its fruits, the beasts of the field, and all the fishes of the sea, to be his food . . . there is food enough for every thing that lives . . . yet are millions of our brethren, in this land of plenty, wasting away under the influence of want."[28] Evans, Jr.'s, "Prospectus" shows very clearly the transmission of this highly specific, Radical ideology through the medium of a newspaper. These ideological communications are the product of a mature political movement with considerable resources of intellectual vitality.

The two-way dialogue of the *Manchester Observer* with London activism makes it an important illustrative example of the Radical press's stamina and the way it bridged two generations. Although not a publisher himself, Evans, Sr., was fully engaged in pamphlet polemics, and Evans, Jr., must have come to the Radical press benefitting from his father's experiences. Evans, Sr.'s, deceptively titled *Christian Policy The Salvation of the Empire* (1816), was published by the veteran pressman and activist Arthur Seale, whose own Radical credentials went back to a fine edition of Volney's *Ruins . . . of Empires* in 1795.[29] Despite the apparent spiritual commitment of *Christian Policy The Salvation*'s call for "a political millenium" (p. 11), Evans, Sr.'s, Spenceanism sought to create a practical Christian socialism guided by a measure of Enlightenment political skepticism.[30] Evans, Sr.'s, related pamphlet, *Christian Policy In Full Practice Among the People of Harmony, A Town in the State of Pennsylvania, North America* (1818), was similarly intended to show how the "projections of More, Harrington, and Spence, are there carried into practical effect" (p. 15). Evans, Sr., thought his Christian agrarianism sound political economy, not merely "Utopian and visionary theories, so long the objects of incessant ridicule as being utterly impracticable" (p. 15). *Christian Policy In Full Practice* is an example similar to his son's expeditions to Paris or Manchester of an attempt to emphasise the revelance of Spencean "Agrarian Fellowship" (p. 15) far beyond the metropolis.

As well as being a veteran of Radical debating clubs, Evans, Sr., was a firm believer in printing's revolutionary potential: "They [priests] have not been able to destroy the press, and the press is now rapidly destroying them, and their pagan employers, and the enormities of their whole system" (*Christian Policy The Salvation*, p. 16). Part of the success of the Radical press lay in its ability to have direct contact with its readership. At the Mulberry Tree tavern, "at least 130 Persons present," "both the Evans spoke at Great Length" on parliamentary reform, but then, "after the Business of the Meeting was over they proceeded to Harmony and Evans Junr read a Publication of Hone's call'd the Political Litany—the Company Chaunting the Responses."[31] This live, working-class response to Hone's *Political Litany To Be Said or Sung At All Fire Sides In England, Wales, Scotland and Ireland. Humbly dedicated to all Archbishops, Bishops, Rural Deans, Prebendaries, Rectors, Vicars, &c.* (1817) gives definitive evidence of how the Radical press delivered itself to its specified audience, very much as Hone had imagined it in his subtitle. The litanies were carnivalesque. While the "order of service" in Hone's *Political Litany* requires a leader and a simple communal response ("O House of Commons, proceeding from corrupt Boroughmongers, have mercy upon us, your should-be constituents. . . . / *We beseech you, & c.*"), other litanies, such as *The Political Pig-Stye, Written by Gregory Grunt, Esq., of Hog's Norton, in the County of Baconshire, President of the Society for the Suppression of Swill Tubs; and Agent to the Auxiliary Bristle Club, Tune— "Black Joke"* (1816), must have been much more raucous when it denounced, to a chorus of grunts, how "At Paris our glorious Allies . . . combined, / To eat up the French and enslave all mankind, / Sing (*Grunt*) Pigs, all of a stye." The insertion of this anti-monarchist, anti-nationalist message within a political litany is a vivid example of how an extreme ultra-Radical position could be adapted to suit a communal context.

It is possible to sketch out a rough social history of this wider Radical press community and create a picture of the Radical bookshops themselves. When half a dozen red-jacketed militia wrecked the Manchester *Observer*'s offices, they "vigorously attacked" with bayonets "the placards hung at the door."[32] In London, Richard Carlile's wife Jane fended off workmen sent to distrain her imprisoned husband's possessions, even as they tried to dismantle the shop and remove its name board, "RICHARD CARLILE PUBLISHER AND BOOKSELLER," along with an interior notice, "OFFICE FOR THE DEIST AND TEMPLE OF REASON."[33] Evans, Sr.'s, Worship Street "Patriotic Coffee House" similarly announced its presence with "seditious writings & Representations in the Windows," including transparencies showing "Britannia . . . seated with her Shield on which is written Universal Suffrage & the Voice of the People the only Freedom."[34] This assertive Radical press inspired loyalists to produce their own inversions of the most successful Radical journals. Carlile recalled how the *White Dwarf,* edited by Gibbons Merle, "lived but a short time, that is, just as long as his patrons thought proper to distribute the publication gratis to all coffee-houses, taverns, and ale-houses; for scarce a copy ever fetched fourpence."[35] Robert Wedderburn foresaw its end ("Sir, I prophesy the fall of your Dwarf") in his, alas, similarly short-lived *Axe Laid to the Root,* no. 5.

In this close-knit community Richard Carlile reckoned he "knew the face of almost every forward man in London, by their coming to my shop for pamphlets."[36] Nevertheless, this did not stop him failing to notice spies in his midst. When the name of the sculptor-spy George Edwards came out at the Cato Street trials it must have caused Carlile considerable embarrassment because he had himself employed Edwards "as a modeller for several figures" during 1819. Carlile met the "Artist" Edwards in February or March 1819, when he had been "in the habit of coming into the shop to purchase my pamphlets." Carlile paid Edwards £5. 3 shillings for the copyright of a remarkable statue of Thomas Paine which he commissioned for his shop, both as publicity for his edition of Paine's theological works and so as to sell miniature replicas as a sideline:

> A whole length figure of Paine in drapery, 3 feet high, with a scroll in the right hand, reclining on a small square pedastal; scroll inscribed "To reason with Despots is throwing reason away. The best of argument is a vigorous preparation." Letter to the People of France. The left hand is pointing to the front pannel of the pedastal, on which is inscribed "Common Sense. Rights of Man. Age of Reason." The side pannel next to the figure, bears a red cap of Liberty, inscribed on a blue boader "LIBERTAS". The off pannel has a figure representing the resurrection of truth from the bottom of a well, onto the "Temple of Reason," agreeable to the saying of Democritus, who said that truth was hid in the bottom of a well, which is as much as to say that he dared not promulgate it in his time. A Globe on the small pedastal, lighted with Gas, represents America illuminated next to PAINE. The whole stands on a large marbled pedestal with the following inscriptions. . . .[37]

By the time this puff for Edwards's gas-lit statue appeared in the *Republican,* the artist had been a spy for nearly two years.[38] Such was the tightly knit nature of the press community that Carlile's shop must have provided an easy *entrée* into the intricate circles of metropolitan Radical pressmen. The diminutive printer and much-prosecuted placard bearer, Samuel "Little Waddy" Waddington, later told the L. C. S. historian Francis Place that Mrs. Alexander Galloway, wife of a Spencean engineer, had commissioned "fifteen" [*sic*] busts of Spence ("for patriotic persons") from Edwards.[39] Embarrassingly, Edwards also sculpted a portrait bust of Carlile, having the gall to put the finishing touches to it while visiting the *Republican* editor in King's Bench prison.[40]

The degree of cultural promiscuity in the Radical press within the few square miles of central London should not be underestimated. After the Cato Street arrests, Carlile used the pages of the *Republican* to (truthfully) distance himself from the conspiracy, but, thanks to spy reports, it is possible to see how closely allied were the community of pressmen with those ultra-Radical activists who wanted to gain ideological objectives through physical force. A few days after Cato Street, Carlile described the circumstances of his first meeting with the soon-to-be executed William "Black" Davidson six months before in the Crown and Anchor tavern.[41] What Carlile cannot have known was that the Fountain Gardens, Lambeth, spy John Shegog (code name "B") was there to report it.[42]

Shegog noted the presence in the Crown and Anchor of "Carlisle" as well as some of London's most committed ultras, including the Spencean tailor Robert Moggridge ("Moggerige"), the tailor and soon-to-be informer Abel Hall, the veteran semiprofessional orator John Gale Jones, the ex-soldiers Harrison and Hartley, and the seditious placard-bearing printer Samuel Waddington—as well as Arthur Thistlewood, "Dr." James Watson and the lame shoemaker Thomas Preston (the latter three already tried—and acquitted—of high treason in 1817). Also present was one of the Evanses (who acted as secretary that night), the ex-sailor "Black" Davidson and, remarkably, the printer Thomas Davison. Shegog carefully distinguished in his report between "Davidson the Black" and "Davidson [sic] I think of the Medusa." This was quite an assembly. Richard Carlile must have very soon realized the volatile potential of the situation because Shegog reported that "the company was in confusion in concequence" of "Carlisle" "leaving the Room."[43] Carlile's exit was probably well-advised, because a few months later a spy would be reporting on how Hartley, "Black" Davidson and Harrison were arriving armed at Cato Street conspiracy meetings.

It is worth pausing to assess this gathering and the extent of its involvement with the press and contemporary Radical politicking. Both of the Evanses were authors. Thomas Preston, in addition to his 1817 autobiography, wrote vituperative letters to George IV and Home Secretary Sidmouth. "Dr." Watson, his son safely exiled in America after Spa Fields, also published occasional pamphlets. In terms of a proven commitment to Radical politics, the group had impressive credentials. Gale Jones shared platforms with John Thelwall as far back as the 1795 "Gagging Acts"; James Watson had been one of the principal orators at the Spa Fields Rising; Waddington would soon be selling "Pamphlets & Pike heads" from his Grays Inn Lane shop.[44] Less ambiguously, some of the others—like Harrison, Hartley and Thistlewood—were more committed to physical force than practical prose. However, the two groups of pressman-ideologues and physical force ultras retained a certain amount of fluidity in the means they employed. In Paris in 1814 the ideologue Evans, Jr., had been particularly directed to seek out the exiled Arthur Thistlewood while, in their local tavern-based communities, the physical force activists Watson and Preston were treated as ideologues.[45]

Crucially, what must have alarmed Richard Carlile was the presence of

146

physical force revolutionaries alongside "Davidson . . . of the Medusa." Working from Duke Street, Smithfield, Thomas Davison printed the *Republican* until his own imprisonment in late 1820 (when his press was taken over by the enigmatic activist Rhoda Helder); he also operated from another press in Lombard Street, Whitefriars, where he was employed by John Murray to print much of Byron's output, at least as far back as *The Bride of Abydos. A Turkish Tale* (1813). Not only would the government have in Shegog's report sufficient information to associate Carlile with well-known (if unconvicted) extremists, the presence in the Crown and Anchor of Thomas Davison would have laid both the production and the editorial functions of the *Republican* open to treasonable allegations. As it turned out, Carlile could hardly have been in worse jeopardy than he encountered at the hands of the Society for the Suppression of Vice, because the authorities eventually got their men. Three months later Carlile's publication of *The Age of Reason* and Palmer's *Principles of Nature* put him in Dorchester gaol for six years while, twelve months later, Davison was sent down for two years to the harsher conditions of Okeham gaol, Rutland.

Printers were prime targets for *agents provocateurs* because they were less likely to be editorially aware. Writing from King's Bench prison in 1817, William Hone related in his *Reformists' Register* how he once received a visit from "several strangers" "who held violent language, and who, I am well persuaded, were emissaries to entrap me," having asked him to print a hand-bill beginning "Britons, Petitioning Avails You Nothing." Hone had the sense to turn them away, but the same strangers next offered the work to Hay and Turner, printers in Newcastle Street, Strand.[46] Once again the degree of promiscuity in the Radical press, as well as the intensity of its surveillance, can be judged. Hay and Turner, who printed Evans, Sr.'s, *Christian Policy In Full Practice* (1818), remained under surveillance. One of the pair, the Lambeth Marsh resident William Turner, was reported in July 1819 by bust-modeller Edwards (alias "W——r") to be "going about the Town, principally on the Surry side, with a very inflammatory Bill of the Spencean Doctrines, and carries with him a new book to sell."[47] This was not an isolated instance. In exactly the same way, a spy-amongst-the-pressmen was on hand in December 1818 at Evans, Sr.'s, Archer Street, Haymarket, debating club to report one of its meetings (typically, a "blasphemous perversion of Scripture, and a general abuse of Government") chaired by James Wade, editor of the *Gorgon,* a weekly printed by ex-St. Mary's Gate, Manchester, Radical pressman, J. Molineux, now working from Bream's Buildings, Chancery Lane.[48]

Within London's Radical print culture circulated the rumours and fledgling oral histories prevalent in any close-knit community. At the Northumberland Arms, Clerkenwell Green, a spy sent to monitor the unsettled situation after the Spa Fields Rising reported that the enigmatic Radicals, William

147

Clark, Sr., and Jr., were delivering what amounted to an alternative Radical historiography.

The Clarks, like the Evanses, were a father and adult son sharing mutual Radical commitments. William Clark, Jr., acted as secretary to Henry "Orator" Hunt at the Spa Fields meetings convened after December 1816's abortive insurrection. Clark, Sr., was also politically active and known to be going "round to the different [public] Houses with the Spa Fields Petition for Signatures." Significantly, Clark, Sr., claimed an involvement with the Radical press dating back to the early 1790s. At the Northumberland Arms "Clarke had a good deal to Say . . . on the examination of a man for Selling Tracks [*sic*] that they were as Liable to be taken as those who sold Cobbetts [*Register*]."[49] Although the spy's report is unelaborated, it evokes the fears engendered in the local community by the arrest of the Evanses, to whom the gathering at the tavern were trying to communicate messages of support and solidarity via Mrs. Jane Evans.[50] The elder Clark declared in this overheard conversation not only "his friendship for Evans," but also a personal acquaintance with Thomas Spence going back to the early 1790s. If true, it is a remarkable set of claims:

> Clark [Sr.] . . . mentioned his friendship for Evans and Said of the Plan which they had Introduced was their own Plan and not Spences as he was very friendly with Spence for he and Spence Rote Hogs Meat but they quarld about the Spencean Plan for he Said it was not Spences Plan for he took it from a Book Written by Dean Swift on the Partition of the Land[.][51]

The importance of this report is not merely that Clark, Sr., claimed a part in formulating the Spencean "Plan" of land nationalization alongside Evans, Sr., but also that "he and Spence Rote Hogs Meat," which is Clark, Sr.'s (or the spy's) disremembering of the title of Thomas Spence's 1793–1795 journal, *Pig's Meat*.[52]

Disentangling Radical pressmen named William Clark (or Clarke) is extremely difficult but they (or he) are important to literary history. The Northumberland Arms Clarks, Sr., and Jr., were "journeymen coach-makers," according to Carlile, who knew them and condemned their parsimonious treatment by "Orator" Hunt, but a man called William Clark was also the first pirater of P. B. Shelley's *Queen Mab* in 1821.[53] It is difficult to know whether *Mab* Clark was one of the Northumberland Arms Clarks. In another issue of the *Republican,* without further distinguishing between the Clarks, Carlile reprimanded *Mab* Clark for having bound himself over to magistrates rather than go to gaol when the Society for the Suppression of Vice prosecuted him.[54] Whatever the later circumstances of *Mab* Clark (who went on to publish pro-Caroline works as well as Bryon's *Don Juan*), he was new enough to publishing in 1821 to have recently graduated from having "long served" as one of Carlile's volunteer shopmen at 55 Fleet Street.[55] Digging deeper into this Radical artisan community, we find that one of the Clarks (Sr., or Jr.), who "Speaks of Kings—praise[s] Buonaparte," was "Calld the Poet of the Court of Acquity" by locals at the Northumberland Arms, in whose neighborhood both father and son lived.[56] However many Clarks there were, they all express a common interest in poetry, the press and Radical politics.

Another frequenter of the Northumberland Arms at that time was the shoemaker poet Robert Charles Fair.[57] Fair had been the enthusiastic excerpter of Shelley's *Queen Mab* when, after its first private printing in 1813, most of it had been reprinted in 1815 in the *Theological Inquirer; or, Polemical Magazine* edited by the shadowy Radical activist and pressman impressario George Cannon. Like Cannon, Fair is something of a pivotal literary figure. He must have known Clark "the Poet of the Court of Acquity" because the government spy noted their presence together in the Northumberland Arms four days after the 1817 Suspension of Habeas Corpus.[58] Fair was sufficient of an early Shelley enthusiast to have written an admiring "Ode To the Author of 'Queen Mab,' " which was published in Cannon's *Inquirer* as well as William Benbow's edition of *Miscellaneous and Posthumous Poems of Percy Bysshe Shelley*.[59] Although it cannot conclusively be shown that the William Clark who pirated *Queen Mab* in 1821 is the same man Robert Charles Fair drank with in the Northumberland Arms in 1817, the involvement in the local press community and the interest in poetry is common.

Recently, William St. Clair has linked *Mab* Clark with both George Cannon and Richard Carlile.[60] This considerably extends the range of likely circles of acquaintance of those Radical pressmen associated with the early printings of *Mab*. Not only would this circle include Thomas Davison of the *Medusa* (who worked for Cannon as well as for Carlile) but also some of the poet-activists on the fringes of the Thistlewood-led physical force ultras.[61] To both William Clark "the Poet of the Court of Acquity" (and possible publisher of *Mab*) and to Robert Charles Fair (the eulogist of Shelley) on the basis of their likely mutual acquaintance, there is a direct link to the indicted poet Edward James Blandford and the shoemaker, debator and poet, Allen Davenport, both of them activists who recommended physical force. Blandford was involved with the armed group centered on Thistlewood, while Davenport spoke at the Hopkins Street Chapel debating club, which was, effectively, the populist wing of the Cato Street conspiracy. These men must be counted amongst the earliest group of Radicals likely to have had a knowledge of *Queen Mab*.[62]

This small community supported each others' writings. Davenport wrote a poem dedicated to Robert Shorter, editor of the *Theological Comet; or, Free-Thinking Englishman,* while his "The Poet's Mite" for the *Republican* was enclosed with a donation to help the gaoled Richard Carlile, his son Thomas Paine Carlile and sister Mary-Anne.[63] Fair's skeptical "Ode to Religion" ("what art thou, phantasm of caprice[?]"), printed in Cannon's *Theo-*

149

logical Inquirer, was swiftly followed by his near-blasphemous poem "Scripture Soliloquies: Our Blessed Saviour on Mount Calvary" ("Why am I here? . . . / O bitter cup! that his lov'd only son / A father's power to save has thus forsaken!").[64] Another Fair poem, "Ode to Poetry," was printed in William Benbow's *Ramblers Magazine, or Man of Fashion's Companion.*[65] Such supportive publication was a two-way process. Allegedly writing from Dorchester gaol where he was imprisoned at the same time as Carlile, the black orator and ex-*Axe Laid To The Root* editor Robert Wedderburn attacked the clergy in his pamphlet *High-Heel'd Shoes for Dwarfs in Holiness* (1821), honoring Clark's bravery for publishing *Mab,* reviewing the rest of Shelley's work and, for good measure, citing the poetry of Fair.

According to *High-Heel'd Shoes,* the "young madman" Shelley's *Queen Mab* "had become very scarce" until a "young desperado, who aspires to the crown of martyrdom . . . had the temerity to publish this amalgam of infamy."[66] Nevertheless, the real author of *High-Heel'd Shoes* is more likely to be George Cannon than the semiliterate Wedderburn. *High-Heel'd Shoes* has all the hallmarks of Cannon's lionizing of Shelley, with Cannon now exploiting the poet's growing reputation from the modest beginnings he had helped foster with *Mab*'s excerption in the *Theological Inquirer. High-Heel'd Shoes* not only recommended, ironically, *Queen Mab* as "the Bedlamite ravings of Atheism and Democracy" but also quoted (without naming the author) the "Soliloquy of our blessed Saviour on Mount Calvary"—Cannon's disremembering of the title of Fair's "Scripture Soliloquies: Our Blessed Saviour on Mount Calvary," which he recollected from, as he put it, "Perkins's *Theological Inquirer.*"[67]

In short, such was the cohesiveness of the Radical press that Shelley's *Queen Mab* was rapidly incorporated into the tropes of Radical writers. Seven months before Clark's *Mab* was published in May 1821, Thomas Preston— then in Tothill-fields prison pending (unforthcoming) charges of high treason following Cato Street—began a satirical letter to Home Secretary Sidmouth which related an "extraordinary dream" occasioned by "several noctural visits from Queen Mab." Shelley's poem could have been known to Preston either directly through Cannon's *Theological Inquirer* or else through Preston's contact with the Clark/Fair circle. *Mab* provided the idiom within which Preston could beatify his "inestimable friend Arthur Thistlewood," executed six months earlier.

Preston's manuscript describes at length how "a luminous halo e[n]veloped his [Thistlewood's] whole form, a Crown of blazing Laurels discended and encompassed his head, the Scaffolding and the whole frightful apparatus of destruction vanished, [amid] the scattered fragments of the mangled carcases of his oppressors, . . . in the midst of these, towering above the rest in all the splendour of manly magnanimity, stood my friend Arthur." In "a voice surpassing the loudest thunder," Thistlewood declares that " 'Tyranny shall

be annihilated, and Man shall rise to the summit of universal friendship!' "
There then follows a vision of Radical martyrology in which appear the
"Ghosts of Brandreth, Turner, Ludlam, Cashman, together with those of all
the other victims of treachery and espoignage [*sic*]."[68] In a counter vision of
lynched policemen, spies and informers, "strung with ropes by the neck in a
bunch like Herrings on a string," Preston names the spies Edwards and
"Shego" whose "piece-meal carcases were sacrificed to the fury of the betrayed, insulted and enraged people who trampled them to the earth, the groan-
ing bosom of which revolted even to sickness at the loathsome filth of
corruption which besmeared and disgraced its surface." Then, "while my
friend Thistlewood stretched forth his hand towards the West, I saw your Lord-
ship loaded with heavy chains, and . . . dragged through the public streets
without respect or ceremony to a loathsome Jail." Finally, Preston dreams he
visited Sidmouth in prison "when horrible to relate, I found you dead and
stiff, hanging by a strong blue ribbon round the neck to a hook in the prison
door! black in the face and your eyeballs started from their sockets! I left the
place and having uttered a piercing shriek, at which the Massy buildings fell
in hideous ruin, at the dreadful crash I started,—and awoke,—and lo! I found
that but a *dream* that with such violence had roused my senses to excessive
fright!!!"[69]

Preston's Gothic vision of Queen Mab with its beatification of Arthur
Thistlewood and casual appropriation of Shelley's poem is indicative of the
strength and intellectual community of Radicalism. Wherever one looks,
whether at ephemeral handbills, fugitive tracts, occasional poems or tavern
gatherings, the Radical press was both the product and the reflection of Regency England's unenfranchised artisan class.

NOTES

1. "WP" to J. Moore, 12 December 1792, BM Add MS. 16922. 53. The keeper
of the Chancery Lane pamphlet stall was almost certainly Thomas Spence.

2. Iain McCalman, *Radical Underworld: Prophets, Revolutionaries and Pornographers in London, 1795–1840* (Cambridge: Cambridge University Press, 1988), hereafter McCalman (1988); David Worrall, *Radical Culture: Discourse, Resistance and
Surveillance, 1790–1820* (Hemel Hempstead: Harvester Wheatsheaf, 1992); hereafter
Worrall (1992).

3. *The Manchester Mercury; and Harrop's General Advertizer,* 31 August 1819.

4. "Yet even in their [newspapers] mutilated and garbled accounts of the speeches
of men who were never bred to the trade of speech-making, but have worked hard all
their days for an honest livelihood, there is much more sound sense, aye, and good
language and eloquence too, than in the harrangues of many an heriditary legislator";
White Hat 1, No. 1 (16 October 1819): 3.

5. *At a Special Meeting of Members of The Committee of Sunday-Schools in
Manchester and Salford, Belonging to the Established Church;* handbill enclosure, 24
September 1819; HO 42/ 198. 135.

6. 23 August 1819; HO 42/ 193. 323.

7. 13 November 1817; HO 40/ 7 (3). 17.

8. 23 March 1817; HO 42/ 162. 280. For Radicalism's agrarianist appropriation of Robert Southey's recently pirated *Wat Tyler* (1794), see David Worrall, "Agrarians against the Picturesque: Ultra-Radicalism and the revolutionary politics of land," *The Politics of the Picturesque: Literature, Landscape and Aesthetics since 1770*, ed. Stephen Copley and Peter Garside (Cambridge: Cambridge University Press, 1994), pp. 240–60.

9. 26 October 1819; HO 42/ 197. 155.

10. McCalman gives as the lifetimes of the journals: *Theological Comet* (24 July–13 November 1819); *Medusa* (20 February 1819–1 January 1820); *Cap of Liberty* (8 September 1819–4 January 1820); McCalman (1988), pp. 298–301.

11. It is not clear whether the report refers to Newcastle upon Tyne, in northeast England, or to Newcastle under Lyme, in the northwest Midlands; HO 42/ 197. 719.

12. "Ode to George the Fourth, and Caroline his Wife, Now Queen Consort of Great Britain" by "John Bull"; printer: J. Thomas, Penzance. 3 August 1820; HO 40/ 14. 84. Of course, at this juncture, the Radical cause was firmly in favor of the Queen and against King George IV.

13. HO 40/ 10. 271, c. March 1817; letter from Kendal, Westmoreland, c. March 1817. William Cobbett, *To the Journeymen And Labourers of England, Wales, Scotland, and Ireland, On the Cause of their present Miseries; on the Measures which have produced that Cause; on the Remedies which some foolish, and some cruel and insolent, men have proposed; and of the line of conduct which Journeymen and Labourers ought to pursue in order to obtain effectual Relief, and to assist in promoting the Tranquillity, and restoring the Happiness of their Country* (Manchester: J. Molineux, Ridings Court. St. Mary's Gate, 1816). "As to the cause of our present miseries—it is the enormous amount of the taxes. . ." (p. 3).

14. 22 July 1820; HO 40/ 14. 63.

15. *Axe Laid to the Root* 6 (c. 1817). This issue of Wedderburn's short-lived journal is reproduced in Iain McCalman, *"The Horrors of Slavery" and Other Writings by Robert Wedderburn* (New York: Markus Wiener Publishing, 1991), pp. 105–10. John Brittain, 14 February 1820; HO 44/ 2. Brittain was a low-grade informer. His reference to "India" is more likely to be a misunderstood reference to the West Indies.

16. *Patriot* 1 (6 November 1819); HO 42/ 198. 112. The *Patriot*'s loyalist-sounding title was more than a (much-used) device to flabbergast the authorities. The ownership of the concept of nationhood was strongly contested by Radicals. A poem in the *Patriot* made clear its attempts to redefine patriotism: "We will spurn that base-born thing / Who can now in triumph sing / 'King and Constitution!' "

17. *To the Editor of the Lichfield Mercury* (printed by J. Amphlett). A handwritten note identifies Amphlett as "Editor of the Lichfield Mercury"; enclosure HO 42/ 198. 567.

18. 25 October 1816; HO 40/ 9. 506. The printer's name is given as "Legg . . . Gosport." *The Voice of Nature: a play, in three acts . . .* is a translation by James Boaden of "Le Jugement de Salomon" by Louis Charles Caigniez (London: James Ridgway, 1803).

19. *Declaration and Rules of the Political Protestants* [printer: J. Marshall, Newcastle], c. 1819.

20. Identifiable or representative texts include John Wade's *Black Book, or corruption unmasked* (1820); William Cobbett's *Paper Against Gold; the history and mystery of the Bank of England* (1821); Jeremy Bentham's *Plan of Parliamentary Reform, in the form of a catechism . . . with an introduction, etc.* (1817); and works of George Ensor, such as *Radical Reform, restoration of usurped rights* (1819) or *An Inquiry concerning the Population of Nations: containing a refutation of Mr. Malthus's essay on Population* (London, 1818).

21. *Republican* (18 January 1822): 86–88.

22. *Republican* (15 March 1822): 331–34. Carlile was jailed in 1819 for publishing Paine's *Age of Reason* and Eliu Palmer's *The Principles of Nature, or a Development of the Moral Causes of Happiness and Misery amongst the Human Species* (1807). The contents of the latter had already been modestly excerpted in George Cannon's *Theological Inquirer* (20 August 1815): 486–90, when "J. S." of Islington sent in extracts of the Charlestown printing of this "curious work . . . quite common in the United States of America."

23. 29 March 1820; HO 44/ 1. 194. Although Hazard was not charged with treason, an informer wrote in to "state that Hazard establish[ed] a Society who met at his house called the Union Society at which he gave lessons in Politics"; 17 March 1820; HO 44/ 5. 374.

24. c. October/November 1818; HO 42/ 182. 116.

25. 25 August 1819; HO 42/ 193. 216.

26. Thomas Evans to T. J. Evans, Jr., 18 September 1814; HO 42/ 168. 353.

27. *Manchester Observer* (19 February 1820).

28. *Manchester Observer* (12 August 1820). Compare Evans, Jr.'s, "National Prayer" with Dr. Watson's precipitate speech at the Spa Fields Rising in December 1816, "The Earth is capable of affording us all the means of allaying our wants and of averting starvation. . . . There is not a day in which we pass the street that we do not see our miserable Countrymen starving to death"; quoted in Worrall (1992), pp. 101–2, "A National Prayer."

29. The full title is *Christian Policy The Salvation of the Empire. Being A Clear and Concise Examination Into The Causes That have Produced The Impending, Unavoidable national Bankruptcy; And the Effects that must ensue, unless averted by the Adoption of this only real and Desirable Remedy, which would elevate these realms to A Pitch of Greatness Hitherto Unattained by any Nation that ere Existed* (1816).

30. 18 September 1814; HO 42/ 168. 353. Evans, Sr., had written to his son in Paris that, on meeting the English exiles there, he was to "acquaint . . . [them] of an institution to propogate the opinions of Spence and state its progress[,] virtues, justice, and practice in the cristian church."

31. 30 January 1817; HO 42/ 158. 13. "Harmony" was the festive closing session on debate nights.

32. *Manchester Observer* (28 August 1819). The editor at that time was James Wroe.

33. *Republican* (30 June 1820): 340–41.

34. October/November 1818; HO 42/ 182. 116.

35. *Republican* (8 December 1820): 530.

36. *Republican* (3 March 1820): 218–19. Carlile was giving his account of meeting William "Black" Davidson, the Cato Street conspirator.

37. *Republican* (8 October 1819): 100–102. Carlile later claimed that "a gentleman . . . was determined to bid £100" for Paine's statue. Its present whereabouts are unknown. *Republican* (30 June 1820): 340.

38. Worrall (1992), p. 125.

39. Samuel Waddington to Francis Place, BL Add. MS. 16922. 322. Waddington's declaration of a print press is located at 15 March 1819; HO 42/ 185. 143.

40. *Republican* (28 April 1820): 3–7.

41. Carlile recalled being "not a little surprised at being accosted, in a very free and open manner, by this black man . . . who appeared from his vivacity to keep the whole company alive"; *Republican* (3 March 1820): 218–19.

42. For Shegog's address, see 4 October 1817; HO 42/ 170. 64.

43. 30 August 1819; HO 42/ 193. 341.

44. Thomas Preston, *The Life and Opinions of Thomas Preston, Patriot and Shoemaker* (1817). Preston's letters are in the *Black Dwarf* (19 April 1820): 518–20; HO 44/ 3. 33a, 20 October 1820, to Lord Sidmouth; HO 44/ 3. 34, 18 November, to the king; see below. James Watson, *More Plots, More Treason, More Green Bags: A Letter to Viscount Sidmouth* (1818); 16 October 1819; HO 42/ 197. 387.

45. Thomas Evans to T. J. Evans, Jr.; 18 September 1814; HO 42/ 168. 353.

46. *Hone's Reformists' Register* (28 June 1817).

47. 14 July 1819; HO 42/ 190. 40.

48. 15 December 1818; HO 42/ 182. 424. Molineux was the printer of the edition of Cobbett's *To the Journeymen And Labourers* (1816) found on the seventy-three-year-old Westmoreland vagrant.

49. 1 March 1817; HO 42/ 162. 275. A series of letters in the *Black Dwarf* between William T. Sherwin and T. J. Wooler suggests that both thought William Clark, Sr., and Jr., owned "manuscripts" which would have been relevant to Thomas Clio Rickman's *The Life of Thomas Paine* (1819), although Rickman promptly denied it; see *Black Dwarf* (21 April 1819): 255, (28 April 1819): 269–70, (5 May 1819): 279–80. Later comments by Wooler about the same incident imply that "Wm. Clark" had recently returned to England from New York: *Black Dwarf* (16 February 1820): 216.

50. 22 March 1817; HO 42/ 162. 280.

51. 1 March 1817; HO 42/ 162. 275. Spence died in 1814. The book by Swift might be *Some Thoughts on the Tillage of Ireland: humbly dedicated to the Parliament. To which is prefixed, A Letter to the Printer, from the Reverend Doctor Swift, . . .* [by Alexander Macaulay], London, 1737, and Dublin, 1738.

52. *Hog's Wash, or A Salmagundy for Swine* was the title of Daniel Isaac Eaton's journal before it became *Politics for the People,* 1794–1795.

53. For Clark the publisher of *Queen Mab,* see McCalman (1988), pp. 220–21; William St. Clair, *The Godwins and the Shelleys: The Biography of a Family* (1989), Appendix 3.

54. *Republican* (1 March 1822): 279; (1 February 1822): 146–47.

55. McCalman (1988), pp. 220; St. Clair, p. 559, n12; *Republican* (1 February 1822): 146–47.

56. 8 March 1817; HO 42/ 162. 274. c. October 1817; HO 42/ 170. 475.

57. 8 March 1817; HO 42/ 162. 277. 22 March 1817; HO 42/ 162. 280.

58. 8 March 1817; HO 42/ 162. 274.

59. Benbow's edition of Shelley's *Miscellaneous Poems,* bound with *Queen Mab* in the British Library, confirms the "Ode to the Author of Queen Mab" as written by "R. C. F.," an enlargement of the *Theological Inquirer's* "F."

60. St. Clair, p. 516. St. Clair notes that Carlile's edition of *Queen Mab* was printed using Clark's types (p. 514). Carlile's accounts of the Clarks, Sr., and Jr., and of *Mab* Clark are given in *Republican* (1 February 1822): 145–48 and (1 March 1822): 279. William B. Todd, *A Directory of Printers and Others in Allied Trades, London and Vicinity 1800–34* (1972) and A. H. Brown, *London Publishers and Printers c. 1800–1870* (London: British Library, 1982) show that W. Clark operated from 201 Strand in 1821. By 1823 the premises were occupied by the pressman Alfred Mead. Carlile described *Mab* Clark's shops as being near St. Clement's Church; *Republican* (1 February 1822): 146. To this list of Radical Clarks must be added William Clark of Webber Street, Blackfriars Road, who donated 2s. 6d. to Carlile's legal expenses; *Republican* (5 November 1819): 166–67. This man (assuming that he is different from the Clarks, Sr., and Jr., already mentioned) may have been sufficiently committed to have become the shopman volunteer and *Mab* publisher Richard Carlile refers to in *Republican* (1 February 1822): 146–47.

61. Thomas Davison printed Cannon's "Prospectus for a New Publication, to be Entitled *Collectanea Sceptica,*" pasted into the BL copy of the *Theological Inquirer.* Davison and Jane Carlile were also publishers of Cannon's *The Trial of Rev. Robt. Wedderburn, (A Dissenting Minister of the Unitarian persuasion,) For Blasphemy, Before Sir Charles Abbott, Knight, Lord Chief-Justice, and a Special Jury, in the Court of King's Bench, Westminster, The Sittings after Hillary Term, 1820; Containing a Verbatim Report of the Defence,* ed. Erasmus Perkins (London: Mrs. Carlile, T. Davison, J. Griffin, 1820).

62. On Blandford and Davenport's careers at this time, see Worrall (1992). Davenport's poem "Words to the Wind" (written before mid-1827) is reminiscent of Shelley's "Ode to the West Wind"; Allen Davenport, *The Muses Wreath: Composed of Original Poems* (n.d.: 1827?), pp. 17–18.

63. A[llen] Davenport, "To the editor, on his recent death, his subsequent resurrection, and his final ascension in the comet," *Theological Comet; or, Free-Thinking Englishman* (7 August 1819); "The Poet's Mite," *Republican* (20 September 1822): 516.

64. *Theological Inquirer* (1815): 142, 144. Both poems are signed "F." The author's identity is confirmed by Fair's letter to ex-London Corresponding Society activist and labor historian Francis Place, in which Fair enclosed a copy of his "Ode to Religion." Fair's letter tells of how he attended part of Thomas Spence's funeral in 1814 but did not stay to hear William Snow's interment oration; R. C. Fair to Francis Place, 9 March 1831; BL Add. MS. 27808.321.

65. R[obert] C[harles] F[air], "Ode to Poetry," *Ramblers Magazine, or Man of Fashion's Companion* (1 February 1822): 93–96.

66. Robert Wedderburn, *High-Heel'd Shoes for Dwarfs in Holiness. Being plain directions to weak Christians, how they may escape the snares of the devil, and the dreadful gulphs of Scepticism and Infidelity. In a Letter to the Rev. Erasmus Perkins, B. A. by the Rev. R. Wedderburn, V. D. M. Author of a Letter to the Jewish High Priest, on the Political Schemes of Moses; A Critical, Historical, and Admonitory Letter to the Archbishop of Canterbury, on the Progress of Infidelity; Cast-Iron Parsons, or a*

Scheme to Dispense with the Clergy, without Injury to Religion; A Shove for a Heavy-Breech'd Christian; Crutches from the Lame in Faith; Dialogues in Hell, Purgatory and Paradise; &c. &c. &c. (n. d.: ?1821), pp. 12–13. The "young desperado" must be Clark. If *Mab* Clark is one of the Northumberland Arms Clarks, then *High-Heel'd Shoes* suggests that he is Clark, Jr.

67. *High-Heel'd Shoes,* pp. 8–9, 13. "Erasmus Perkins" was a favourite pseudonym of George Cannon.

68. Brandreth, Turner and Ludlam were executed as ringleaders of the Derbyshire Pentrich Rising of 1817. Cashman was a sailor executed for his alleged part in the Spa Fields Rising, 1816.

69. HO 44/ 3. 33a, 20 October 1820; letter from Thomas Preston to Lord Sidmouth.

Demonology, Ethos, and Community in Cobbett and Shelley

Kevin Binfield

"Mass movements can rise and spread without belief
in a God, but never without belief in a devil."[1]

Remarking on Percy Shelley's "painful self-examination" during the autumn of 1819, Michael Scrivener writes, "To pursue the Ideal as if it were a personalized Absolute, as if it could be possessed by the individual, is to be self-destructive, to lead oneself to despair, false hope, and irresponsible actions."[2] If Scrivener's assessment holds for Shelley's political writing, and the inability to realize a "personalized Absolute" or a positive Ideal plagued Shelley in his efforts to effect reform, then one might go further, discovering that the failure to find an adequate devil, a personalized antitype, and to build an appropriate polemical style around that devil also plagued Shelley's writing to no insignificant degree. This essay explores the rhetorical device which Shelley failed to master, the *demonology,* and considers its origins in the conflicting demands of Radical discourse, its utilization by two Romantic period reformers, William Cobbett and Shelley, and the causes of the differing degrees of success the two writers achieved using the technique.

Briefly, the demonology might be understood simply as a catalogue of demons, that is, particular people or categories of people representing offensive practices or institutions. The demonology possesses obvious rhetorical significance, but, like any topos, it can also be understood as a socio-intellectual tool. Barry Allen treats demonology as a style of reasoning that presupposes some sense of community, a core of belief and behavior with reference to which deviance and heresy can be evaluated; a community of value must exist prior to the construction of a demonology.[3] The community, even if it lacks communal self-awareness, is able to identify individual behavior which violates its values.

Late eighteenth-century Radicalism seems generally to have expressed the values of its constituent classes in a vocabulary of Enlightenment abstractions—rights, reason, necessity, and the idea to which Thomas Paine gave a new significance in the Second Part of *The Rights of Man,* society. Paine occasionally inveighs against "the Bastard and his armed banditti" and "courtiers, placemen, pensioners and borough-holders," but, for the most part, the eighteenth-century reformers were engaged in conflicts between ideas rather than persons. The difficulty with such a discourse is that even while it names desirable qualities, it maintains them in the ether of language, preventing them from taking shape in what Antonio Gramsci calls "real action."[4] What the nascent Radicalism required was a homeric rhetoric, such as that described by George A. Kennedy, a rhetoric yoking words to personal action.[5]

Some Radical polemicists attempted to preserve the discourse of abstraction, even as they recognized the need to shift toward a discourse of persons. They recognized that even though oppression assumed its form on a national scale, individuals and communities experienced its effects in a variety of ways. Some writers sought a middle ground between abstracting and personalizing discourses in their attempts to persuade the separate elements of an emerging Radical subculture that they suffered in common. For example, William Godwin's expressed outrage over Paine's trial promotes a sense of communal suffering through Godwin's choice not to name Paine, even while he emphasizes, in an almost self-contradictory fashion, the victimization of unspecified persons. In one telling passage, attending to the means of punishment exercised by an abstract and de-personalized "they," and omitting specific mention of any particular Radical martyr, Godwin envelops all Radicals, not just Paine, in a cloud of potential victimization:

> If they are not thus checked, I am persuaded that the contempt, the scurrilities and the obloquy which are now circulated, will speedily be exchanged for those more formidable adversaries of discussion, imprisonment and pillory, banishment, and what its promulgators will denunciate as ignominious death.[6]

Although Godwin's remarks concentrate attention on those who suffer, actually or potentially, this excerpt from *Thoughts Occasioned by the Perusal of Dr. Parr's Spital Sermon* betrays some of the shortcomings of a rhetoric which seeks to negotiate between abstract and specific discourses. Perhaps the most significant weakness is the passive sense which pervades Godwin's text—"are not thus checked," "are now circulated," "will speedily be exchanged." Even the suffering of the martyrs (themselves noticeably unnamed as "martyrs" or "victims") is reduced to an implied predicate of a vague instrumentality of unidentified "promulgators." With a sense of violation, but without naming either those deserving to be impugned or their victims, and without, therefore, advocating personally directed action dependent upon naming, the martyrology becomes merely a rhetorical component of a larger structure of oppression which gains its stability from the balance of victim and abuser.[7]

Radical martyrologies were the first rhetorical steps toward creating a shared sense of individual suffering which might inspire action.[8] John Hampden, Tom Paine, Joseph Gerrald, Thomas Hardy and others were celebrated as part of a Radical strategy of organizing its history around a number of past and present patriot-martyrs, those who suffered to varying degrees under the governmental oppression against which they protested. The martyrology must, however, be understood as functioning in concert with the demonology, for without an identification of demons against whom a Radical community can act, the martyrology deteriorates into a victimology of the helpless oppressed; conversely, without a catalogue of the noble oppressed, demonology either becomes bullying or fails to move beyond abstract polemic.

Discussing the movement from abstraction to personalization, E. P. Thompson writes that after the Napoleonic wars, Radical rhetoric became increasingly specific: replacing the vague discourse of *abuses*—borough-mongering, corruption, fund-holding—with a discourse of identifiable *abusers*—stock-jobbers, gentry, placemen, large masters.[9] The displacement of the general by the specific resulted in the decline of the benevolent, abstract Radical counter-statement—brotherhood, equality, rights of man, the language of Paine and the Society for Constitutional Information. In its place, the specifically negative discourse fostered a practical counter—democratic and popular action. The need to yoke language to action underlies the demonology. The extent to which the Radical writer recognizes and fulfills this practical need helps to determine the success of her or his political writing.

To varying degrees, both Cobbett and Shelley sought to inspire popular action and create a sense of active democratic community; however, their efforts at creating community differed as much in approach as in outcome. For Cobbett, Shelley, and other Radicals of the period, the problem of creating community involved balancing the centrifugal demands of the general (assembling an audience of sympathetic individuals possessing common values and experiences without creating a mob) with the centripetal need to be specific (concentrating on a target and course of action). In their different ways, Cobbett and Shelley attempted to solve the problem by employing the demonology—born of the centripetal need to identify targets of thought and action.

Cobbett's problem was to create a community of individuals, aware of shared suffering and willing to act to alleviate it, while maintaining their independence. Cobbett's demons are known by their membership in "the System." By its own nature, the "System" or "Old Corruption" constitutes a failure of individualism, a lack of independence.[10] Without assembling his readers into an alternative system, destructive of individualism, Cobbett had to make them aware of abuses, abusers, and the need to act against them. Demonology, then, had a ritual significance—affirming a community of values, individually held. Indeed, Thompson describes Cobbett's demonology as a discourse "in which the Prince Regent, Castlereagh, Sidmouth, the spies— Oliver, Castle, and Edwards—the Manchester Yeomanry, Peel and paper-money, and half-hearted or equivocal reformers like Brougham all had ritual parts."[11]

Like Thompson's word "ritual," the next word, "parts," is well-chosen: at times, Cobbett's *Political Register* reads like a playbill, a "List of His Majesty's Ministers, 1815" taking up two columns of the 7 October 1815 edition in the manner of a list of *dramatis personae*.[12] The nearly dramatic function of the demonology enables Cobbett to avoid assembling an audience into some sort of combination (which he distrusted) by effecting a focus which permits more than just class-awareness. That focus must be external to the community. The task seems beyond logical solution, but the demonology makes it possible to suggest action by focusing on targets of that action, the characters whose offensive actions Cobbett records in the *Register*.

In Cobbett's hands, the demonology was an anti-rational device used to create a type of community between himself and his audience. It was anti-rational in that it freed him from the need to construct consistent arguments from first principles, enabling him to substitute a convenient bigotry. Gertrude Himmelfarb has indicated, for example, Cobbett's irrationality in his failure to reconcile his belief in unlimited private property with his objections to the sale of property to Jews, Scots, and other "demons."[13] Most importantly, Cobbett's demonology permitted his audience to rethink political and economic crises in terms of personal conflict rather than institutional processes. In personalizing a battle, Cobbett carefully selected his demons. One example is his description in *Paper against Gold* of the Bullion Committee as consisting of "SIR FRANCIS BARING, for instance, the great loan-maker, and GOLD-SMIDT, the rich Jew, whose name you so often see in the newspapers, where he is often stated to give grand dinners to princes and great men."[14] "GOLD-SMIDT," though printed in capitals, is reduced to a last name. His Jewishness is foregrounded, not only with the immediately subsequent explanatory phrase, but in the very reduction of the man to a Jewish last name.

Ian Dyck links Cobbett's tendency to focus his attention "more upon individuals than upon ideas" to the difficulty a reader has in finding "a coherent political vision."[15] I believe that Dyck misses the point of Cobbett's apparent reduction of political conflict to an individual level. In Cobbett's writings, personal conflict takes the form of relational definition; Cobbett plays the role of "moral entrepreneur," demonizing a few to generate a moral unity among the undemonized, so that they might recognize their own rightness by their moral distance from the demons.[16] This practice is consistent with the period's inclination toward personal invective as a substitute for other forms of political expression. In fact, Cobbett claims for invective the status of political right: a free press, he insists, ensures "a legal right, in any man, freely to examine, in print, into the character, talents, and conduct of any other man" (*Register* 14, 427). However, Cobbett does not restrict his discourse to invective, but, rather, elevates it to the level of a demonology, which has the effect of casting Cobbett as moral guardian. If we call his invective by the name of "demonology," we might very well identify its balancing twin as "hagiology." Demonology becomes a method of describing a moral drama, or perhaps a battle, requiring a suitable *hero.*

Throughout his career, Cobbett wrote politically about Cobbett, exploiting the facts of his humble origin, his self-education, his farming skills, and his subsequent rise in the world. His rhetoric is ethical—that is, based on ethos—but it does not limit itself to arguments from authority. Rather, Cobbett's ethos was tied to working-class pathos, the common desire to rise in the world and overcome obstructions. Despite the fact that his desires were shared by a community of his working-class readers, Cobbett typically did not adopt the "we" of the working-class anonymous letters of the period. Instead, Cobbett set his own ethos, and others like his, in opposition to the demons, revealing that the battle for reform might be fought on personal, individual grounds.[17] In one way, it appears that Cobbett *contracts* the scene of battle by reducing it to a personal level, but a closer look reveals that this contraction to the personal might actually be understood as an *expansion.* Olivia Smith has pointed out Cobbett's great faith in the critical and intellectual abilities of his working-class audiences. In fact, Cobbett used his *Grammar* to wage a war with what he called "refined language," the language of limitation which excludes the general population from considering legal and political questions. Even in his early works, Cobbett expanded discourse to the personal, leaving to his individual readers the apprehension of meaning.[18]

One example of Cobbett's faith in the reader is his 1798 Tory tract, *The Democratic Judge.* In it, Cobbett prints a word-for-word duplication of a libel indictment against him, leaving it for readers to render judgment—hence the title of the tract. Prior to reproducing the bill of indictment, Cobbett asks that his readers "go over" the "ignoramus bills": "The next document, which follows in due course, is THE BILL OF INDICTMENT; the IGNORAMUS Bill of Indictment.—Go over it with attention, I beseech thee, reader; or else, take my word for it, you will be just as wise when you are done, as you are now."[19]

In making his case to his readers, Cobbett relies heavily on his audience's faculties for discrimination and judgment. Even bearing in mind that Cobbett was in this instance writing during his reactionary phase, we can see, nevertheless, the same faith in the independent reader which later led him so strongly to oppose "the System." He writes, "I am much mistaken if the bare sight of [the bill] would not make more converts to [the reformist's] cause than all the means, that their talents and their laudable zeal have hitherto invented or employed" (*Judge,* p. 32). Cobbett's faith that "the bare sight" of the indictment would dissuade reformists from their cause is based on his convictions about the self-sufficiency of language to communicate not so much a clear meaning as a clear purpose, that is, the relative political aspirations of one person or group over another. Cobbett continues to point out how his readers might separate the grains from the "verbose chaff": "The best way of doing this, and of enabling the reader to form a correct judgment both as to their import and their tendency, will be to lay before him the three publications (in which they are to be found) entire and undistorted, marking the pretended libellous parts in *italicks*" (*Judge,* p. 32).

Duplicating the offensive text, and thus allowing it to stand for itself, served two purposes. First, the duplication created, in Kevin Gilmartin's words, "a rhetoric of fact," "an unmediated language, beyond dissent or debate."[20] Second, despite creating this "rhetoric of fact," Cobbett did not use the device to seek a truth but rather to create affinities between himself and his readers.

The fact that Cobbett did not seek a demonstrable, verifiable truth in his use of quotation can be more clearly understood in light of the work of W. V. Quine. In *The Pursuit of Truth,* Quine argues that one might predicate the truth of a sentence merely by removing its quotation marks. This device, which Quine calls "disquotation," stands in direct contrast to Cobbett's use of quotation.[21] Cobbett leaves the indictment in quotation, refraining from analyzing its truth-content, but rather inviting his readers to judge for themselves. Truth becomes communal, though individually apprehended, a situation compatible with the Gramscian spontaneity Cobbett recognized in working-class sensibility.[22] Even during his Radical phase, through the demonology and the use of quotation, Cobbett sought to preserve independence of judgment while still guiding his readers to a common verdict, casting his arguments in personal rather than collective terms. There is, however, one significant departure from the language of independence—his 2 November 1816 *Register,* the "Address to the Journeymen and Labourers." In it, Cobbett puts aside many of his distinguishing rhetorical traits. After deliberately and pointedly personalizing the political and economic conflict through his use of the second person—"And I beseech you not to look upon yourselves as the *scum;* but, on the contrary, to be well persuaded, that a great deal depends upon *your exertions,*"[23] he adopts the collective pronoun—"Let us, therefore, congratulate ourselves, that we have great constitutional principles and laws, to which we can refer, and to which we are attached" ("Address," p. 568).

The "Address" is not Cobbett's only departure from polemic based primarily on egotism and personal ethos, but it is the most significant because of the way it varies—one might say "completes"—the demonology. Even in his most egoistic, individualistic writing, Cobbett assumed an affinity between his values and capacities and those of his audience. In the "Address," that affinity takes an explicit form—"we." Furthermore, Cobbett remarks the first principles of economy, labor, and political right which previously he had left unstated, or certainly unexamined in any thorough fashion.

The effectiveness of Cobbett's "Address," achieved despite departures from his customary style, demands explanation, for which we can turn to the work itself and its context. In the "Address," Cobbett describes a process by which journeymen and laborers, through their accumulated labors, have come to merit an acknowledged stake in British affairs: "For, there can exist no riches and no resources, which they by their labour, have not *assisted to create*" ("Address," p. 560). That stake is treated almost as a commodity or a stock of wealth. The metaphor extends throughout the "Address," but to read it as a metaphor existing solely on the rhetorical axis, conducting a meaning from Cobbett to his readers, would be to deny its full effect and to ignore one of the most remarkable and distinguishing features of Cobbett's rhetoric— self-reference. Cobbett regularly refers the reader to past and future texts. We ought, then, in reading the "Address," to understand it not only in terms of Cobbett's prior writings but in terms of his future writings, too. Cobbett thinks in terms of building up a stock of credibility, piling up ethos, which he can expend as he chooses. On 26 November 1816, one week before publishing his "Address," Cobbett defines the conditions under which he will approve and disapprove others' republishing of the *Register:* "What I have an objection to is, first, the *garbling* of what I write; and the next is to the being robbed of my fair title to whatever degree of merit shall be thought to belong to my productions" (*Register* 31:520). Cobbett jealously guarded his productions (not only his texts but also the Cobbett ethos). Only the fact that Cobbett already had established an ethos allows him, in his "Address," to depart from his usual style and embrace a more conventional style, even while retaining his effectiveness.

Throughout his career, Cobbett employed demonologies, linking them not to millenarian or apocalyptic wishes but rather to the potential for practical, individual action, such as self-improvement or shouting down ministerial representatives at local meetings—actions permissible within the ethical parameters of the constitutional reform movement. When Shelley used the demonology, on the other hand, most notably in *The Mask of Anarchy,* he varied it and blunted it, primarily by abstracting a discourse which earlier he had personalized, by reducing the consequences of hatred, and by straying from the practical into the apocalyptic.

Shelley selected as targets particular hated individuals who were within range of the practical effects of hatred. In *The Mask of Anarchy,* he demonizes Castlereagh, Eldon, and Sidmouth, describing them in caricature as hypocritical and evil: the character Murder, masked like Castlereagh, throws human hearts to his accompanying bloodhounds; Fraud, in ermine like Eldon, weeps tears which turn to millstones, knocking out children's brains. Although the demonology begins with great promise, Shelley thwarts his own apparent purposes by joining Eldon and Sidmouth to systemic abuses—murder, fraud, and anarchy; not (as Cobbett might have done) by inscribing an unequivocal attribution of responsibility, but by employing simile ("like Castlereagh," "Like Eldon," "Like Sidmouth").[24] The connection is easily broken, dismissed; the poem becomes a catalogue of immoral qualities competing with another catalogue of ascending abstractions—freedom, justice, wisdom, peace, and love (*SPP*, pp. 306–07). The hatred of the three demons which Shelley taps early in the *Mask* dissipates at the appearance on the scene of freedom and its companion spectral forms; the effect of the demonology is lost.

The three demonized ministers might be, like Perceval was, targets of violence, within its range, but Shelley replaces violent with non-violent action, thereby reducing the consequences of hatred and, in turn, reducing the personalizing, demonizing tenor of the first several stanzas.[25] Shelley elevates non-violent action to apocalyptic rather than practical significance, positing Hope's self-sacrificing non-violence as a trigger for millenarian events wrought by "rising" apocalyptic agency—in *Mask,* "a mist, a light, an image . . . a Shape" (*SPP*, p. 304) or the "glorious Phantom" of "England in 1819" (*SPP*, p. 311).

Shelley's efforts to use the demonology and its accompanying devices to create a community of readers occasionally succeeded or at least they possess rhetorical merit, as Stephen Behrendt has demonstrated in *Shelley and His Audiences*.[26] In *An Address to the People on the Death of Princess Charlotte,* for example, Shelley demonstrates that he can perform a part of the Radical ritual, the martyrology, by summoning the images of the executed Pentrich rebels—Jeremiah Brandreth, William Turner, and Isaac Ludlam.[27] Furthermore, he is able to re-enact a second part of the ritual, the demonology, by conjuring an image of the spy, Oliver (*CW,* VI, 81). Notwithstanding the favorable reception his address has subsequently found among scholars of Romantic rhetoric, Shelley in fact found himself absolutely unable to re-enact the final part of the ritual, the hagiological component, the summoning of a hero to counter both martyrs and demons through exemplary personal action. The hero-saint becomes lost in his eulogy for the dead Princess, who is hardly heroic and who is, in any event, certainly incapable of action. In her, Shelley blurs victims, demons, and saints. As a potential saint, Charlotte was kind, embodying the hopes of reformers of all classes that she could counteract the excesses of the Prince Regent and the ministers; as Shelley said, "She was amiable and would have become wise . . ." (*CW,* VI, 82). As a victim, however, she was incapable of acting; indeed, according to Shelley she had not acted for good or evil during her life. Worse, in comparison to Brandreth and the other revolutionaries and in the hopes left unrealized by her death, she remained a member of the oppressing classes. If she was not one of the demons, she was at least suggestive of them. Recognizing that his argument has consumed a promising initial personalization, Shelley finally strays into the ideal, lamenting a personified "Liberty" and wishing, as he often does, for "glorious Phantoms" (*CW,* VI, 82).

An examination of the rhetorical dynamic involving demonology, martyrology, and hagiology in *An Address to the People on the Death of Princess Charlotte* reveals Shelley's inability to perform the entire communal ritual centered on the demonology. We are left to wonder how, then, Shelley used an incomplete demonology. As he noted in the *Essay on Christianity,* he employed rhetorical devices (such as the demonology) in a Ciceronian fashion as Jesus does, to prepare the mind of the reader for the impact of reason and to deal with abstractions: "Thus like a skilful orator (see Cicero de Oratore), he secures the prejudices of his auditors, and induces them by his professions of sympathy with their feelings to enter with a willing mind into the exposition of his own" (*CW,* 6:242). Rejecting the *sensus communis* and its prejudices, he preferred argument based on irreducible first principles, such as love, reason, or necessity—principles which he nevertheless failed to show having personal, non-fictional significance. Dealing in abstractions, Shelley virtually ignored action.

Most importantly, Shelley reduced the personal authorial dimension of demonology to insignificance. Whereas Cobbett described himself in *Paper against Gold* as energetically battling corruption from prison (*Paper,* pp. v–viii), Shelley writes in *The Mask of Anarchy* that he "lay asleep in Italy" (*SPP,* p. 301). It is difficult to find anywhere a genuinely active Shelleyan ethos. In *An Address to the Irish People,* Shelley vaguely sketches some of his character, mentioning his Irish sympathies and his ideology, cast in negatives ("not an Irishman" and "not a Protestant nor . . . a Catholic" [*CW,* 5:215–16]), but this is rare. Other works exemplify Shelley's tendency to *minimize* ethos when he does not ignore it altogether. His 3 January 1812 letter of introduction to Godwin exhibits less the young Shelley's own ideas than his ability to reproduce the language of an admired author.[28] *A Philosophical View of Reform,* with its Cobbettesque catalogue of "attornies and excisemen and directors and government pensioners, usurers, stock jobbers, country bankers, with their dependents and descendants"—Shelley's "new aristocracy"—contains no ethical counter to the list of demons (*CW,* 7:28–29). In a heroic age which overvalued heroes (Wellington, Nelson, Ludd, Cartwright) doing battle for good, Shelley failed in that he offered no champion other than ideas or the Ideal. He offered only progressive historical forces carrying political reforms against contemporary oppression.

Mere use of the demonology does not ensure success in Radical polemic. Under what circumstances, then, might it be an effective Radical tool? An answer may be found in Cobbett's decision to take the rhetoric of communal sense back to its foundation—ethos. *The Periodical Press,* the conservative

1824 review of the British press, acknowledges that no one used invective against its greatest master, Cobbett.[29] Notwithstanding the accuracy of the acknowledgment, Shelley, who read and admired the *Register,* nevertheless recognized that personal moral objections to Cobbett might reasonably and effectively be made. In a 23–24 January 1819 letter to Thomas Love Peacock, Shelley writes, "Cobbett is a fine [hymnwriter]—does his influence increase or diminish. What a pity that so powerful a genius should be combined with the most odious moral qualities" (*Letters,* 1:75). Shelley's observation is ironic in light of Cobbett's use of primarily ethical devices and, more particularly, his exertions to create an ethos immune to the moral objections of government apologists. One pauses in considering how Cobbett's "odious moral qualities" might have escaped the notice of truly humane scholars like Thompson and Raymond Williams.[30]

Shelley's remarks indicate not only skepticism about Cobbett but also the poet's larger doubts about ethos as the foundation of any political writing. Only a writer who could envision battles as taking place between ideas rather than between persons could see through the screen of ethos which Cobbett had created for himself. Cobbett succeeded against "Old Corruption" because he established the rules of engagement which the government and its press apologists embraced, locating the battle on the field of the personal, then immunizing himself against attacks upon his character by emphasizing his low birth, agricultural skills, and rise in society, a rise in accord with the values (individualism, capitalism, Anglicanism) held by the public at large and by advocates of "the System" in particular. Cobbett's repetition of the British pandemonium of stock-jobbers and pensioners works together with his ongoing autobiography to re-enact socio-political ritual, to affirm the boundaries of what A. W. Metcalfe calls the sacred and the profane.[31]

NOTES

1. Eric Hoffer, *The True Believer* (New York: Harper and Row, 1966), p. 86.

2. Scrivener, *Radical Shelley: The Philosophical Anarchism and Utopian Thought of Percy Bysshe Shelley* (Princeton: Princeton University Press, 1982), p. 282.

3. Allen, "Demonology, Styles of Reasoning, and Truth," *International Journal of Moral and Social Studies* 8.2 (Summer 1993): 95–122.

4. "Real action" is distinct from theoretical, verbal formulae. It deals with the actions of "real men, formed in specific historical relations, with specific feelings, outlooks, fragmentary conceptions of the world, etc., which were the result of 'spontaneous' combination of a given situation of material production with the 'fortuitous' agglomeration within it of disparate social elements." See Gramsci, *Selections from the Prison Notebooks of Antonio Gramsci,* ed. and trans. Quintin Hoare and Geoffrey Nowell Smith (New York: International Publishers, 1971), p. 198.

5. The homeric orator, exemplified by Achilles in Book Nine of the *Iliad,* must be "a speaker of words and a doer of deeds." Homeric speech involves pitting ethos

against ethos—in this case, Achilles' character against Agamemnon's. See Kennedy, *Classical Rhetoric and Its Christian and Secular Tradition from Ancient to Modern Times* (Chapel Hill: University of North Carolina Press, 1980), pp. 10–13.

6. Godwin, *Thoughts Occasioned by the Perusal of Dr. Parr's Spital Sermon: Preached at Christ Church, April 15, 1880* (London: Taylor and Wilks, 1801), p. 79. See Olivia Smith's discussion in *The Politics of Language, 1791–1819* (Oxford: Clarendon Press, 1984), p. 206.

7. On "self-stabilization" in styles of reasoning, see Allen, p. 98.

8. E. P. Thompson uses the terms "martyrology" and "demonology" in *The Making of the English Working Class* (New York: Vintage, 1966), p. 604; hereafter cited as *Making*. With reservations, I follow Thompson in using "martyrology" to describe the discourse which serves as an early marker of group awareness in the formation of Radical rhetoric. My reservations stem from my discovery that existing scholarship makes no adequate distinction between martyrs and victims of state persecution. The problem is especially important in understanding how constitutional reform writers who mention such victims of state persecution as the Derbyshire rebels conceive of those rebels, especially when the rebels violate the values of constitutional reform. More study is necessary. For a sense of how such a study might proceed, see James Epstein's chapter on the trial of Thomas J. Wooler and the "canonization" of the Leveller John Lilburne in *Radical Expression: Political Language, Ritual, and Symbol in England, 1790–1850* (Oxford: Oxford University Press, 1994), especially pp. 30–35, and Linda Colley's "Radical Patriotism in Eighteenth-Century England" in *Patriotism: The Making and Unmaking of British National Identity,* ed. Raphael Samuel, 3 vols. (London: Routledge, 1989), 1:169–87.

9. *Making,* p. 603. Following Thompson, Donald Thomas, in *A Long Time Burning: The History of Literary Censorship in England* (New York: Praeger, 1969), describes a general tendency in Regency political writing toward personal attacks (Thomas, p. 146). Michael Scrivener demonstrates that Thompson's observation about the increasing specificity of Radical writing applies even to the upper-class exile Shelley (Scrivener, p. 135).

10. In *The Question of Class Struggle: Social Foundations of Popular Radicalism during the Industrial Revolution* (Chicago: University of Chicago Press, 1982), Craig Calhoun distinguishes between individualism and independence: "Individualism and economism, key features of liberal or bourgeois ideology, offered a national analysis which could be of little benefit to workers at a local level. Individualism meant not independence but common subjection to capital or, more crudely, to 'the master' " (Calhoun, p. 15). See also Adrian Randall's *Before the Luddites: Custom, Community and Machinery in the English Woollen Industry, 1776–1809* (Cambridge: Cambridge University Press, 1991), p. 31.

11. *Making,* p. 604. On the ritualistic component of demonology, its use as "moral terror," see A. W. Metcalfe, "The Demonology of Class," *Critique of Anthropology* 10 (Summer 1990): 53.

12. *Cobbett's Weekly Political Register* 29 (1815): 3–4; *Cobbett's Weekly Political Register* is cited hereafter as *Register.*

13. Himmelfarb, "William Cobbett: 'an English episode'," *New Criterion* 1.2 (October 1982), p. 46.

14. *Cobbett's Paper against Gold* (London: W. Molineux, 1815), p. 2; hereafter cited as *Paper.*

15. Dyck, "From 'Rabble' to 'Chopsticks': The Radicalism of William Cobbett," *Albion* 21 (Spring 1989): 58.

16. Metcalfe, p. 52.

17. Cobbett's 29 June 1816 *Register* is especially noteworthy for the way in which Cobbett represents the "The Men of Kent" heroically to themselves for their rejection of an announcement by a Crown representative that certain benefits, at public expense, were to be settled upon Cobbett's newest demon, "a German prince," Princess Charlotte's new husband, Prince Leopold of Saxe Cobourg Saalfeld (*Register* 30:803–5). Readers unfamiliar with Cobbett's works might refer to this number of the *Register* for a typical Cobbett catalogue of "Courtiers, Colonels, borough-mongers, sinecure placemen, pensioners, and tax-gatherers" (p. 819), to which he adds "clergy, contractors, silk-gown gentlemen . . . and all other persons living out of the taxes . . ." (p. 824).

18. Epstein's observations on T. J. Wooler's performance during his 1817 trials for seditious libel apply just as well to Cobbett in his rejection of "refined language": "The citizen-hero stood in counter-distinction to lawyers and judges; the citizen spoke the nonspecialist language of civic virtue, the language of all citizens, including the jury" (p. 55).

19. Cobbett, *The Democratic Judge: Or the Equal Liberty of the Press* (Philadelphia: William Cobbett, 1798), p. 27; hereafter cited as *Judge*. In former days, "Ignoramus"—Latin for "We ignore it"—was written across a bill of indictment after a grand jury determined that an accusation against a prisoner was groundless.

20. Gilmartin, " 'Victims of Argument, Slaves of Fact': Hunt, Hazlitt, Cobbett and the Literature of Opposition," *Wordsworth Circle* 21 (1990): 90.

21. Quine, *The Pursuit of Truth* (Cambridge, Mass.: Harvard University Press, 1990), p. 80.

22. "Spontaneity" is the term Gramsci uses to describe certain class movements or feelings: " 'Spontaneous' in the sense that they are not the result of any systematic educational activity on the part of an already conscious leading group, but have been formed through everyday experience illuminated by 'common sense,' i.e. by the traditional popular conception of the world—what is unimaginatively called 'instinct,' although it too is in fact a primitive and elementary historical acquisition" (Gramsci, pp. 198–99).

23. *Register* 31 (1816): 565; hereafter cited as "Address."

24. In *Shelley's Poetry and Prose,* ed. Donald H. Reiman and Sharon B. Powers (New York: Norton, 1977), pp. 301–2; hereafter cited as *SPP.*

25. "To S——th and C———gh" also contains a reduction of the personal, despite the overtures of the title, as Shelley chooses to depict carnivorous animals rather than ministers. See *Shelley: Poetical Works,* ed. Thomas Hutchinson, corr. G. M. Matthews (Oxford: Oxford University Press, 1971), p. 573.

26. Stephen C. Behrendt, *Shelley and His Audiences* (Lincoln: University of Nebraska Press, 1989).

27. *The Complete Works of Percy Bysshe Shelley,* ed. Roger Ingpen and Walter E. Peck, 10 vols. (New York: Gordian Press, 1965), 6:76; hereafter cited as *CW.*

28. *The Letters of Percy Bysshe Shelley,* 2 vols., ed. Frederick L. Jones (Oxford: Oxford University Press, 1964), 1:219–20; cited hereafter as *Letters.*

29. *The Periodical Press of Great Britain and Ireland: Or An Inquiry into the*

State of the Public Journals, Chiefly as Regards Their Moral and Political Influence (London: Hurst, Robinson, and Co., 1824), p. 106.

30. This is not to suggest that Thompson, Williams, and the author of the most recent and complete Cobbett biography, George Spater, entirely overlook Cobbett's racism, for instance (but not the cowardice that made him flee to America in March 1817, just when the government was beginning to move against the Hampden Clubs and to take into custody their leaders—including Thomas Evans, Gravener Henson, and Samuel Bamford). What ought to be noted, however, is the fact that a Radical such as Shelley could in fact make some moral objections against Cobbett and that other recent biographers, Karl W. Schweizer and John W. Osborne, devote several pages to Cobbett's racism. See Schweizer and Osborne, *Cobbett in His Times* (Leicester: Leicester University Press, 1990).

31. Metcalfe, p. 51.

"RADICAL TRASH":

American Emigrants in the Quarterly Review

KIM WHEATLEY

I n 1824 James Mill, in the first number of the liberal *Westminster Review,* set out to analyze the rhetoric of the two major reviewing periodicals in early nineteenth-century England, the *Quarterly* and *Edinburgh* reviews. In his article Mill contrasts what he perceives to be the straightforward bigotry of the Tory *Quarterly Review*—expressed in a fiercely anti-jacobinical tone—with the more complex *"seesaw"* language of the Whig *Edinburgh Review,* a language designed to appeal contradictorily both to aristocratic and popular political views.[1] Mill evidently found the *Edinburgh*'s style more of a force to be reckoned with, since in a lengthy article, continued by John Stuart Mill in the next number of the *Westminster,* he gives multiple examples of that periodical's vacillation over such topics as religion, education, morality, and of course politics. By contrast, he presents his analysis of the *Quarterly* in a shorter article, in the form of a scathing response to a single essay in the *Quarterly:* a review of a book about emigration from Britain to the United States. This review, he asserts, reveals the "process by which" the *Quarterly* "fabricates a representation calculated to flatter the passions and prejudices" of its reactionary readers.[2] The differing treatment of the two periodicals suggests that the *Quarterly* can be easily dismissed, while the very inconsistency of the *Edinburgh* gives it an insidious power hitherto unacknowledged until this exposure in the *Westminster.*[3] The writers seem to assume that now that they have identified the *Edinburgh*'s rhetoric as inconsistent, it will collapse under the weight of its contradictions.

I have argued elsewhere however that the rhetoric of the *Quarterly* and the *Edinburgh* alike is characterized by contradictions, which enhance rather than undermine its effectiveness. Both periodicals derive their air of authority from a heightened language which combines a tone of persecution with expressions of facetious contempt. This "paranoid style" aggrandizes the reviewers' shared political opponents—Radicals and reformers—by casting them in a demonic role, but at the same time it disempowers those same opponents by locking them into a cycle of mutual denunciation.[4] In this essay I will look more closely at the *Quarterly*'s violent and unstable treatment of Radicals. I will show that the *Quarterly,* in manipulating the "passions and prejudices" of its elite readers, appeals not only to their sense of outrage, but also to their sense of humor—a twofold strategy which itself contradictorily projects both alarm and confidence. Several recent critics have examined the use of satire and burlesque in the works of Radical writers, but the—admittedly heavy-handed—comic impulse of the elitist press has been less often noticed. Taking my cue from the *Westminster,* I have chosen to focus on the topic of emigration from Britain to the United States, because responses to books on this topic exemplify the at once vituperative and playful rhetoric of the *Quarterly.* I see this rhetoric as a source of strength rather than weakness. My concern here is not with the actual political efficacy of the *Quarterly,* but with the specific maneuvers by which this periodical created an *impression* of hegemonic power. The prospect of mass emigration in the years after Waterloo might have been a source of conservative anxiety, since it suggested the success of a democratic government, but I would claim that the controversy over the issue is a matter of what the *Edinburgh Review* calls "paper shot."[5] Writers in both the *Quarterly* and the *Edinburgh* devoted considerable space to this issue in the immediate postwar period, but that does not necessarily mean that they felt threatened by the "radical trash"[6] of the pro-American books under review. The *Quarterly* reviewers certainly appear dismayed by the implications of what they claimed was a mass exodus, but I will argue that their attacks on the proponents of emigration functioned less as a political argument than as a form of entertainment for an elite audience, a move which was itself ultimately a political statement.[7]

Although it may not shed light on real power relations between conservatives and Radicals, the topic of emigration foregrounds the question of the supposed impact of the Radical press, since the Tory reviewers insisted that the proponents of emigration were influenced by British Radical journalists. Radical political views are invariably found to underlie the unpatriotic impulse to desert one's native land. Stephen Fender claims that although most British emigrants between 1815 and 1832 went to Canada or Australia, during this period the British press was more preoccupied with emigration to the United States, because the issue of emigration had become politicized by pressures for domestic parliamentary reform.[8] The *Quarterly* identified emigrants themselves as victims of the "outrageous panegyrics on America"[9] published by reformers such as William Cobbett, Thomas Wooler and W. T. Sherwin;

by the same token, Americans were the dupes of "the polluted trash of our Jacobinical press."[10] Advocates of emigration were demonized in the same fashion as Cobbett, who himself lived in the United States from May 1817 to October 1819 and who advocated emigration to New England.[11] Cast in the role of Satanic seducers of their innocent readers, these writers were made to appear diabolically powerful even while they were inevitably subordinated to the establishment God the Father. On one level the *Quarterly* tells a story of Satanic outcasts who inspire fascination as well as disgust. But at the same time these reviews repeat what Marjorie Levinson calls "the lesson we first learned from the Romantics. Namely, that Satan is always God's product, structural complement, and support-system."[12] For the Tory reviewers and their readers, British reformers and the aliens with whom they were ostensibly in league were villains for whom no insults were too strong—yet at the same time comic figures in an ongoing farce.

The reviewers countered the supposedly seductive effect of "outrageous panegyrics on America" by setting out to dissuade their readers from emigrating. Who these readers were is never clearly defined, however; the actual audiences of the *Quarterly* can hardly have been the same people allegedly fleeing in droves from their native land. The *Quarterly*'s purchasers would have been members of the professional and upper classes who expected its reviews to confirm their aristocratic bias; even if not landowners themselves, they would have identified with the ideal of gentrified leisure.[13] As we will see, the reviewers made routine appeals to their readers' class snobbery by treating both emigrants and Americans themselves as doomed to futile efforts at upward social mobility. And although the reviews purported to deter would-be emigrants, their responses to books on America instead attempted to beguile upper-class British readers with an amusing spectacle: the antics and mishaps of disenchanted emigrants, would-be emigrants, and the Americans encountered on their travels. In its critique of the *Quarterly,* the *Westminster* accuses that periodical of presenting negative information about America with "a fiendlike exultation" (255).[14] But in condemning the reviewer's diabolically gleeful tone, the *Westminster* indirectly pays tribute to the *Quarterly*'s liveliness and readability. The *Quarterly*'s "exultation" may indeed be "fiendlike," but its fiendishness (caught as if by contagion from the writers under attack) coexists with a certain tongue-in-cheek element, at which the *Westminster* reviewer refuses to be amused because he is not a member of the *Quarterly*'s conservative audience. In what follows I will look closely at selected articles from the *Quarterly* which exploit the issue of emigration to create an ongoing narrative in which the Miltonic plot of the fall from heaven is Romantically and humorously rewritten.

The *Quarterly* article singled out by the *Westminster* in 1824 for its bigotry was merely the most recent in a series of reviews about emigration to the United States. The impetus for the flurry of publications on this topic—and thus for the flurry of reviews—came from Morris Birkbeck's *Notes on a Journey in America, from the Coast of Virginia to the Territory of Illinois* (1818) and his follow-up volume, *Letters from the Illinois* (1818). I would suggest that the article that set the terms for the *Quarterly's* treatment of postwar emigration is its attack on Birkbeck in April 1818. The *Quarterly's* review of Birkbeck's *Notes* was quickly followed by reviews in both the *Quarterly* and the *Edinburgh* of various other publications evaluating the prospects for emigrants to the United States. The writers of these books responded to each other, correcting each other's accounts and in most cases specifically setting out to verify the truth of Birkbeck's claims. Morris Birkbeck (1764–1825) emigrated to Illinois (then a territory and not yet a state) in 1817; clearly his settlement achieved enough publicity to attract a number of curious visitors.[15] Birkbeck is usually relegated to a footnote of Romantic literary history: John Keats and his brother George both read Birkbeck's *Letters from Illinois,* which was issued by Keats's publishers Taylor and Hessey, before George Keats emigrated to the United States in 1818.[16] George initially intended to join Birkbeck's settlement, but he ended up instead in Kentucky. In what follows, this figure from the margins of Romanticism will momentarily take center stage: I will first discuss the *Quarterly's* review of Birkbeck's *Notes* before turning to several other articles from the *Quarterly* for which its account of Birkbeck serves as a prototype.

The context of the *Quarterly's* April 1818 number suggests some of the ideological continuities between its review of Birkbeck and its essays on other subjects. Among the *Quarterly's* literary reviews in April 1818 were John Wilson Croker's attack on Keats's *Endymion* (the review immortalized in *Adonais*) in which Keats is punished for his association with Leigh Hunt. Alongside this attack readers would have found Walter Scott's positive account of Byron's *Childe Harold's Pilgrimage,* Canto IV, a review in which the *Quarterly's* aristocratic bias temporarily overrides both its political affiliation and its disapproval of the morals of the poet who will later be dubbed the leader of the "Satanic School." This number of the *Quarterly* also featured "On the Means of Improving the People," an essay in which Robert Southey makes his almost routine argument that the Radical press is endangering "the happiness of the British nation" by spreading "pernicious" ideas.[17] The review of Birkbeck, drafted by John Barrow and revised by William Gifford, relies on the same assumptions that underlie Southey's claim about the corruptive effect of Radical publications, though at the same time it presents itself as more than a match for Birkbeck, despite the alleged seductiveness of his descriptions of the United States.[18] The *Quarterly's* public stance against Birkbeck is in fact more dismissive than the private view of its editor: a letter from Gifford to John Murray states that "[Birkbeck] appears to me the most dangerous man that ever yet wrote from America, & is likely to do us much mischief."[19] By "us" Gifford presumably refers to the conservative establishment; the way in which the review of Birkbeck at once downplays and retains a hold on this paranoid view points to the rhetorical manipulations by which the *Quarterly* perpetuates its attitude of superiority. Although the sardonically humorous element that I will be focusing on can be found in many *Quarterly* articles, the topic of British-American emigration offers an irresistible opportunity to develop a simple moral fable in which the Otherness of the New World reinforces the association between Radicalism and evil.

The *Quarterly* begins its attack on Birkbeck by immediately objecting to his political opinions. Birkbeck is sarcastically introduced as "happily relieved from all manner of 'prejudices' on the score of religion and civil polity, except indeed a vehement one against all religions, and all governments" (54). The reviewers accuse "Friend Morris" (55) as they facetiously call him (Birkbeck being a former Quaker) of fleeing from his farm in England in response to unfavorable postwar economic conditions. Birkbeck's companion, "a young man of the name of Flower" (55), a former sheep farmer, was, according to the reviewers, speciously persuaded against his best interests that "to be happy and contented under such a government as that of Great Britain was contrary to all sound reason, and that for his credit's sake he must be transplanted into a more philosophical soil; accordingly the ill-starred Corydon sold off his sheep, and consented to seek an abode in a country where sheep cannot thrive" (55). This sentence treats ironically the efficacy of Radical rhetoric, while figuring "Great Britain" as an idyllic pastoral realm; the reviewers go on to mock Birkbeck's support of the French Revolution, a stance apparently shared by the "ill-starred" George Flower.[20] In response to these obnoxious political views, the reviewers will later implicitly cast Flower in the role of Beelzebub to Birkbeck's Satan.

Despite making their attitude to Birkbeck plain from the outset, the reviewers open their critique of Birkbeck's book in a way that does not prepare their audience for what is to follow. Their mode of attack in this and later reviews is to give Birkbeck power and then take it away again. They begin an apparently objective summary of the travelers' journey in the United States, describing Norfolk, Virginia, as "a large town, with spacious streets, well paved causeways, and clean and good-looking houses" (56). The effect of this move is to put the hypothetical reader in the improbable position of one of Birkbeck's ill-starred traveling companions, a captive to Birkbeck's wiles, unwittingly led astray and quickly disillusioned. The first actual quotation from Birkbeck is very negative; at Norfolk Birkbeck found "the worst meat I ever saw" and "most wretched horses"; he added, "this first glimpse of a slave population is extremely distressing" (56). A second, longer quotation from Birkbeck mentions the "filth" of Virginian taverns and the "lax" morals of Virginian plantation owners and expatiates on the "evil" of slavery (56). As analysis of later reviews will show, the fact that opposition to slavery cut across British party lines did not deter Tory writers from tarring Radicals with the same brush as slave-owners.[21] But instead of lingering over the issue of slavery, the reviewers next list the high prices encountered by Birkbeck at Richmond, Virginia, and surprisingly conclude the account of this first stage of the journey by quoting Birkbeck on his "esteem for the general character of Virginians" (58). The strategy of the review at first seems to be to let Birkbeck speak for himself, but the reviewers go on to point out "contradictions" in Birkbeck's prose, claiming that Birkbeck's "facts and his opinions are . . . continually at issue" (58). In highlighting these discrepancies, the review establishes an archetypical scenario: the writer of the work under consideration—whether a traveler to the United States, an emigrant, or someone sent out to examine the prospects for would-be emigrants—is presented as disappointed by what he encounters but determined to cast things in the best possible light. The conflict between the off-putting information Birkbeck provided and his pro-American stance is foregrounded for comic purposes throughout the review, but a conflict between assertions and evidence emerges in the reviewers' own writing. Birkbeck's negative descriptions of America are dwelt upon at so much length that the reviewers betray their fascination not only with America, but also with the troubled figure of Birkbeck himself. Although he is the target of a flow of sardonic jibes, he emerges as unexpectedly compelling due to his very perversity.

Birkbeck's alleged tendency to exaggerate and inflate—a tendency which seems to conflict with what the reviewer concedes is his "natural shrewdness and turn for observation" (58)—is shown to be caught from the Americans:

> The next stage was the "city of Pittsburgh, the Birmingham of America," where Mr. Birkbeck expected to have been enveloped in clouds of smoke issuing from a thousand furnaces, and stunned with the din of ten thousand hammers; but he soon found that he had been deceived by an American figure of rhetoric of extensive use in description; he calls it *anticipation,* by way of softening down the vulgar and proper term, and explains it by informing the reader that "it simply consists in the use of the present indicative, instead of the future subjunctive." (61)[22]

This idea of an "American figure of rhetoric"—implicitly contrasted with the supposed plain speaking of the reviewer—is exploited for humorous effect by the writer of this and subsequent reviews: "Mr. Birkbeck is an apt scholar; he is already familiar with 'the American figure of anticipation,' and, like his adopted countrymen, 'contemplates what *may be,* as though it were in actual existence' " (62).[23] The reviewer takes for granted his own and his audience's immunity to such delusions, but by suggesting that this figure is easily learned or even contagious, he unwittingly opens up the possibility that he himself may be vulnerable to contamination. Whether making Birkbeck seem threatening or laughable, the *Quarterly* is itself liable to exaggerate. We will see that the figure of "anticipation" is ultimately connected with the Satanic.

In the course of presenting what amounts to an extended character analysis of Birkbeck, the reviewers exploit Birkbeck's picture of a decidedly unedenic America to exalt British sanity, health, taste, good manners, and civilized behavior. A quotation about the bad complexions of Americans, for example, becomes an implicit statement about the moral degeneracy of their society. In this respect the attack on Birkbeck takes its place in a longstanding tradition of exploiting the shortcomings of both American nature and culture for satiric effect.[24] Nevertheless the reviewers are less interested in scoring political points than in taking pleasure in the excesses of Birkbeck's self-delusions:

> On the way to Vincennes our Friend loses himself, and is obliged, in the phraseology of the country, "*to camp out,*" that is, to sleep in the woods. The night, as Mrs. Wilkins says in Tom Jones, happened to be "very fine, only a little windy and rainy," and our travellers contrived by dint of oil and brandy, and gunpowder and cambric handkerchiefs, to kindle a fire, and pass it as they could. This agreeable adventure, which would sicken an English gipsy of "camping out," leads quite naturally to a lofty panegyric on the superior advantages of travelling "in that vast western wilderness" compared with those to be found in this country. "Let," says Mr. Birkbeck "a stranger make his way through England—let him keep at a distance from every public road," (made for his accommodation,) "avoid all the inns," (established expressly for his convenience and comfort,) and perversely scramble over hedge and ditch "in quest of such entertainment only as the hovel of the labourer can supply, and he would have more cause to complain of the rudeness of the inhabitants" than of the weir-wolves of the wilds of Indiana! If we could conceive a traveller to be guilty of such gratuitous folly, we should then say, that as his application to the day-labourer for "entertainment" could only be looked upon as a deliberate insult on his poverty, he would deserve whatever rudeness he might chance to experience. In somewhat of a similar spirit, Mr. Birkbeck adds—"when we have been so unfortunate as to pitch our tent near a swamp, and have mismanaged our fire, we have been teased by musquitoes [*sic*]; but so might we, perhaps, in the fens of Cambridgeshire." The traveller must have a strong predilection for the *teasing* of musquitoes [*sic*] who would sleep in the fens of Cambridgeshire, when by turning a few yards to the right or the left he might obtain shelter under a roof—and this, too, without the hazard of being, like Mr. Birkbeck and his party, driven out again "by the innumerable tormentors which (says he) assail you in every dwelling, till at length you are glad to avoid the abodes of man, and spread your pallet under the trees." p. 167. Certainly these are pleasant proofs of the inferiority of England to America. (67–68)

Through the use of sarcasm ("leads quite naturally to a lofty panegyric"); comic embellishment ("perversely scramble over hedge and ditch"; "the weir-wolves of the wilds of Indiana") and understatement ("a few yards to the right or the left"), the reviewers render Birkbeck's claims ludicrous. The tone of the last sentence in this paragraph is cynically dismissive. Yet the overall point of the passage rests on shaky logic: Birkbeck is somehow held personally responsible for the uncultivated and deplorably uncivilized wilderness. Moreover, the reviewers pay so much detailed attention to Birkbeck's wording that they give the impression of being intrigued.

The summary of Birkbeck's journey builds to a climax as he reaches the site of his future settlement in Illinois. The reviewers mention that "Beyond the little Wabash, every mark of civilization was lost" (69); they go on to quote Birkbeck's own description of a hunter's wretched log cabin and its unhealthy inhabitants. The reviewers' comment on this passage takes the form of a quotation from *Paradise Lost:*

> "Is this the region, this the soil, the clime,"
> Said then the lost Archangel—(70)

Birkbeck is here explicitly identified with Milton's Satan, who speaks these words on arrival in hell; America's settlers are equivalent to the angels who fell with Satan, and the land itself is equated with the fallen angels' place of banishment. (Birkbeck himself, in blissful ignorance of any literary associations, called life in a forest "incarceration" [69].) The invocation of *Paradise Lost* might at first seem to be a routine allusion to a well-known text[25]; but the reviewers' later emphasis on the Birkbeck-Satan analogy demonstrates that the emigration controversy is to be read in Miltonic terms. The metaphor reappears a few pages further on in the *Quarterly*'s article: Birkbeck, once settled "in the pestilential swamps of the Wabash," is described as looking at England "(like another great 'anticipator') *with jealous leer malign"* (77). The phrase is quoted from the passage in Book IV of *Paradise Lost* in which Satan is described as watching Adam and Eve embrace (1. 503). If America is hell, then England must be Paradise as well as heaven. The notion of America as a place of fallenness was traditional (the inevitable flip-side of the idealization of the New World as prelapsarian), but with their allusion to Milton the reviewers here give the trope a Romantic twist. This goes two ways: the comparison with Satan is a little unfortunate if one remembers Satan's success in the Garden of Eden, but on the other hand Birkbeck is left to wallow in the pestilential swamps.[26]

There is of course discord in hell: reviews of several other books on travel to the United States gave the *Quarterly* ample opportunity to develop the implications of its emphasis on the infernal. I turn now to the *Quarterly*'s January 1819 review of Henry Fearon's *Sketches of America* (1818), the subtitle of which advertises *"Remarks on Mr. Birkbeck's 'Notes' and 'Letters' "—* remarks which the reader later discovers are not favorable. The review of Birkbeck began by insinuating that "Friend Morris" had left England more in response to falling profits due to the "sudden change from war to peace" (55) than to political disaffection. Likewise, the review of Fearon starts by attacking those who, "having grown inordinately rich" under the "protecting shield" of England, "while the rest of the civilized world lay exposed to the ravages of war," now "rudely trampling over the graves of their forefathers . . . rush in crouds to deposit their wealth where it may be safe from the claims of their native land" (125). The *Quarterly Review*, unlike the *Edinburgh*, never acknowledged that people emigrate out of poverty, but this attack is so hyperbolic that it almost begs to be contradicted.[27] The diatribe was provoked partly by the fact that Fearon was sent out to investigate the prospects for trade in America by "forty families, principally resident, we believe, in the neighbourhood of Southwark" (125). The reviewer makes plain his attitude to these bourgeois Cockneys: "Had the amiable confraternity of whom we are speaking been agriculturalists, they would have transported themselves at once, and blindly plunged into the insatiable gulf which has already swallowed up so many thousands of their countrymen: but they were traders—cold-blooded, calculating men" (125).[28]

This melodramatic distinction between "blindly" trusting farmers and "cold-blooded" cautious traders ultimately breaks down: the *Quarterly*'s attack on Fearon resembles its article on Birkbeck in that it plays off the discrepancy between Fearon's expectations and the bleak reality that he encounterd in the United States, a discrepancy that while glaringly obvious to the *Quarterly*'s audience is not apparently evident to Fearon's intended readers.

Fearon, figured throughout the article as a more naive version of Birkbeck, is regarded as a victim of "all the rancorous abuse of this country" (126) by Cobbett and others.[29] His political views were of course objectionable to the *Quarterly:* "A democrat fieffe, Mr. Fearon joined to a sovereign contempt for the civil and religious institutions of England, of which he knew little, a blind and sottish admiration of those of America, of which he knew nothing at all" (125–26). The *Quarterly* accounts for Fearon's limited knowledge by explaining that he is a reader of "the enlightened pages of the Examiner and the Black Dwarf" (132). Fearon—said by the *Quarterly* to possess "the simplicity of a sucking child" (128)—is "the dupe of words" (127); the strategy of the article is to expose the ways in which Fearon's preconceptions, derived from the British Radical press, are thwarted at every turn by practical observations. The "gullibility" (126) of Fearon is implicitly linked with the openness to persuasion of those who are lured to "the land to which the artifices . . . of the Birkbecks and the Fearons are eagerly propelling them" (150). The *Quarterly*'s initial review of Birkbeck accused him of seeking companionship in misery: he was described as "attempting to seduce [England's] capitalists to follow his steps, and partake in his wretchedness" (77). Similarly, Fearon is described as trying to "entice" from England "poor wretches . . . by perverting their understanding by flattering promises, by fallacies and lies" (146).[30] Although on the one hand Fearon is accused of trying to delude potential emigrants, on the other hand he is judged to be "incapable of advancing an untruth" (136). According to the reviewer, Fearon's "sincerity" continually overpowers his democratic "prejudices" (166). Hence the documentary value of his *Sketches,* which are, concludes the reviewer, "pregnant with information of the most valuable kind to every one who meditates a removal to America" (166).

The *Quarterly* provides a very lively summary of Fearon's long journey through the United States, satirizing the so-called "liberty and equality" of the "land of promise" (129). The "republican independence" of the Americans is revealed to be nothing more than "impudence" (127), while their "enlightened government" (137) is declared to be full of *"place-hunters"* (158). As in the review of Birkbeck, the physical ill health of Americans becomes a metaphor for their lax morality. In Philadelphia, Fearon observed that, "Neither sex possesses the English standard of health—a rosy cheek" (143). The reviewer heavily underlines the significance of this statement by describing the corruption in Pennsylvanian local politics as *"all bruise and wound and putrifying sore"* (144, his italics). In line with this tone of relish, the reviewer finds a certain enjoyment in Fearon's "interesting and amusing" book (166), relating, as in the review of Birkbeck, instance after instance of the author's defeated expectations. The reviewer pokes sardonic fun at the "splendid accommodations" (128) of American boarding houses, the high house rents of New York, and the lack of provisions available in taverns. He uses anecdotes from Fearon to show that American "religious liberty" (148) is a euphemism for the practices of what Fearon himself called "maniacal fanatics" (148). "It cannot have escaped the reader," comments the reviewer, "that Mr. Fearon has been in a state of perplexity and amazement ever since he left his home: nothing falls out as he expected it to do" (137). But as in the review of Birkbeck, by quoting and summarizing at such length the reviewer appears mesmerized by the very material that he claims he scorns. Moreover, by exploiting Fearon's contradictions for their entertainment value, the reviewer de-emphasizes his own political agenda, even while his treatment of Fearon as a figure of fun ultimately reinforces the security of the *Quarterly*'s conservative stance. In mocking everything described by Fearon—from the "cadaverous appearance" of the residents of Ohio to the serving of "bread and butter" in "huge hunks piled zig-zag" (143)—the reviewer places all aspects of America on the same level. His exposure of the "heart-sickening" racism (130) and casual violence of Americans thereby loses some of its potential impact. He quotes from Fearon advertisements for slaves, together with stories about the "barbarous practice of *gouging*" out of eyes and the *"scalping"* of native Americans in Kentucky (155). But these pieces of evidence are undercut by the generic expectations that the reviewer has already set up: comedy and "horrors" (156) do not mix.[31]

Whereas Fearon is made to look merely buffoon-like—even when (or especially when) aghast at what he encountered—the reviewer directs more scathing language against the English reformers from whom Fearon is said to derive his political opinions. The reviewer ridicules Fearon's admiration for

179

the "*celebrated* Mr. Cobbett" (134) and his sentimental account of the supposedly "*self-banished*" Cobbett (135), whom he imagines "leading an isolated life in a foreign land—a path rarely trod—fences in ruin—the gate broken—the house mouldering to decay" (135). The reviewer insists on the political resonances of this description by commenting tartly, "We know no parallel to such sinking of the heart, except that which Mr. Hobhouse declares he felt at hearing of the victory of the English at Waterloo" (135). He goes on to denounce Cobbett as a " 'triple-turned' renegade," an "unprincipled miscreant" and a "sculking vagabond" (136) who fled to America not to escape political persecution but to elude his creditors. Just as this reviewer will later mockingly announce the news of a falling out between Birkbeck and Flower, he is pleased to report that Fearon's visit to Cobbett on Long Island was not well received. He quotes Cobbett's own comments on the encounter, in which Fearon is described as a "blade" and "a slippery young man"—"(a thief, we presume)," adds the reviewer (136). The *Quarterly* continues, "We take no interest in the dispute between these strenuous advocates of liberty and equality, nor, we believe, do any of our readers" (136). Why then discuss it at all? Because dissension between Radicals is of course an integral element of the *Quarterly*'s portrait of America—and by extension democracy—as hell; Fearon played into the reviewer's hands first by antagonizing Cobbett and later by criticizing Birkbeck (161). While Fearon, unlike Birkbeck, is described as being merely led astray, the Satanic role conferred on Birkbeck in the earlier review is here displaced onto Cobbett, of whose character "falsehood is known to be the essential part" (136).[32]

The reviewer does however quote from Cobbett's own "Letter to Birkbeck" in order to help refute Birkbeck's claims about the "pleasing prospects" of his "delightful *prairie*" (161). One might expect Birkbeck to be consigned to the oblivion of "the woods and swamps of the new Eden" (161), but a footnote to the article on Fearon provides updated news of Birkbeck and Flower, attempting to titillate readers with information about the emigrants' private lives. Initially the note revises the *Quarterly*'s earlier statement about Birkbeck's motives for emigrating, claiming now that Birkbeck in fact left England after failing at soap-manufacture, "not satisfied with the vast profits" (162) of his farm. The note—and the saga—continues:

> Soap-boiling is not the only speculation of friend Morris which has turned out ill. He appears to have tried to do something in *the female line,* and to have taken out a young lady with his family, as a venture. This fair creature, soon after their arrival at the Wabash, asserted her natural claim to liberty, and revolted to Mr. Flower, who, having left his wife in England, very considerately took her to his bed *ad interim.* Mr. Birkbeck was very unaccountably nettled at this arrangement; and the friends now glare at each other across the swamp like two angry comets "denouncing war and ruin." (reviewer's italics, 162)

Not content with condemning the economic motives underlying Birkbeck's obnoxious efforts at social mobility, the reviewer now accuses him of conflating the sexual and the economic: Birkbeck's marriage to the "young lady" would be a business "venture." At first sight it seems as if Birkbeck is being ruthlessly punished for offending the reviewer's class bias by ironically turning into a victim of the kind of political rebellion that he himself advocated (needless to say, the *Quarterly* does not find the desire for "liberty" to be "natural"). But Birkbeck also has to be punished for his initial seduction of Flower, whose youth and feminine-sounding name make him a particularly gullible version of the sort of person that Birkbeck tried to persuade to revolt with him against his native land. The resulting dissension is, it is implied, a fitting conclusion to the tale of the self-banished inhabitants of the hellish Midwestern swamp.[33] But as we will see, the story does not end here.[34]

Recurring themes in the reviews of Birkbeck and Fearon are further developed in another *Quarterly* article in which attacks on proponents of emigration reach something of a climax.[35] Ironically the story of disillusionment with America eventually incorporates Birkbeck himself. This article reviews four books, two of which—by William Tell Harris and Adlard Welby—set out to verify the claims of Birkbeck; one of them, by Richard Flower, George Flower's father, "pompously" (72) includes a "Letter from Mr. Birkbeck" (71) and a "Refutation" of Cobbett; and finally one by "an Englishwoman," which the *Quarterly* dismisses as a "most ridiculous and extravagant panegyric on the government and people of the United States" (72–73). The reviewer comments on the last author as follows:

> An Englishwoman, with the proper spirit and feeling attached to that proud title, would blush to be thought the author of such a work. We will not, we cannot possibly, believe that one so lost to shame exists among us; and are rather disposed, therefore, to attribute it to one of those wretched hirelings who, under the assumed names of "travellers," "residents in France," "Italy," &c. supply the Radical press with the means of mischief. (73)[36]

In taking for granted the ability of the "radical press" to bring about subversion, this hypothesis implies that the travel narratives that effect such "mischief" are fictitious, whereas the *Quarterly* has privileged access to the truth, not because of first-hand knowledge but because of an ability to read between the lines. In connection with the work of this "pseudo-Englishwoman" (73), the *Quarterly* makes a standard—and unsubtle—rhetorical move: the book would be "too stupidly outrageous" (73) to comment on, except that "it becomes a duty to rise up and expose [its] fallacies" in order to prevent "credulous people" from being "deluded by them" (73). Again the implied audience of the *Quarterly*—defenders of the establishment—is conflated with the readership to which the travel books are directed. The *Quarterly* takes the trouble to refute a few historical points made by "this abandoned prostitutor of the name and character of an 'Englishwoman' " (75), as if to crush that crime against nature, a self-proclaimed female Radical. Meanwhile its treatment of the other three authors follows another familiar pattern in which, by contrast, ridicule outweighs hostility: the travelers are characterized by comically unsuccessful attempts to hide their disillusionment with the hell that is America. Behind them lurks the shadowy but as usual demonically influential figure of Cobbett, "a writer whose name is synonymous with falsehood" (72).

The first of the authors under review, William Tell Harris, is initially imagined as an "agent . . . of a provincial branch of the same surly sourheaded faction which sent forth the well known Fearon" (71)—well-known perhaps only to readers of the *Quarterly,* one might add—but he is figured as less hapless than his "predecessor" (76) and therefore, by contrast, at least potentially threatening. Harris is of course accused of being "in spite of every indication to the contrary . . . strongly disposed to find all things as they should be" (83). After using extracts from Harris to denounce slavery and the "brutal practice of gouging" (85), the reviewer follows "this poor driveller" (86) to his inevitable destination, "the swamps of the Wabash" (86). Harris himself obligingly provided a description of his journey to Illinois: "The dismal appearance of these swamps, whose trees seem to be thus mantled with the emblems of death; the dark sluggish streams tinged by decayed roots, and ruffled only by the alligator and the frog; together with the stillness that prevails; lead [sic] my recollections to the descriptions of the fabled Styx and Lethe" (87).

In passing, Harris is condemned as a "heartless democrat" (88) and dubbed "this callous-hearted radical (for he is one of that pernicious set)" (87) for refusing to sympathize with "numbers of his fellow countrymen in distress, (seduced from their hearths and homes by the flattering reports of wretches like himself)" (87). As usual, the *Quarterly* assumes that misleadingly attractive "reports" can easily be seen through by its own readers. Harris's eventual "silence" on the subject of Birkbeck's and Flower's "western paradise" is said to speak "volumes" (89); even the omission of information on a subject in which the *Quarterly* is so invested is read as complicity in guilt. Fortunately for the reviewer and presumably for his captivated readers, Welby's book supplies details which enable the *Quarterly* to extend the ongoing saga of life in the swamps.

Welby, depicted as a "plain country gentleman" (89) from England, provided yet another narrative of progressive disappointment. After encountering "green stinking puddles" and "putrifying carcasses of dead dogs" in Philadelphia (77), he found "rogues and rudeness" (79) in Ohio. "He still however consoled himself," continues the *Quarterly,* "with the hope that the Illinois and the 'English settlement' would set all right; but while thus engaging in daydreams, a severe blow was given to the sanguine expectations he was forming of this western paradise, by 'a party on their return from it to New York' " (79). Finally arrived at " 'the swamps of the Wabash;' or, as Messrs. Birkbeck and Flower are pleased to call it, the 'English settlements of Albion and Wanborough,' in the 'Prairies of the Illinois' " (89), Welby was "wofully disappointed, but he tells the truth" (89). He visited a "poor victim of Birkbeck's knavery" (91), who had been "induced by Mr. Birkbeck's 'Notes' " to 'repair to the Prairies" (90). The reviewer adds, "Our Lincolnshire squire is justly indignant with this and several similar instances of bad treatment by friend Morris, and leaves him 'to settle with his *conscience* the bringing people out thus far by his misrepresentations to hopeless banishment' " (91). Again Birkbeck is imagined as capable of luring countless emigrants to their doom.[37] Once more the Miltonic scenario of the fall from heaven is implicitly evoked:

> There are thousands of our poor countrymen who have been seduced from their homes by these artificers of fraud, and have embarked their little all in their journey to these gloomy wilds, that are at this moment pining in despair, and hastening to a strange grave with broken hearts. They cannot return, and the land of their birth will know them no more. (91)

Birkbeck's fellow-emigrants begin to assume the shape of the third part of heaven's host who accompanied Milton's Satan; while the crowds who were seduced to join Birkbeck in his "Eden" (92) may have been simply deluded, the *Quarterly* flatters its readers by taking for granted their resistance to seduction.

"It would seem, however," continues the reviewer, "that friend Morris is not altogether free from the danger of a reprisal from those he has deluded" (91). This threat of punishment sounds at once fitting and ominous, but the only evidence the reviewer can produce from Welby is that "the angry feelings of the poor people who had been trapped by the deceptive colouring of his writings, flashed out in true English threats of tossing him in a blanket!" (91–92). Despite this anticlimax, the reviewer persists in characterizing Birkbeck's " 'town' of Albion, as it is proudly called" (90) as a place of fallenness, notorious for "the lawless and licentious manners of its inhabitants" (93), which Richard Flower in his book describes as "an infidel and wicked settlement" (93). Upon introducing a Unitarian prayer service, Flower, according to his own account, was proclaimed as "the saviour of the place" (93). Birkbeck—perhaps from "a spirit of opposition to Mr. Flower, (for these two friends and fellow-travellers are no longer one)" (93)[38]— apparently then "opened a place of worship at Wanborough; he officiates himself, and reads the *Church of England service*" (reviewer's italics, 93). The *Quarterly* announces this fact only to pour scorn upon "the Reverend Morris Birkbeck" (94). The reviewer claims, appealing apparently more to the *Quarterly*'s lengthy portrait of Birkbeck than to any factual evidence, "it was a matter of perfect indifference to Mr. Morris Birkbeck whether he officiated as an 'orthodox divine,' or as an Imaun, Bonze, Lama, Fetish-man, or Mumbo-Jumbo" (94).[39] It is ironic that this accusation is made as part of a polemic against the "exaggerated statements" (72) of Harris et al.: even while the *Quarterly* relies on "friend Morris" as an easy whipping-boy, Birkbeck by this point has assumed larger-than-life proportions. But in treating him this way, the *Quarterly* continues to dictate the highly simplified terms—good versus evil—in which the emigration controversy is to be read.

I turn finally to the article criticized by the *Westminster* for its bigoted view of emigration, the *Quarterly*'s review of William Faux's *Memorable Days in America, being a Journal of a Tour to the United States, principally undertaken to ascertain, by positive Evidence, the Condition and probable Prospects of British Emigrants; including Accounts of Mr. Birkbeck's Settlement in the Illinois* (1823). A kind of sequel to the Harris review, this article is organized similarly in that it builds up to the climax of Faux's inevitable visit to "that paradise of prairies, the Illinois territory" (356). This one, however—belatedly, one might think—claims that "The bubble . . . appears to have burst at last" (360).[40] Yet again the author of the book under review—"our simple farmer" (349)—is seen as a naive reporter of horrors.[41] A hot day in Washington is another rendering of hell: "The breezes, if any, are perfumed by nuisances of all sorts, emptied into the streets, rotting carcases, and the exhalations of dismal swamps, made vocal and alive with toads, lizards, and bellowing bull-frogs. . . . [P]itiable the fate of the poor emigrant sighing in vain for comforts, cool breezes, wholesome diet, and the old friends of his native land" (346). Likewise the description of "the cold, wet, marshy prairies, over which hang dense, pestilent fogs and steaming heat" (366) debunks any lingering notion that the western territory is edenic. Upon reaching the "Paradise of Fools" (363), emigrants suffer the "Indian summer, which partakes of the vulgar idea of the infernal" (362), and living conditions summed up as "barbarizing in a little log hole" (363). After the usual anecdotes in which slavery, eye-gouging, dirt and mosquitoes assume equally dire proportions,[42] Faux and his reviewer reach the "end" of their "destination" and their "hopes"—"the English prairie" (364). The *Quarterly* continues,

> Our farmer of course visited Flower and Birkbeck, and was civilly treated by both. These dear friends however dwelt at opposite sides of the prairie, and were not on speaking terms; indeed one of the Flowers observed to Mr. Faux that he avoided seeing Birkbeck, "because, if I come near," said he, "I must lay violent hands on him, I must knock him down" (364).

Birkbeck refused to be knocked down, however, or rather, the *Quarterly* refuses to let him alone. The reviewer repeats the story about the "young lady" whom Birkbeck "intended . . . for himself, but Flower got the start of him, and Birkbeck's plea of quarrel is, the immorality of Flower, in marrying a second wife while his first was still living in England" (364). But even though he refused to sanction bigamy, there can be no sympathy for Birkbeck: the reviewer merely remarks, "As we hear nothing of the Reverend Morris Birkbeck preaching, we suppose that he has laid aside his canonicals" (364). However unsubtle the *Quarterly*'s jibes, as here, they work to reinforce its readers' self-congratulatory feelings of superiority; the *Quarterly* accords its own image of Birkbeck more authenticity than eye-witness accounts. Birkbeck remains laughably oblivious that he has been reduced to the role of an expelled rebel in a preordained plot.

Despite its at once dismissive and fascinated account of Birkbeck, the *Quarterly*, as we have seen, ascribes to Birkbeck and other Radical writers the ability to find readers everywhere. Birkbeck is imagined throughout these reviews as desperately attempting to attract followers. One might expect this endeavor to be exposed as ineffectual, but the *Quarterly* prefers to report widespread success followed by widespread disillusionment: the review of Faux claims that as a result of Birkbeck's *Letters from Illinois,* "emigrants in abundance flocked" to join him; but "all were disgusted" and departed "with hearty curses on Morris Birkbeck and his prairie" (365). The problem with this accusation is that it makes Birkbeck's writing seem almost preternaturally effective—especially since so little positive information about America is supplied—and he himself thus something more than a mere figure of fun. Yet the *Quarterly* continues to play the game of giving power to Birkbeck and taking it away again. The idea of Birkbeck's victims returning home in disgust conflicts with the notion developed in a previous review that Birkbeck's fellow-settlers had been lured out to suffer "hopeless banishment," but the *Quarterly* reviewers are happy to have it both ways. The review of Faux reports that the "settlers visited by our farmer" included " 'Orator Hunt's son and his deaf and dumb brother" (365)—a reference which perhaps indicates the emigrants' tangential relationship to mainstream Radicalism. This passage is singled out for attack by the *Westminster,* which is particularly offended by what it terms the *Quarterly* reviewer's "mirth" over the subject of American taxes: "This writer, on extracting from Faux, that land in the Illinois belonging to Orator Hunt's brother was uncultivated, and selling for the *payment of taxes,* appears absolutely dancing in a transport of joy. 'Avast reading there!' he cries . . . '*Taxes,* did you say? *Taxes,* in this last retreat of suffering humanity, and the land selling to pay them!' " (reviewer's italics, 257). Unmoved by the *Quarterly*'s would-be humorous use of sarcasm, the *Westminster's* writer comments acidly, "Yes, *Taxes!* With any man in his senses, the question is, not whether there are taxes, but what is their *amount*" (reviewer's italics, 257). The writer in the *Westminster* apparently fails to understand that the effectiveness of the *Quarterly* rests on its lively, anecdotal style—its effectiveness, that is, not so much as a propaganda machine but as a source of amusing reading material for a leisured audience.

The fate of those who emigrate, concludes the review of Faux, is "hopeless misery" (370). But if the case were closed, this particular source of amusement for the *Quarterly*'s audience would be removed, so the reviewer, improbably enough, addresses his readers as if they are still "in a state of hesitation whether to embark their all on a speculation to the back-woods of America" (370). As I have already implied, there never was a state of hesitation, since the *Quarterly*'s readers were not the people addressed by the proponents of emigration; the notion that their audience might be open to persuasion on this point is a useful fiction which allows the reviewers to assume their characteristic tone of urgency, but which is also exploited for humorous effect. The idea of being persuaded to emigrate by the grim picture of America that emerges in these reviews is self-consciously absurd. The suggestion that the *Quarterly*'s own readers could be enticed to flee abroad by the seductive artifices of Birkbeck and his fellow Radicals is part of the *Quarterly*'s elaborate joke at the Radicals' expense. The heavy-handedness of the *Quarterly*'s humor could backfire; and as I have shown, at moments the *Quarterly* displays its own investment in the diabolical. But the *Quarterly* could afford to make Birkbeck and others demonic because it remained capable of playing with its political opponents like pawns. In the days of a revived reform movement and social agitation after Waterloo, there was every reason why the Tories should appear under threat. But because the *Quarterly* addressed a select audience, it preached to the converted. It invented a space in which a politically-charged issue—emigration—was repeatedly toyed with for its readers' amusement. The fact that the *Quarterly* could make this move is itself evidence of a sense of political stability that is not necessarily possessed either by the reviewers as individuals or by their actual readers—but which the reviews collectively succeeded in projecting, because they took for granted the invulnerability of their *implied* audience. This elite periodical projected such a secure impression of itself that it was able, first, to control its Radical opponents with vituperation—since vituperation engenders nothing but more of the same even while it recoils on its users—and second, to contain those opponents by making them into actors in a farcical travesty of the fall from heaven. Through implicit and explicit allusions to *Paradise Lost,* these reviews transformed a topical issue with consequences in the real world into a replaying of a familiar literary scenario, and in doing so granted its participants only the semblance of political agency, since the outcome of their rebellion was scripted in advance. The Romantic move here was to recognize the glamour of the Satanic and simultaneously to expose the Satanic as derivative. A further Romantic move was to transcend partisan conflicts in order to produce pleasure, a gesture that in this case only confirms the self-sustaining power of that Tory stronghold, the *Quarterly Review.*

Notes

1. [James Mill], "Periodical Literature: 1. *The Edinburgh Review, Vol.* 1, 2, &c," *Westminster Review* 1 (January 1824): 206–49 (reviewer's italics, p. 218).

2. [Peregrine Bingham], "Periodical Literature: *The Quarterly Review,* No. LVIII," *Westminster Review* 1 (January 1824): 250–68 (p. 250).

3. The *Westminster* did however go on to attack the *Quarterly* in more general terms, while claiming that "The Quarterly Review has always displayed much more of the character of a bookseller's catch-penny, than the Edinburgh Review." See [James Mill], "Periodical Literature: *The Quarterly Review,*" *Westminster Review* 2 (October 1824): 463–503 (463).

4. Kim Wheatley, "Paranoid Politics: The *Quarterly* and *Edinburgh* Reviews," *Prose Studies* 15 (1992): 319–43. In that article I suggest that vituperation is an unwieldy tool across the political spectrum: the rhetoric of William Cobbett, for example, remains caught within terms set by the elitist press. The phrase "paranoid style" is borrowed from Richard Hofstadter, *The Paranoid Style in American Politics and Other Essays* (New York: Alfred A. Knopf, 1965).

5. [Francis Jeffrey], "Dispositions of England and America," *Edinburgh Review* 33 (May 1820): 395–431 (399). The reviews that I will be examining illustrate on one level the political partisanship of the *Quarterly* in that they provide a ready opportunity for Tory vindications of domestic policy, just as the ones on the same topic in the *Edinburgh* give rise to Whig attacks on the postwar government. But against Radicals, the Tories and Whigs present what amounts to a united front. While the *Quarterly* is admittedly more extreme than the *Edinburgh,* ideologically the two display more similarities than differences: as William Hazlitt once commented, these periodicals "travel the same road and arrive at the same destination"; Hazlitt, Preface to *Political Essays,* in *Works,* ed. P. P. Howe (London and Toronto: J. M. Dent and Sons, 1930–1934), 7:20.

6. [John Barrow and William Gifford], "Faux—*Memorable Days in America,*" *Quarterly Review* 29 (July 1823): 338–70 (339). Further references in parentheses. The anonymous contributors to the *Quarterly Review* are identified by Hill Shine and Helen Chadwick Shine, *The Quarterly Review Under Gifford: Identification of Contributors 1809–1824* (Chapel Hill: University of North Carolina Press, 1949).

7. In de-emphasizing the overt political argument of these texts I disagree with Walter Graham, who, in *Tory Criticism in the Quarterly Review 1809–1853* (1921; rpt. New York: AMS Press, 1970), asserts that the "vilification of America in the *Quarterly Review* . . . seems to have had a definite political end to serve" in that "Canning and other ministers countenanced the irritating propaganda to lessen emigration to the United States" (p. 10). As I suggest below, this assumption is problematic because the *Quarterly*'s own readers were not likely to consider emigrating.

8. Stephen Fender, *Sea Changes: British Emigration and American Literature* (Cambridge: Cambridge University Press, 1992), pp. 38–41. Fender says that about 206,500 people emigrated from Britain to the United States during this seventeen-year period. His invaluable book places the reviews that I will be focusing on in the much larger cultural context of the ongoing discourse on British emigration to (and "back-migration" from) the United States.

9. [John Barrow], "Fearon's *Sketches of America,*" *Quarterly Review* 21 (January 1819): 124–67 (126). Further references in parentheses.

10. [William Jacob], "Bristed—*Statistical View of America,*" *Quarterly Review* 21 (January 1819): 1–25 (8).

11. Cobbett wrote *A Year's Residence in the United States of America* (1819)

during his stay, and he continued to publish his *Political Register* in Britain during that period; as we will see, the authors reviewed engage in various forms of dialogue with him.

12. Marjorie Levinson, *Keats's Life of Allegory: The Origins of a Style* (Oxford: Basil Blackwell, 1988), p. 41.

13. See Marilyn Butler, "Culture's Medium: The Role of the Review," in *The Cambridge Companion to British Romanticism,* ed. Stuart Curran (Cambridge: Cambridge University Press, 1993), pp. 120–47, on the discrepancy between the reviewers' actual status as professional writers and their studied "tone of social superiority" (p. 136); the quarterlies' prose elides its own economic underpinnings.

14. The *Westminster* also deplores the *Quarterly*'s acceptance of hearsay and anecdotal evidence, although the strategy of presenting lengthy quotations from the book under discussion with minimal comment was the standard reviewing method in the early nineteenth century. This strategy is of course equivocal in that gaps open up between assertions and supporting details, but I would suggest that, in the case of the *Quarterly* articles I will be discussing, such discrepancies ultimately reinforce this periodical's vehement anti-Americanism.

15. That the reviews served as a form of publicity may be suggested by the fact that both of Birkbeck's books rapidly went through multiple editions, though again this raises the question of whether Birkbeck's audience overlapped with the *Quarterly*'s. According to Wilbur S. Shepperson, *Emigration and Disenchantment* (Norman: University of Oklahoma Press, 1965), the Birkbeck-Flower colony in Edwards County, Illinois, numbered 400 people by August 1819 (p. 43).

16. Disappointed by his brother's initial difficulties in America, John Keats later wrote to Georgiana Keats in a letter of 15 January 1820: "[Thomas Campbell's] Gertrude of Wyoming and Birkbeck's book should be bound up together like a Brace of Decoy Ducks—One is almost as poetical as the other. Precious miserable people at the Prarie" (quoted from Hyder Edward Rollins, ed., *The Letters of John Keats 1814–1821* [Cambridge, Mass.: Harvard University Press, 1958], 2:243).

17. [Robert Southey], "On the Means of Improving the People," *Quarterly Review* 19 (April 1818): 79–118 (93).

18. [John Barrow and William Gifford], "Birkbeck's *Notes on America,*" *Quarterly Review* 19 (April 1818): 54–78. References in parentheses. Robert M. Sutton, in his edition of Birkbeck's *Letters from Illinois* (New York: Da Capo Press, 1970), makes the bizarre suggestion that this review "may well" have been written by William Cobbett (p. ix).

19. The quotation is taken from Shine, *The Quarterly Review Under Gifford,* p. 61.

20. George Flower (1788–1862) actually preceded Birkbeck to the United States.

21. Birkbeck, in his *Notes on a Journey in America,* 5th ed. (London: James Ridgway, 1819) claims that a desire to avoid slavery motivated his emigration to Illinois.

22. An earlier attack on America in the *Quarterly* had already commented that "Amplification indeed is . . . a favourite figure with this infant community." See [John Barrow], "Inchiquen's Favourable View of the United States," *Quarterly Review* 10 (January 1814): 494–539 (p. 527).

23. Although my purpose in this essay is to analyze the rhetoric of the reviews

and their treatment of their implied audience, rather than the persuasiveness or otherwise of actual accounts of America by reformers, it is true that Birkbeck's tone in his *Letters from Illinois* is optimistic; it is uncertain whether he intended to delude his readers, but his claim at the end of his *Notes* that he is not a land speculator (p. 154) seems disingenuous.

24. See Fender, *Sea Changes,* pp. 225–27.

25. See "Inchiquen's Favourable View of the United States," where an American scheme to rework the English language is condemned with the quotation "to raise / Quite out their native language, and instead / To sow a jangling noise of words unknown" (p. 528).

26. For the *Edinburgh*'s review of Birkbeck, see [Henry Brougham], "Birkbeck's *Notes on America,*" *Edinburgh Review* 30 (June 1818): 120–40. This article purports to take a stance diametrically opposed to that of the *Quarterly,* but it ultimately conveys a similar impression of Birkbeck and the issue of emigration, partly because it presents the same negative information about America—taken from Birkbeck—that is provided by the *Quarterly,* and partly because it goes on to contradict its own initial stance in favor of emigration. The reviewer discourses at some length on what he claims is a providential human "instinct" against emigration: "After all . . . man is, of all luggage, the most difficult to be transported. . . . We find him rebuilding his cottage upon the half cooled lava which has swept all his possessions away" (p. 135). The latter highly exaggerated illustration would seem to overbalance the reviewer's praise of Birkbeck, especially since he next asserts, "Not even the pestilential swamps of Guiana and Java can frighten [man] from his home, and dissolve the most powerful of all ties—local attachment" (p. 135). The *Edinburgh* here displaces to an even more alien setting the "pestilential swamps of the Wabash" mentioned in the *Quarterly.* But for most people, concludes the *Edinburgh,* "those feelings [of local attachment] are too strong even for the ruder hand of the Government and its agents,—what shape soever they may assume—whether of inquisitors, or spies, or mercenary troops, or collectors of taxes" (p. 135). This last statement is an unsubtle jibe at the Tory government; on the other hand, in granting the power of "local attachment" the *Edinburgh* echoes the *Quarterly*'s review of Birkbeck. The latter had made a derogatory reference to Americans' compulsive traveling, adding, "they have few or none of those local attachments and fixed habits, which make it in Europe so painful a task to separate from those objects which time and memory have endeared" (p. 59). These quasi-Wordsworthian "attachments," made dear by "time and memory," are invoked throughout the reviews on emigration, regardless of party affiliation: even the *Westminster*'s attack on the *Quarterly*'s review of Faux mentions the difficulty of giving up "scenes and connections" (p. 105). By seeming to agree that individual identity is grounded in a particular place, the *Edinburgh* implicitly sanctions the *Quarterly*'s emphasis on the quasi-subversive rootlessness of Americans.

27. The *Quarterly* implies that the move to America is an inevitable step down on the social scale, but as Shepperson claims in *Emigration and Disenchantment,* "The British were . . . the most heterogeneous of all immigrant groups" (p. 6).

28. According to Shepperson, *Emigration and Disenchantment,* Fearon was himself a wine-merchant, but the thirty-nine families from Essex who sent him out were farmers (p. 46).

29. The review of Fearon comments on the author's description of Baltimore as a city which "occupies the foremost rank in deadly animosity towards England":

We are not surprised at this; for the inhabitants are not merely democrats, but furious Jacobins. A spirit of hostility towards England, however, is but too prevalent throughout the United States,—a spirit which is industriously kept up by the Cobbetts . . . and, above all, by the editors of newspapers, who are generally Scotch or Irish rebels, or felons who have defrauded the gallows of its due. (p. 160)

With this claim the *Quarterly* returns to its paranoid preoccupation with the power of the Radical press, yet at the same time, with his dismissive plural ("Cobbetts") and his absurdly sweeping generalization about the editors, the reviewer contrives to give the impression that such writers are beneath contempt.

30. The *Quarterly* misrepresents Fearon's book in order to fit it into the pattern established by the review of Birkbeck: Fearon actually concludes by stating that he "cannot make up [his] mind" whether to recommend emigration; Henry Bradshaw Fearon, *Sketches of America,* 2nd ed. (London: Longman, Hurst, Rees, Orme, and Brown, 1818; rpt. New York and London: Benjamin Blom, 1969), p. 419. In his attack on the *Quarterly* in the *Westminster,* James Mill pointed out the contradictoriness of the *Quarterly*'s treatment of Fearon: "They begin by describing Mr. Fearon as a person wholly unfit to be trusted for an observation or an opinion; but finding him afterward very much disposed to find fault with . . . America, they treat him as an oracle" (2:486–87).

31. The reviewer in fact makes an abrupt shift from the "disgusting scenes" witnessed by Fearon in the "plague-spotted State" of Kentucky (p. 156) to an advertisement warning widows of a "remarkably ugly and ill-natured" bigamist (p. 156).

32. The review ends as if on a note of triumph with an old quotation from Cobbett praising England's aristocratic and monarchical government. But given that the review has already cast doubt on the validity of anything written by Cobbett, this joke at Fearon's expense perhaps backfires.

33. According to Gladys Scott Thompson, *A Pioneer Family: The Birkbecks in Illinois 1818–1827* (London: Jonathan Cape, 1953), Flower's marriage to Eliza Julia Andrews was not the sole cause of the feud (p. 63).

34. The *Edinburgh*'s review of Fearon's *Sketches of America,* like its review of Birkbeck's *Notes,* begins by taking a stance diametrically opposed to that of the *Quarterly,* but ends by undermining its own defense of America, and by extension of emigration. See [Sydney Smith], "Travellers in America," *Edinburgh Review* 31 (December 1818): 132–50. The *Edinburgh* concludes, "it is not pleasant to emigrate into a country of changes and revolution, the size and integrity of whose empire no man can predict" (p. 149). And in the last paragraph of the article the reviewer exclaims, "What a dreadful disease Nostalgia must be on the banks of the Missouri! Severe and painful poverty will drive us all anywhere; but a wise man should be quite sure he has so irresistible a plea, before he ventures on the Great or the little Wabash" (p. 150).

35. [Unidentified author], "Views, Visits, and Tours in North America," *Quarterly Review* 27 (April 1822): 71–99.

36. The review of Faux the following year however identifies the "Englishwoman" as a "sad reality": a "Miss Wright," an "adopted daughter (as she says) of Jeremy Bentham" (p. 339). Frances Wright was a friend of Frances Trollope, author of *Domestic Manners of the Americans* (1832).

37. In contrast with these images of emigrants rushing to join Birkbeck, the reviewer supplies statistics in a footnote to prove that emigration is on the decline—but needless to say by this point the actual facts of the case seem unimportant.

38. The reviewer here seems to conflate the two Flowers, a move which simplifies the feud between the Flower family and Birkbeck.

39. The reviewer does however quote from Birkbeck's *Letters from Illinois* his statement that he *"did not believe"* in the *"doctrines"* of the Anglican Church (reviewer's italics, p. 94).

40. Predictably, just as Faux's book is grounded in "a strong desire to ascertain the naked truth in all particulars relating to emigration" (p. 339), the *Quarterly* hopes that his book—and presumably the review—will give "a check to hasty and thoughtless emigration, and thereby diminish . . . those scenes of heart-rending distress, which the alluring misrepresentations of English land-jobbers, in particular, have brought upon many respectable families, who were weak enough to be the dupes of their artifices" (p. 340).

41. See the review of Faux's book in *Blackwood's Edinburgh Magazine* 14 (Nov. 1923): 561–72, which calls Faux a "simpleton of the first water" (562) who writes satire in spite of his intentions.

42. The *Westminster* claims that the reviewer suppresses Faux's positive evidence while quoting at length "details of individual instances of ferocity, violence, knavery, boasting and vulgarity, disappointment, failure, despondency, bad soils, bad climates, bad food, discomfort, dirt, and barbarism" (p. 251). The issue at stake is more the *Quarterly*'s own reading of Faux than the question of Faux's accuracy.

WILLIAM HONE, JOHN MURRAY,
AND THE
USES OF BYRON

KYLE GRIMES

In the middle of July 1819, the first two cantos of Byron's *Don Juan* were published in London. Though these cantos appeared without Byron's or the publisher John Murray's name (and with a few of the more slanderous stanzas deleted and replaced by asterisks), there was little doubt in the literary community about who had written and who had published the controversial work. Nonetheless, the anonymity of the publication opened the door for numerous imitations and spurious continuations.[1] William Hone, the Radical publisher, parodist, and antiquarian, was quick to see the opportunity, and, within a few months of the July publication, Hone had written and published a work he called *Don Juan, Canto the Third!* In Hone's continuation of the story, Juan marries Haidee, the couple have twelve children (six pairs of twins born in consecutive years), and the whole family moves to London, where Juan establishes himself as the chief writer and editor of a newspaper called *The Devilled Biscuit.* Juan's motivation for taking up journalism is primarily financial: he knows that "twins can't live on air,"[2] and he comes to England in order to "find some folk so apt to cram a lie / That he might feed his wife and family" (st. 6). To satisfy this thrill- and scandal-seeking audience, Juan makes sure that his sensational paper is "concocted / Of every hot or savoury Ingredient" (st. 25), and he devises an unusual mode of circulation for *The Devilled Biscuit.* Rather than distributing the paper through the conventional network of booksellers and patterers, Juan stands in the doorway to his shop and—to the accompaniment of his Spanish guitar—sings the columns of his newspaper to any passersby who happen to be in the street. Eventually, Juan's search for the sensational story involves him in the political divisiveness that marked 1819 London, and, more by accident than commitment, he becomes a Radical journalist, bent on disseminating his interpretation of the news to a broad-based audience while simultaneously trying to fend off the repressive apparatus of a paranoid and reactionary government. Taken as a whole, then, Hone's poem begins with the elegant and expensive Murray/Byron production and then transfers the narrative to the world of London's Radical publishers. That being so, the poem straddles the divide between the elite and largely leisure class (even if scandalous) literature of the period and the active political work of the Radical press.

In effect, Hone's poem co-opts the comic-Byronic voice and impresses it into the service of popular politics. This discursive strategy affords Hone a platform from which he can both criticize what he saw as squeamish cowardice on the part of John Murray—"Drab John" in the poem—and simultaneously publicize his own status as a Radical writer and publisher. (Not surprisingly, Hone's Juan is the transparent representative of Hone himself.) Indeed, Hone's opening stanzas are merciless in their parodic lampooning of Murray. Stanza one, for instance, explains the circumstances surrounding the apparent shift of publishing houses from Murray to Hone for this titular third canto of *Don Juan:*

> Miss Haidee and Don Juan pleaded well;
> At least my publisher *of late* so tells me,
> Although the world he does not chuse to tell,
> Yet every body knows 'tis he who sells me:
> To sing what furthermore the *pair* befel,
> (As he declines my book and thus compels me,
> Because my *"guinea trash"* he will not own,)
> I send this Canto into Mr. Hone.

Part of the joke here is that Hone's narrator identifies Murray's publication as "guinea trash"—a parodic recasting of the phrase "twopenny trash" with which the Radical press had been denigrated ever since 1816, when Cobbett cut the price of the *Political Register.* What is more, Hone quite pointedly usurps the authority of Byron's voice, both in the direct ascription of the stanza's closing line and also in the easy adoption of the tone, style, and even personal pronoun of Byron's famous narrator. Clearly, Hone was quick to recognize and exploit the revolutionary potential of Byron's quixotic narrator. In fact, Hone uses the narrator to found a claim on *Don Juan* itself, mockingly establishing his own narrator's voice as the "true one" and relegating Murray to the status of a cowardly and now superseded pretender to the admiration of the reading public.

Situated as the poem is on the border between the popular press and the literary elite, the comical parrying for authority inscribed into *Don Juan,*

Canto the Third! takes on an added significance. Hone's poem is founded on a kind of discursive power struggle that mirrors the socio-political struggle between, on the one hand, a deeply committed, politically motivated Radical press and, on the other hand, a more conservative oligarchy of "respectable" publishing houses (Longman's, Murray's, Rivington's, and so forth) that together—and often with the assistance of church and state—sought to resist the Radicals' egalitarian claims and thereby maintain their own economic and cultural ascendancy. In this context, it is entirely fitting that the opening stanzas of Hone's *Juan* should pit Hone himself against Murray as the representatives of these economic, political, and cultural adversaries. Hone, after all, had become famous as a consequence of the widely reported libel trials of December 1817, in which he had succeeded almost single-handedly in embarrassing Lord Ellenborough and the attorney general and, more broadly, momentarily foiled the Tory government's attempt to stifle reformist and/or revolutionary discourse. Hone was, in short, the iconic figure of both the persecution and the eventual triumph of the Radical, popular press.[3] For his part, Murray (who was, among other things, the London publisher of the conservative *Quarterly Review*) was probably the most prestigious publisher/bookseller in England. His fashionable Albemarle address was the gathering place of the Regency literati, and his expensively produced books, with their ample margins and fine paper, were nothing short of the book-arts avatars of aristocratic elegance. In 1819, especially in the months following Peterloo, the Radical and respectable presses were engaged in a kind of cultural skirmish, fighting for authority with the reading public. The respectable press often treated the Radicals (when they noticed them at all) with a patrician disdain for things vulgar.[4] The Radicals, of course, saw the respectable press as little more than government lackeys, the very mouthpiece of an oppressive and morally defunct dominant culture. In the context of this broader struggle, then, both Hone and Murray found Byron to be a useful writer and *Don Juan* a useful poem.

I

As both a Radical (of sorts) and an aristocrat, Byron was an ambiguous figure in the political battles that divided England, especially in the wake of the Manchester Massacre. The name "Byron" signified a social stance marked by both aristocratic elitism and Radical iconoclasm—and, as is well known, the blend captured the attention of extremely large audiences. For Murray, of course, these audiences translated into profits. "Byron," as Jerome Christensen has recently argued, had all the cachet of a brand name;[5] like "Calvin Klein" or "Giorgio Armani," "Byron" was a carefully constructed marketing label that served to maintain the high price of the commodity in question and thereby to demarcate the whole product line into the high-status "genuine article" and the knock-off "cheap imitation." Thus, even if Byron's poetry had in 1819 become so morally suspect and politically risky that he did not wish to be publicly associated with it, Murray still knew very well that the "Byron" brand was good business. Indeed, despite his apprehensions about the manifold freedoms of *Don Juan*'s discourse, Murray wrote to Byron in March 1819 claiming that he had the "greatest expectations" concerning the poem, expectations that he "long[ed] to realize."[6] And after the publication Murray directed his lawyer Sharon Turner to seek a legal injunction barring other publishers from pirating the cantos. Though complicated by the poem's loose morality and by Murray's unwillingness to proclaim his interest in the publication, the successful appeal was clearly an effort to gain legal protection for Murray's property rights and the profits that went with them.[7]

For Hone, however, *Don Juan* offered the opportunity to enlist this influential literary brand name specifically on the side of the Radical press, thereby inverting the very class divisions within the expanding British readership that Murray and other such publishers were trying to maintain. To explain the dynamics here, it will be helpful to step back a few years to sketch in some publishing history.

Hone's attitude toward Murray had begun to establish itself at least as early as 1816 when Hone was the first and most important of the several pirates who published Byron's *Poems on His Domestic Circumstances.* Murray had printed some of these poems in a small edition for private circulation, but poems of this sort by such a prominent poet would not likely remain private, and indeed on 14 April the *Champion* newspaper printed "Fare Thee Well" and "A Sketch from Private Life." Hone quickly followed with a one-shilling collection which, despite competition from numerous other pirates, rapidly went through as many as twenty-four printings in at least three different editions, in effect forcing Murray to issue his own (belated) edition for public sale. The episode inevitably strained relations between the two publishers.[8] Then, in 1817, Hone produced and marketed a prose version of Byron's *Corsair,* largely—suggests Peter Manning—for its symbolic currency in the context of the sedition trials following the Pentrich uprising, but also as an effort to extend the audience for the tale beyond those few wealthy readers who could lay their hands on Murray's expensive edition.[9] To this point in the affair, Hone is probably most accurately described as an opportunist. One might argue—with some justification—that, by producing and widely circulating inexpensive editions of works that had previously been available only to a wealthy few, he was seeking ways to destabilize the stratifications in the reading public and thus to blur the distinctions between the elite and the vulgar, the respectable press and the Radicals. More likely, however, Hone had more humble motivations. Early in 1817, the perpetually impecunious Hone was living with his wife and eight children in very cramped quarters behind his tiny shop in Fleet Street. Like most persons associated with Regency print culture, he was fascinated by Byron's popularity, and he saw that he might be able to profit financially by issuing his own editions of the poems. If he could also use Byron's work in the service of popular politics, so much the better. But the primary impetus was nonetheless financial.

Hone's feelings about Murray and the respectable press hardened considerably in 1817, however, when he was tried on three libel charges for parodying sections of the English Church liturgy—libels which, he contended, would have slipped past the attorney general unnoticed had they issued from the press of a more respectable publisher. Hone was certainly correct in his assessment. During the famous libel trials of 1817, the prosecution spelled out precisely this double standard as it applied to readers of the printed word. Discussing Hone's *Political Litany,* Attorney General Samuel Shepherd contended that "the express purpose of the book is clear from its being circulated at a cheap rate, so as to be within the reach of the common and ordinary people. . . . There may be many writings which sensible men may read in their closets; some of them may be highly improper for general circulation."[10]

And it follows that, if the readership is to be divided between "common and ordinary people" and "sensible men . . . in their closets," then so too should publishers cater to the specific needs and roles of these very different audiences. Hone's trial here was a case in point. Despite prosecution arguments to the contrary, Hone was not really being tried for having written and printed a text that the attorney general deemed dangerous to the English church; rather, he was in the dock for having issued and popularized works that, if published at all, ought properly to have remained available only to a more select audience of "sensible men." In essence, his offense was that he had transgressed the boundary between the elite and the common, and now he had to fight for his life before the King's Court, which sought to enforce that boundary. More respectable publishers like Murray enjoyed relative freedom from such official harassment, partly because their politics tended to be more conservative and partly because the high price of their wares (Murray's edition of *Don Juan,* for instance, was an ostentatious quarto that sold for £1. 11s. 6d.) placed them out of the reach of "common and ordinary people."

In any event, the discrepancy in the government's treatment of Murray and Hone was very much on Hone's mind just after the publication of Byron's *Don Juan.* On 19 July 1819, just four days after the publication of Byron's poem, Hone issued a forty-page pamphlet called *Don John, or Don Juan Unmasked,* in which he launched a blistering attack on what he took to be Murray's cowardice and hypocritical behavior in publishing such a risqué and politically suspect poem. At the same time he guarded in a cloak of anonymity his status as the leading London publisher of conservative social commentary and left his printer to face any potential legal consequences. Hone complained bitterly, for instance, that, while Murray might suppress a few stanzas of personal, political slander, he had not felt it necessary to suppress the two stanzas from Canto II in which Byron parodies the ten commandments. Hone had been prosecuted for precisely this offense, and even now he was assisting another printer—Joseph Russell of Birmingham—who was to go to trial in August 1819 for republishing Hone's parodies—Hone's acquittals on these same charges notwithstanding.[11] This bitterness also found comic expression in Hone's *Juan,* where Murray is repeatedly represented as a publisher whose relative success is founded on good fortune and an embarrassing *lack* of principle, or at least a willingness to set aside principle in callous grasping after social clout and greater profits. As Hone's narrator puts the case:

> You're witness here I don't get passionable,
>   I never yet was cooler in my life;
> But all men know, Drab John was rendered fashionable
>   When my son Harold took the Muse to wife:
> I flatter me I still am dash-on-able,
>   And so I scorn to lengthen out our strife:
> I am a decent *judge* of Nerve and Bone
> I'd rather *try* Drab John than Mr. Hone. (st. 4)

The emphasis here is quite deliberately on the language of law—the italicized "*judge*" and "*try*" in the stanza's closing couplet, for instance. The implication, of course, is that, in the eyes of this Byronic narrator (ostensibly Byron himself, the father of Harold), Murray is more reprehensible and more deserving of the ordeal of a libel trial than Hone. The former is a hypocrite, who thrives on good fortune rather than principle; the latter is, by contrast, a man of character and principle, who is thus to be favored with *Don Juan*'s third canto.

II

But there is more to Hone's use of *Don Juan* than simply an opportunity to express his sour grapes complaints about Murray's financial success and "fashionability." More important from a literary point of view is that Hone recognized very quickly and then exploited the revolutionary potential of Byron's comic, Shandyan narrator. It is mildly disconcerting in passages like the ones quoted above to hear those familiar ottava rima stanzas and the outrageous polysyllabic rhymes and to realize simultaneously that these lines are *not* Byron's. True, Hone's text is a parodic continuation of Byron's, and parody, by definition, demands a stylistic similarity. But this is a parody of a very peculiar kind. A contrasting example will perhaps clarify the point: When one thinks of, say, Wordsworth's poetry, one thinks of a characteristic elevation of tone that can bestow on even the most lowly objects a "sense sublime / Of something far more deeply interfused." And there are, of course, numerous parodies which imitate—usually to comic effect—this distinctive quality of Wordsworth's writing. Indeed, there are whole anthologies of such comic imitations of poetical standards, and for the most part they are identifiable by a consistent orientation toward the original text upon which they are based.[12] Whether they adopt an ethos of respectful homage or of satiric and contemptuous ridicule, these parodies necessarily distance themselves *from* the original in order to comment, at least implicitly, *on* the original. In all such cases, despite the telltale formal similarity, conventional parody effectively maintains, and even thrives on, a clear demarcation between the original, name-brand, genuine article and the cheap imitation. After all, a parody of, say, "Tintern Abbey" achieves its effects through an intertextual bouncing between the parody and the original text, the latter of which must be playing in the background of the reader's mind, so to speak. The division between the genuine and the imitation, between the elite and the vulgar, which is the source of the comic effects of conventional parody, is inscribed directly into its dialogical form, and conventional parody thus formally reinforces precisely the class divisions that are so evident in the clash between the respectable press and its Radical opposition.

Hone's parody, by contrast, strives to annihilate this distance; in fact, rather than producing a parody that is oriented toward some (external) original, Hone claims that his text *is* the original, now being continued with a different publisher.[13] It is Byron's narrator, I would argue, that makes possible this discursive incursion. Conventional parody requires a kind of identifiable and stable center—the Wordsworthian "voice" in the "Tintern Abbey" example—which has become ossified into a predictable, repetitive "discourse machine." And, as Bakhtin and others have pointed out, one of the key functions of parody is to reveal with laughter this ossification of discourse, thus making room for new voices and new forms to emerge. The identifiable and stable center is also the driving force behind the name-brand marketing that had converted the earlier Byron into such a profitable commercial property for Murray. Each of Byron's Oriental Tales, for example, was in effect a repetition of the Byron brand, a redaction of the Byronic Hero, and Murray could count on each new version to be a money- and reputation-making best-seller. Murray knew very well that the Byron name over his own imprint was the exclusive mark of aristocratic authenticity, and he exploited this exclusivity to build the status of his publishing house as well as to profit financially.

But the narrator of Byron's *Don Juan* undermines the stability of the "Byron" brand and with it the brand's ability to divide the literary field into the elite and the common. Here is a narrator marked not by fixed and predictable repetition but rather by a kind of "mobility." He contradicts himself; he becomes himself the butt of his characters' slapstick gags; he wanders through a freewheeling account of his freewheeling hero, all the time offering passing commentaries on the quirks of contemporary culture and exposing his own fleeting, comic idiosyncrasies. (Most dangerous to Murray, he offers an ironic and disarming context in which to place all those earlier poems with their brooding and oh-so-serious Byronic heroes.) Indeed, about the only stable and predictable aspect of *Don Juan* is the insistent prosody of the ottava rima stanzas and the hudibrastic rhymes—a consistency at the level of the signifier that belies a sliding "mobility" at the level of the signified. And this, when combined with the anonymity of the poem's publication, gives Hone his opening: by copying the form of Byron's poem Hone can sound enough like the original to claim that originality for himself, and then he can turn the poem with its full aristocratic authority toward the purposes of his Radical social criticism.

One way Hone manages this shift is fairly straightforward: he simply alters the setting, steering the narrative away from its exotic Spanish and Greek milieux and using it instead as the vehicle for a Radical interpretation of the intensely politicized world of post-Peterloo London:

> It was a time when England's robe was rent,
>   And famine's curse was blistering on her tongue;
> When thro' her every limb strange shiverings went,
>   And suffering had her every nerve unstrung;
> When passion vainly strove to find a vent,
>   When helplessly her mania arms were flung
> To Heaven, and Heaven allowed unscathed to go,
> The monsters who had wrought such utter woe. (st. 23)

The poem also includes *The Devilled Biscuit*'s accounts of the relatively incendiary speeches by Sir Francis Burdett and John Cam Hobhouse delivered to a large, open-air meeting in Palace Yard, which, like Peterloo, was broken up by a confused charge of alarmed royalists. And Hone's *Juan* ends with the hero (in an allusion both to Hone's incarceration in 1817 and to the plight of other Radical publishers in 1819) languishing in prison on ambiguous, *ex officio* charges of seditious libel for attempting to report on these proceedings. But the poem does not merely engage thematically the contemporary plight of English Radicalism; by slipping into Byron's narrator's voice and chastising Byron's own publisher, the poem also offers a unique and ironic commentary on relations between the Radical and respectable press. It presents itself, after all, not in the typical parodic mode of imitation-with-difference. This is not some writer who *sounds like* Byron; instead, the poem claims that this *is* Byron now come back to satirize his former publisher and take up Hone's cause. Clearly, this parody does not so much imitate the original as sift through it to find what it can use to further its own agenda—and what it finds is Byron's iconoclastic yet still authoritative narrator waiting to be animated into the cause of the Radical press.

III

At the time he was writing his parodic continuation of *Don Juan*, Hone was also engaged in an extended sort of research project in the British Library which, he hoped, would eventually lead to his contemplated magnum opus—a large volume long advertised as *A History of Parody*. Though Hone never completed this work, he did leave behind a few sketches of a theoretical section in which he distinguishes between three different types of parodies. The first is roughly what I have been calling conventional parody; in Hone's terms, such parody strives "to ridicule the article parodied." The second borrows the form of the original "for the purpose of conveying some useful moral or political or religious instruction & doubly imprinting it on the mind"; this parody, in other words, harnesses to its own didactic purposes the rhetorical force of the original text. The third is a satirical version of the second, in that the form of the original text is used "on acct. of its notoriety as a vehicle for humour or ridicule upon some other thing or person."[14] *Don Juan, Canto the Third!* clearly belongs in Hone's third category; it borrows Byron's notorious narrator and uses it as a vehicle for satirical commentary on Murray's cowardice and on the situation of the Radical press in general. And Hone's *Juan* takes this form of satirical parody even further than his definition would imply, for the anonymous publication of Byron's poem allows Hone not just to *use* Byron but to *be* Byron. As a result, the poem is a unique kind of political parody, one that cannot be labeled and dismissed as a kind of hectoring Radicalism that, by definition, lies outside the mainstream (as defined by the respectable press) of English political discussion. Rather, in an act of symbolic uppityness, the poem formally claims for itself the "Byron" brand as well as the aristocratic heritage and the social and economic status on which it is founded. In so doing, the poem proves itself to be truly revolutionary: it ironically levels the ground between peer and commoner, between Murray and the respectable press and Hone and the radical press, and—perhaps most profoundly—between those "gentlemen in their closets" and the "common and ordinary people."

Despite this impulse toward a kind of empowering and leveling populism, it is not finally clear how widely Hone was able to distribute his *Don Juan, Canto the Third!*. The scarcity of surviving copies would suggest only a limited circulation. Perhaps the court order protecting Murray's copyright prevented Hone from pursuing his ironic claim on the poem; more likely, Hone's energy and attention turned increasingly to those parodies—*The Political House that Jack Built, The Queen's Matrimonial Ladder,* and so on—that could and did attract a huge popular readership. These latter pamphlets did much to extend the influence of the Radical press and thus wrest control over British print culture from the oligarchy of fashionable, wealthy presses and give it instead to such independent artisans as Hone. The success of these popular parodies is in many ways prefigured by the formal wrestling for authority so evident in the conflicting uses both Murray and Hone found for Byron's masterpiece. In effect, thanks to Hone's parody, *Don Juan* became in 1819 a field of cultural struggle wherein the Radical press—armed with its devastating weaponry of parodic wit—could, at least for a moment, symbolically seize control of the elite and exclusive literature of the day.

NOTES

1. A description of some of these *Don Juan* spinoffs can be found in Samuel Chew, *Byron in England: His Fame and After-Fame* (1924; rpt., St. Clair Shores, Mich.: Scholarly Press, 1972), 27–75. An account of the appearance of Byron's poem is available in Hugh J. Luke, "The Publishing of Byron's *Don Juan*," *PMLA* 80 (1965): 199–209.

2. *Don Juan, Canto the Third!* (London: William Hone, 1819), stanza 8. Citations to the poem will hereafter be indicated parenthetically by stanza numbers. I am grateful to the Lilly Library at Indiana University for providing me with a photocopy of Hone's rare poem.

3. The best accounts of Hone's trials are Marcus Wood, *Radical Satire and Print Culture, 1790–1821* (Oxford: Clarendon Press, 1994), pp. 96–154, and Olivia Smith, *The Politics of Language, 1791–1819* (Oxford: Clarendon Press, 1984), pp. 154–201. Smith's overarching distinction between "refined" and "vulgar" language underlies my more concrete distinction between the respectable and the Radical press.

4. To cite just one example: the *Quarterly Review*'s notice of Hone's *Apocryphal New Testament* (1820) begins with a kind of apology—"Nothing but the execution of a public duty would have tempted us to defile one line of our Journal with the notice of a wretch as contemptible as he is wicked." Then, as if to clear a space for its own scathing commentary, the review claims "we may at once dismiss Mr. Hone from our consideration. He is described to us as a poor illiterate creature, far too ignorant to have any share in the composition either of this, or of his seditious pamphlets." *Quarterly Review* 25 (July 1821): 348.

5. Jerome Christensen, *Lord Byron's Strength: Romantic Writing and Commercial Society* (Baltimore: Johns Hopkins University Press, 1993); I am much indebted to Christensen's claim that the "circumstantial gravity" of Byron's *Don Juan* effectively dismantled the whole commercial system of "Byronism" that Murray had so carefully constructed. See especially Christensen's Chapter 7, "The Circumstantial Gravity of *Don Juan*," pp. 214–57.

6. Quoted in Luke, "The Publishing of Byron's *Don Juan*," p. 200.

7. Lord Eldon's ruling in favor of Murray's copyright surprised Byron, no doubt because Eldon had, in 1817, denied copyright protection to Southey's *Wat Tyler* on the grounds that libelous writing could not be legally protected. But the result of the *Wat Tyler* ruling was to facilitate the publication of Radical writing, since such works could be pirated with impunity. (Hone, incidentally, was the most prominent among several Radical publishers who issued editions of Southey's poem.) It may be that the ruling in favor of Murray's claim to *Don Juan* was an effort on Eldon's part to use copyright law to regain some control over the spread of Radical writing.

8. The episode is documented in Ann Bowden, "William Hone's Political Journalism, 1815–1821" (Ph.D. diss., University of Texas at Austin, 1975), 72–75. See also Chew, *Byron in England,* pp. 19–20, and Jerome McGann's notes to his *Lord Byron: The Complete Poetical Works,* vol. 3 (New York: Oxford, 1981), pp. 493–95.

9. See Peter Manning, "The Hone-ing of Byron's *Corsair*" in *Reading Roman-*

tics: Texts and Contexts (New York: Oxford, 1990), pp. 216–37, and Marina Vitale, "The Domesticated Heroine in Byron's *Corsair* and William Hone's Prose Adaptation," *Literature and History* 10 (1984): 72–94.

10. *Three Trials of William Hone* (London: William Hone, 1818), Second Trial, 6.

11. Hone had travelled to Birmingham in March and April of 1819 to be present at Russell's trial, but the trial was then delayed until August. The fact that Russell could be tried for precisely the same offense for which Hone had been found innocent is a mark of the government's aggressive efforts to stifle popular Radicalism. Russell was found guilty (country juries were typically far less tolerant than London juries), but the publication of his trial achieved some currency in Radical circles.

12. Readers will recognize my reliance here on Linda Hutcheon, *A Theory of Parody: The Teachings of Twentieth-Century Art Forms* (New York: Methuen, 1985).

13. Wood accurately describes the poem as a "fully fledged Byronic forgery" (p. 268). Hone went to amusing lengths to defend his ironic claim to *Don Juan*. Apparently, while his *Don Juan, Canto the Third!* was in press, yet another version of the poem was advertised. Hone's tongue-in-cheek response appears in a footnote on his first page:

> Don't think you can bamboozle folks—
>> Whatever merit lies in it,
> You know, *your* Canto's all a hoax
>> So don't be advertising it.
> But should you call—which Heaven forbid!
>> *My* Juan a nonentity,
> He'll come as Blackwood's Welchman did,
>> To prove his own identity.

I have not been able to locate the specific advertisement to which these rhymes respond. Of course, it is not Byron's since Byron did not send his third and fourth cantos to Murray until the summer of 1820.

14. Hone Papers, BL, Add. MSS 40108, fol. 71. Hone first elaborated these distinctions during his 1817 trials; his acquittals, in fact, depended on convincing the jury that his parodies of liturgical texts were not in his first category and thus did not necessarily ridicule the original liturgical text.

The *Black Dwarf* as Satiric Performance; or, the Instabilities of the "Public Square"

Steven Jones

January 1817: At the culmination of a year of intense popular unrest, an angry crowd attacked the Regent's coach on its way to the opening of Parliament, and a stone or other projectile—some thought a bullet (or, so one joke ran, a potato)—broke one of the coach's windows. This familiar incident has become a symbolic narrative crisis in almost every history of the period, in part because of its emblematic qualities—the shattered fragile barrier between the ruler and the faceless rabble—and in part because the year that followed became so important in the history of Radical Reform that it inevitably casts a weighty shadow back over the opening January scene.[1] In fact, it is arguable that for the first months of 1817 Parliament and the ministry did little but react to this event. In the wake of the attack on the Regent but also of the longer-term effects of demobilization after Waterloo—the general economic crisis, the Corn Law of 1815, Spa Fields, the march of the Manchester Blanketeers, government spies and executions—a resurgent English Radicalism was under enormous pressure from above and below. When Habeas Corpus was suspended at the first of March, a number of legal actions were brought immediately. With William Cobbett out of the picture in America, Thomas Wooler's new journal, the *Black Dwarf*—which appeared for the first time on the day after the attack—took over as the dominant Radical organ, giving its large readership (by 1819, certainly more than twelve thousand)[2] a potent "mixture of heavy-handed satire and libertarian rhetoric."[3]

This contradictory mixture of the satiric and the sincere is my primary focus in this essay. Whereas E. P. Thompson calls Wooler's satire "heavy-handed," Jon Klancher has more precisely detected in the *Black Dwarf* "moments of heightened discursive anguish," in which "the language of satire merges with the excessive language of melodrama itself."[4] I intend, in what follows, to outline one basis for this mixture of modes: the material carnivalesque, as it is invoked by Wooler's totemic figure the Black Dwarf. In the context of a situated *satire*—a *satura* or mixed feast of unstable modes—we can more precisely situate the effects of Wooler's generic mixtures and begin to see how they might have been useful for Radical discourse during the period, as the conflict of modes inscribes in the pages of the journal the conflicted heterogeneity of its potential audiences.[5]

The *Black Dwarf* is an especially powerful example of such Radical productions because it so openly engages in a troubling display of the *volatility* of the modes it incorporates—sentimental and satirical, those associated with "high" as well as "low" discourses—and thus dramatizes the instability of representation itself. This is true in part because Wooler *must* write, edit, compose pages, and publish from the position of pariah-satirist. His work, therefore, deliberately capitalizes on its own relation to a moment of cultural instability by representing instability back to itself—and it is in this sense that we can begin to appreciate its powerful satiric performance.

Who was the Black Dwarf? In Wooler's hands he appears to be a caricature out of prints and cartoons, and, indeed, caricaturists quickly moved to represent the figure. In effect, Wooler preempted his own satirists by adopting such a persona: black in the sense that he is exotically African or vaguely "oriental," the Dwarf is also "black" in the sense of occult or diabolical, as well as simply dangerously low: a blackguard. Through association—for example with his companion persona in the journal, the "Black Neb" (or crow)—the Dwarf is connected with Jacobinism. In a frontispiece engraved for the first collected volume of the journal in 1818 (fig. 1), a large Satyr holds the hand of the dancing Black Dwarf, whose misshapen head bears a turban decorated with black pen-feathers—"radical crow quills," as Wooler called them.[6] The Satyr in the foreground gestures to a smoking heap of the signs of authority, a bonfire of political vanities, while the Dwarf himself remains a kind of exotic shadow-partner in the background. It is the diabolical Satyr (read "satire") who makes the defining gesture at center stage.

Wooler is often assumed to have taken his Black Dwarf from Walter Scott's novel of the same name, published in early December 1816. But so far as I know, no one has pursued the implications of this highly suggestive intertextual link, not so much to a literary "source"—Wooler's sources are surely legion—but to a specific "romantic" milieu into which Wooler was attempting to tap for his own purposes. Scott's dwarf is first of all an unmistakable *country* type, a misanthropic fairy or brownie of the Border living wild on the moor, the picturesque relative of the local devil himself (who was sometimes known as "the Black Man"). Scott takes him straight out of antiquarian folklore, oral tradition, and ballads, as his notes to the novel indi-

Frontispiece to the First Volume of the Black Dwarf.

Published by T. J. Wooler 58 Sun Street.

Fig. 1. Frontispiece, *The Black Dwarf,* Vol. I (1818).
Courtesy of the Newberry Library, Chicago.

cate. But he also cites a particular informant for his version of the local-color character and seems to have visited a real-life model—one David Ritchie—in 1796 or 1797.[7]

In the *Scots Magazine* for October 1817 there appeared an "Account of David Ritchie, the Original of the Black Dwarf," which fails to mention

Wooler's publication but attempts to flesh-out the "singular person . . . whose real history . . . has already excited the curiosity and contributed to the entertainment of the public in no extraordinary degree" in Scott's fiction.[8] The reportedly misanthropic and "satirical" (or caustic) Ritchie (1740–1811), known locally as "Bowed David," lived in a cottage on the grounds of Sir James Waysmyth in Peebleshire and became, especially after the appearance of Scott's novel, "one of the most interesting curiosities of the country" (*Scots Magazine,* p. 208). When it comes to describing his appearance, the magazine resorts to the *fictionalized* description in Scott (p. 209), and then offers a truly remarkable example of Romantic idealization: Ritchie, the article speculates, may have had some prescience of his approaching apotheosis, under the plastic hands of a mighty magician—a still more extraordinary and mysterious personage than himself—one who has not only raised up the spirits of the departed, but, by disrobing them of the more vulgar and prosaic *rags* of their mortal state, and investing them with imposing and poetical qualities, has restored them to the world in a guise a thousand times more pleasing and picturesque, and yet scarcely less true to nature, than the reality itself (p. 211).

Scott is allowed to take over the mysterious magical powers associated with his anthropological specimen, through a process of idealization and the addition of the "poetical." The result is that his portrait is a mirror of the *true* nature behind the distorted physique of the dwarf.

Not Ritchie, but the kind of idealized, picturesque dwarf of North-country legend that Scott helps (re)construct, is clearly a scapegoat-figure for the rural community, an outcast who lives just beyond the pale but binds the social group together by serving as the focus of its superstition and xenophobia. This is obviously one way in which the people of Peebleshire mythologized and transformed David Ritchie (and others like him) into legend. Ritchie's associations in the popular mind with witchcraft and magic appear in Scott's cultural milieu as mere anthropological curiosities, but their implications are clear.[9] Both feared and respected for his presumed supernatural powers (over cattle as well as people), any such figure is shunned and yet prized—at a distance— and is presumed to be able to cure as well as to taint. Ambiguity of effect is a source and consequence of his power. Here is Scott's first description of his version of the dwarf, "Canny Elshie" (or "the Brown Man of the Moor"), "in all his native deformity":

> His head was of immense size, covered with a fell of shaggy black hair, partly grizzled with age; his eye-brows, shaggy and prominent, overhung a pair of small, dark, piercing eyes, set far back in their sockets, that rolled with a portentous wildness, indicative of partial insanity. The rest of his features were of the coarse, rough-hewn stamp with which a painter would equip a giant in romance, to which was added, the wild, irregular, and peculiar expression so often seen in the countenances of those whose persons are deformed. (Scott, p. 29)

206

Scott's dwarf is the kind of picturesque invention readers would immediately recognize as "romantic." Like Wordsworth's Idiot Boy or the leech gatherer, his deformity sets him apart, provokes a sentimental response, and stands as a sign of his proximity to nature's power.

The political plot of Scott's novel concerns the Jacobite uprising of 1708, a story of the kind of internecine political violence widely treated at the time as analogous to conflicts in England in 1817. Scott's Black Dwarf is at the center of the conflict, is even appealed to at one point as a kind of stabilizing force. Like all natural prodigies, according to tradition he is a sign of instability in the social realm; his symbolic "sacrifice" (being ostracized and reviled) serves to ward off further troubles. In this context it is helpful to remember that the *satirist*'s role in society, especially in so-called "primitive" society, can be seen as analogous to the role of the scapegoat.[10] Given these interconnected strata of cultural tradition, Wooler's choice of persona in the Black Dwarf seems an inspired act, perhaps even a deliberately parodic gesture of re-appropriation from the famous Tory novelist who so successfully reproduced a Romantic *popular* culture for his *mass* audience. Taking over the Black Dwarf from Scott may have been Wooler's attempt to return to the frightening Otherness of the figure—and in effect his first satiric gesture in his new journal. This would make Wooler's frontispiece an emblem: the Satyr takes in hand and leads the figure of the dwarf (who capers innocently) toward the site of incendiary, Radical satire.

In any case, audiences in 1817 would have quickly been made aware of both dwarfs, and the comparison could only have intensified the oppositional effect of Wooler's dangerous form of popular *satire,* its reclamation of an ancient popular version of the scapegoat, recently reintroduced into fiction by one of the nation's best-known *literary* authors, in the context of contemporary political troubles as Wooler represents them in his "sub-literary" publication.

From the beginning, with the journal's "Prospectus," Wooler plays on the conflict behind his figure by exploiting the Dwarf's ambiguous relation to customary superstition.

> It may be required of us to declare whether the Black Dwarf emanates from the celestial regions, or from the shades of evil—whether he be an European sage, or an Indian savage. . . . We are not at liberty to unfold all the secrets of his prison-house, to ears of flesh and blood . . . these disclosures we must reserve, until better times ensure the civil treatment of so singular a stranger. (*BD*, Prospectus, 1817)

In the meantime, Wooler declares, the Black Dwarf "intends to expose every species of vice and folly, with which this virtuous age, and enlightened metropolis abounds. . . . Secure from his invisibility, and dangerous from his power of division, (for like the polypus, he can divide and redivide himself, and each division remain a perfect animal)."

207

Notice how this passage begins with uncertainty over the opposition of high and low ("celestial regions" versus "shades of evil"), maps that uncertainty onto the division of 'civilized' "European sage" from 'primitive' "Indian savage," and then ends by claiming for the Dwarf the kind of "dangerous" magical powers that go with blurring or transgressing such essential divisions: "invisibility" and the monstrous ability to divide and redivide himself, to become an unstable quantity. In this way, Wooler exploits what is truly fearful, because volatile, about his outwardly absurd, cartoonish character. As with the figure on the masthead of another Radical journal, the *Gorgon,* Wooler's Dwarf plays on the fear that such slipperiness is dangerous because it can quickly and unpredictably multiply itself: one Black Dwarf can metamorphose suddenly into a "mob" like the one engulfing the Regent's coach.

It will have been obvious from the start to any historian of the period that Wooler's Dwarf also has family relations to yet another kind of stock character, one more at home in the London crowd, perhaps also descended from ancient peasant lore but transplanted, modernized, and urbanized: what we might call "the Grotesque Plebeian Radical." The *Black Dwarf* would have evoked for its readers simultaneously *both* strands of plebeian culture: the ancient rural tradition of "superstitious" beliefs and scapegoat-figures, and the modern London underworld—as it is described by Iain McCalman, for example—made up of grotesquely self-parodic and subversive Radical orators, writers, artisans, and printers; the infamous satirical orator Samuel Waddington, for example, as McCalman reminds us, was known as "the Black Dwarf."[11] Wooler's Black Dwarf exists at the confluence of these two traditions and reveals their interdependence, while fusing the two in the potent farrago of a printed satiric performance.

The heteroglossic style of the journal has rightly been identified as an instance of the Bakhtinian carnivalesque, in its "riotous panoply of voices, speeches, quotations, answers, questions, mockeries, parodies, and harangues."[12] With this I would agree, but would add (following Bakhtin) that parody, satyr play, and eventually satire itself have the deepest roots in the collective rituals of carnival, its mix of "high" and "low" languages, transgressions, violations, and metamorphoses.[13] In other words, there is something intrinsically *satiric* about Wooler's practice of heteroglossia.

When considering the ramifications of "the carnivalesque" in 1817, it is worth keeping in mind that *actual* Black Africans and dwarfs (and, indeed, "Black dwarfs" or pygmies) were among the numerous "prodigies" that made up the staple sideshow exhibits at London carnivals well into the nineteenth century. For example, the 1815 Bartholomew Fair included one Mr. Simon Paap, "the celebrated Dutch Dwarf," only twenty-eight inches high, presented with full ceremony to the Regent and the entire Royal family before beginning his popular run at the Fair.[14] But even closer to Wooler's icon is the earlier advertisement from Queen Anne's reign, in which the Smithfield Fair boasts of displaying a "little Black Man, being but 3 foot high"—put on display at the teeming center of the carnival: that loaded "site" (real as well as virtual) which Bakhtin calls "the public square where the folk gather."[15] The point is that in the eighteenth and nineteenth centuries this was a troubling site of conflicts, distortions, multiple colonizations, moral ambiguities, and blatant exploitation, as well as a site of potentially liberatory inversions and instabilities.

Materially speaking, the English carnival is, however, the one site contemporary with Wooler's publication at which the urban-artisanal and plebeian-rural cultures actually jostled together in "the public square," a space at once economic marketplace and cultural theatre, where commodities were traded and melodramas performed. It was also a site where the relational and conjunctural nature of social and discursive categories was publicly dramatized and potentially opened to questioning. If we re-materialize the carnival, bringing the Bakhtinian abstraction down to earth in Smithfield, as it were, we can catch a glimpse of an important part of the *Black Dwarf*'s constructed and hybrid (satiric/sentimental, low/ high) milieu.

One letter of the Dwarf to the Prince Regent himself ends with this postscript thematizing carnival directly:

> Your Royal Highness may not be aware of the *general alarm* felt by the *cowards* who pretend to watch for the public safety. *If you were,* you, who are certainly a *brave man,* would hesitate to adopt the *suspicions* of your ministers, which are merely the result of their *fears,* and a modest consciousness of what *they deserve.* *Bartholomew Fair,* Sir, has *terrors* for your advisers; and they would have probably prevented its being held, under the bill for regulating *seditious* assemblies, had an *earlier intimation* of *their danger* been forwarded to them, by the wag who announced the *intended insurrection* on Saturday last. Every thing, Sir, was stated to be ready to give a *mortal* wound to the constitution "*as by law established,*" by a combined force of *gingerbread Punches, wooden dolls, and pasteboard soldiers.* Two or three *Jack-in-the-boxes* were named as ring-leaders; and a *monkey,* escaped from Polito's collection, was suspected of having organized *the plot.* (*BD,* 10 September 1817)

As the Dwarf goes on to report in mock concern, "the Punches, dolls, and pasteboard rebels never moved from their stalls! But, what of that? They *would,* no doubt, had they not been intimidated by the preparations made to defeat their seditious machinations!" In future, oaths of loyalty will be required not just of persons but of "all and every imitation of men, women, and children, that are admitted into the fair."

"Seditious machinations"? At the fair? Given the history of the English carnival, the answer would have to be yes—which is what adds the true sting to Wooler's burlesque. His contemporary readers would well know that it was no joke to associate insurrection and riot with the carnival. While it is true that "there is no a priori revolutionary vector" to carnival, as Stallybrass and White have rightly argued, on the other hand "it was only in the late eighteenth and early nineteenth centuries—and then only in certain areas—that one can reasonably talk of popular politics *dissociated* from the carnivalesque at all"; in fact, as they contend, it is probably most useful to treat carnival as a *"catalyst and site of actual and symbolic struggle."*[16]

Ostensibly mocking the government's confusion of reality with representation ("every imitation"), Wooler's 1817 passage actually ends by reinforcing the potential danger of "mere" representations—and by emphasizing the Radical instability of the relation between representation and reality. In this way it makes its own pages into a site of symbolic struggle and a struggle over symbols. For many of his middling and artisanal readers, references to the commerce and craft of the fair would be familiar, homey. But to the authorities (and to some respectable tradesmen in his audience, we may imagine) the satiric fair would be a frightening, uncanny place of hidden conspiracies, where nothing is as it seems and even the gingerbread simulacra may revolt.

In a more conventionally Romantic strain, Wordsworth responded to the same deep-seated fear, in the well-known lines of *The Prelude* VII describing the "anarchy and din, / Barbarian and infernal"[17] of Bartholomew Fair.

> with buffoons against buffoons
> Grimacing, writhing, screaming . . .
> The silver-collared Negro with his timbrel,
> Equestrians, tumblers, women, girls, and boys,
> Blue-breeched, pink-vested, with high-towering plumes.
> All moveables of wonder, from all parts,
> Are here—Albinos, painted Indians, Dwarfs,
> The horse of knowledge, and the learned Pig. (ll. 698–708)

The proximity of slave and dwarf is notable in the present context. But note as well, as the catalogue continues, how the moral (and political) revulsion of the author increases as the line between representation and reality becomes less and less stable:

> Giants, Ventriloquists, the Invisible Girl,
> The Bust that speaks and moves its goggling eyes,
> The Wax-work, Clockwork, all the marvellous craft
> Of modern Merlins, Wild Beasts, Puppet-shows,
> All out-o'-the-way, far-fetched, perverted things,
> All freaks of nature, all Promethean thoughts
> Of man, his dullness, madness, and their feats
> All jumbled up together, to compose
> A Parliament of Monsters, Tents and Booths.
> Meanwhile, as if the whole were one vast mill,

Are vomiting, receiving, on all sides,
Men, Women, three-years Children, Babes in arms. (ll. 710–21)

The human beings spewed from the London Fair are finally indistinguishable from the uncanny robot-bust and wax-work, what man has *made* of man. At the opening of the next book, Wordsworth contrasts this nightmare with an idyllic "rustic fair" at Grasmere. Here, we are told, there are no booths offering sideshow freaks and diversions, only healthy livestock in a sublime natural setting and, significantly, a "sweet lass of the valley" selling her honest and unalienated wares—the "Fruits of her father's orchard" (ll. 38–40). This is a marketplace under full control, not open to the inversions, instabilities, and class confusions of the London carnival.

At the very least, if we can see in both Wordsworth and Wooler images of the fair as a site of struggle and instability, then we are given a salutary counterweight to the many more happy pictures of carnival as a *locus amoenus* of organic England, where different classes intermingle for the day. Take this commemorative verse on Bartholomew Fair from the mid-eighteenth century:

Each wooden house then groans to bear
The populace that croud the Fair. . . .
The chambermaid and Countess sit
Alike admirers of the wit:
The Earl and footman *tête-à-tête*
Sit down contented in one Seat.
The Musick plays, the Curtain draws
The Peer and 'prentice clap applause.
The house is filled with roaring laughter
From lowest pit, to highest rafter.[18]

There *were* no doubt royal visitors to the stalls at the fair, but these are quite possibly the exceptions that prove the rule; they may already in the eighteenth century represent a kind of fashionable slumming. Certainly by 1817, the "roaring laughter" of the harmonious theatrical audience pictured above—had it continued—might well have covered nervousness about the dangers of such a dangerous class intermixture.

It is significant that the representative carnival crowd in this scene is a theatrical audience. The carnival as a whole is obviously a metatheatrical experience comprised of slapstick farces, Punch plays, pantomimes, interludes, melodramas, scenes from Shakespeare—all available at once in the stalls along the lanes of the urban fair, forming in fact a kind of stage-set for the larger play of plays, the carnival itself. In the performance of this larger play, the audience is involved as actors.

In one of Wooler's many theatrical conceits, he announces in the 26 January 1820 issue that the King's Theatre, St. Stephens, will no longer mount

211

performances of classical English drama, "it having been ascertained to *shock* the *delicate nerves* of the people of fashion." Instead, Wooler says (engaging in some shocking Swiftian imagery of his own), from now on, costumes will be "entirely military" and real cannon will be fired "for effect." In the final scene, these guns will be "turned upon the gallery spectators, and discharged with grape shot." "In the combats, the people are to be really killed, and wounded in the Manchester method: and in all cases, nature will be copied as closely as possible." (The drama of Peterloo is more frighteningly real than any play Wooler can imagine, as he reminds us.) Additionally, Wooler adds, due to the egregious "inattention of the underlings," which so badly distracts from the onstage performance, "the *public* are respectfully informed, that in future they will be all made of wood, of the best mechanism, to sit upright, and nod, or shake the head, as may be required." These model spectators possess the same disturbing, uncanny quality as Wooler's gingerbread Punches and Wordsworth's automaton-bust at Bartholomew Fair. The actual effect of Wooler's satiric performance here is a kind of figurative terrorism: he blurs rather than reinforces the boundary between representation and reality, nature and artifice, actor and audience, playing upon social instabilities with his destabilizing imagery.

Indeed, it is difficult not to sense in the violence of this passage an impatience with the passivity of the people as spectators in the national drama. This accords with Wooler's expression of frustration from one of the earliest issues of the *Black Dwarf*: "We sometimes go to the theatre, and sit there with the utmost astonishment, at the indifference we see around us. . . . What an invaluable school would the stage be, if it were quite unfettered. What a powerful engine to correct the abuses; and lash the follies of the times" (*BD*, 20 February 1817). Clearly Wooler's wish is for the theatre to play the role conventionally assigned to satire—the correction of abuses and the lashing of follies—and it is difficult not to hear in both passages a frustration with the limited effects of his own satiric performance. Such frustration culminates in his despairing remark in October 1824: "The nation is asleep, as dull as tortoises in winter, and nothing can stir them from their trance." Only months later, he announced the end of the *Black Dwarf* "to the friends of Reform . . . if there are any left?"

Back in 1820, however, when during the Queen Caroline affair a popular insurrection seemed a real possibility, Wooler depicted Parliament in these satiric terms:

> These *legislators* are really amusing animals. The world would run melancholy without having them to laugh at. They keep a national puppet-shew, and are constantly playing their antics in *front of their booth*, as well as in the interior. . . . [E]very now and then the gaping multitude are entertained by one of the performers stepping out to announce that the performances are about to begin. (*BD*, 28 June 1820)

In its own way, Wooler's satire is also a kind of theatre without footlights, a performance in front of the booth that crosses the line into its audience's conflicts. Rather than cover over such conflicts, Wooler exposes them in performing them. Rather than merely joining debate or participating in public discourse, he takes the risk of turning his pages into a symbolic battleground. In its medley of unstable modes, the *Black Dwarf* inscribes in its mixed-media satiric texts the opposing readings of its heterogenous audience. In this way, it represents the volatility of representation itself and performatively produces a volatility that is not only discursive.

NOTES

1. My historical narrative is based on Elie Halévy, *The Liberal Awakening 1815– 1830,* trans. E. I. Watkin (New York: Peter Smith, 1949), pp. 22–34, and E. P. Thompson, *The Making of the English Working Class* (New York: Vintage Books, 1966), pp. 631–69.

2. 12,000 is the estimated circulation given by Richard D. Altick, *The English Common Reader* (Chicago: University of Chicago Press, 1957), p. 326; but of course such publications were frequently handed from one reader to another, read in lending libraries, and read aloud in groups. The actual audience for the journal was surely much larger than 12,000.

3. Thompson, pp. 674–75.

4. Jon P. Klancher, *The Making of English Reading Audiences, 1790–1832* (Madison: University of Wisconsin Press, 1987), p. 119. In one sense, my essay is an extended meditation on Klancher's astute observations. The most lucid analysis of the stylistic vectors of the *Black Dwarf* remains an article to which I am indebted, Richard Hendrix's "Popular Humor in 'The Black Dwarf'," *Journal of British Studies* 16 (Fall 1976): 108–28. More recently, Michael Scrivener has shed light on Wooler's discursive position in "The *Black Dwarf* Review of Byron's *The Age of Bronze,*" *Keats-Shelley Journal* 41 (1992): 42–48.

5. For a summary of the revisionist debate over Habermas' hegemonic public sphere (versus heterogenous audiences and counter-publics), and the *myth* of a unitary public sphere, see Kevin Gilmartin, "Popular Radicalism and the Public Sphere," *Studies in Romanticism* 33 (1994): 549–57. I would suggest, however, that the fact that the *Black Dwarf* uses as its motto lines from Pope may indicate not, as Gilmartin says, the "unexpected return of a relatively polite and unitary political ideal at the heart of a movement known for its division and divisiveness" (p. 556), but instead a kind of parodic citation-as-appropriation common among Radical satirists—like Wooler's taking over the figure of the dwarf from Scott.

6. The *Black Dwarf,* 12 January 1820; hereafter cited in the text as *BD.*

7. See the Edinburgh Edition of Walter Scott's *The Black Dwarf,* ed. P. D. Garside (Edinburgh and New York: Edinburgh University Press and Columbia University Press, 1993), pp. 132–33. All quotations from the novel are from this edition.

8. *Scots Magazine* (October 1817): 207–12. As this article observes, Ritchie's existence had been mentioned in previous reviews, in both the *Quarterly* and the *Edinburgh.*

9. The *Scots Magazine* goes out of its way (protesting too much, we might suspect) to deny that Ritchie was himself a warlock, but also notes that he was superstitious and practiced talismanic magic against witchcraft. According to the oblique logic of scapegoating, it is enough that the dwarf be mysteriously associated with such supernatural things. As the article observes, "a certain degree of fearful respect and awe was felt toward" Ritchie by his neighbors (p. 211). The *Quarterly Review* for January 1817 (published April) reviews Scott's fiction and in effect anticipates my thesis here, noting that the Black Dwarf is the kind of outcast often attached to country estates, and even suggesting (through a reading of the novel) that community superstitions about such figures act as a displacement of social violence—dueling, revenge pacts, and so forth—endemic (so the reviewer says) to the North.

10. See Robert C. Elliott, *The Power of Satire: Magic, Ritual, Art* (Princeton: Princeton University Press, 1960).

11. Iain McCalman, *Radical Underworld: Prophets, Revolutionaries and Pornographers in London, 1795–1840* (Cambridge: Cambridge University Press, 1988), p. 150.

12. Klancher, p. 114.

13. M. M. Bakhtin, *The Dialogic Imagination,* ed. Michael Holquist, trans. Caryl Emerson and Michael Holquist (Austin: University of Texas Press, 1982), pp. 158–224.

14. Details of the London carnival are from Henry Morley, *Memoirs of Bartholomew Fair* (London: Chatto and Windus, 1880).

15. *The Dialogic Imagination,* pp. 159–60.

16. Peter Stallybrass and Allon White, *The Politics and Poetics of Transgression* (Ithaca: Cornell University Press, 1989), pp. 16, 14.

17. William Wordsworth, *The Prelude 1799, 1805, 1850,* ed. Jonathan Wordsworth, M. H. Abrams, and Stephen Gill (New York and London: W. W. Norton, 1979), pp. 263–65 (1850, ll. 686–87); hereafter cited in the text.

18. Published in *Farrago or Miscellanies in Verse and Prose,* as quoted in Sybil Rosenfeld, *The Theatre of the London Fairs in the 18th Century* (Cambridge: Cambridge University Press, 1960), p. 46.

INDEX